MW01054529

Tiger in the Sea

Tiger in the Sea

The Ditching of Flying Tiger 923
and the Desperate Struggle for Survival

Eric Lindner

Guilford, Connecticut

An imprint of The Rowman & Littlefield Publishing Group, Inc.
4501 Forbes Blvd., Ste. 200
Lanham, MD 20706
www.rowman.com

Distributed by NATIONAL BOOK NETWORK

British Library Cataloguing in Publication Information available

Library of Congress Cataloging-in-Publication Data

Names: Lindner, Eric, 1958- author.
Title: Tiger in the sea : the ditching of Flying Tiger 923 and the desperate struggle for survival / Eric Lindner.
Description: Guilford, Connecticut : Lyons Press, [2021] | Summary: "September 1962: On a moonless night over the raging Atlantic, 900 miles from land, the engines of Flying Tiger flight 923 burst into flames, one by one. A crash into the sea was inevitable. Tiger in the Sea is the story of that harrowing ordeal."
Identifiers: LCCN 2020052657 | ISBN 9781493031566 (cloth) alk. paper | ISBN 9781493031573 (electronic)
Subjects: LCSH: Aircraft accidents—North Atlantic Ocean—History—20th century. | Search and rescue operations--North Atlantic Ocean—History—20th century. | Airplane crash survival—United States—History—20th century. | Constellation (Transport planes)—History.
Classification: LCC TL553.9 .L56 2021 | DDC 363.12/493—dc23
LC record available at https://lccn.loc.gov/2020052657

∞™ The paper used in this publication meets the minimum requirements of American National Standard for Information Sciences—Permanence of Paper for Printed Library Materials, ANSI/NISO Z39.48-1992.

To Ellen Murray,

my love, my pilot.

CONTENTS

PART I

MISSING PLANES

Escort being scrambled: the most welcome words in the English language.

—*Capt. John Murray*[1]

Chapter 1

Trouble above the North Atlantic

Four miles above the North Atlantic
Aboard Flying Tiger Line Flight 923
September 23, 1962, 8:07 p.m.

Capt. John Murray finally felt like he could breathe a sigh of relief. Though he'd just moments ago passed the point of no return, so he no longer had enough fuel to return to Gander International Airport some thousand miles away, he no longer felt he'd need to.[1] Since leaving Newfoundland three hours earlier, his Lockheed Super Constellation had encountered pounding hail and periodic wing icing. But by stair-stepping 10,000 feet above his intended flight plan and threading the seams of the rocky air, he'd eluded the storm.[2]

The 44-year-old Oyster Bay, Long Island, resident reached into his shirt pocket, pulled out a crinkled pack of Pall Mall cigarettes, and lipped one out, spilling a few tobacco flakes onto his seat cushion. Since the pilot had one hand on the yoke, the copilot sitting to his right clicked his own lighter and held it out: Murray turned his head, engaged the tiny flame, took a drag, closed his eyes, and let the nicotine go to work. The smoke added to the claustrophobia in the flight deck, with its seats for the captain and first officer, fold-down desks and chairs for the navigator and flight engineer, manuals and personal belongings lying about, and an archaic maze of floor-to-ceiling electronics.

Murray throttled back from climb power, then told his engineer to set cruise power. The plane's roar decelerated into a 330-mph purr on pillowy air. Wanting to give inexperienced first officer and copilot Robert Parker more flying time, the pilot said, "Your plane," let his hands fall from the yoke, then took another drag.[3]

In the cabin, the Fasten Seat Belt—No Smoking sign dinged and darkened, indicating it was okay for the four stewardesses to resume handing out snacks, drinks, and air sickness bags to the 68 passengers. Some unbuckled their seat belts and raced to the lavatories. Others returned to their books or magazines, gin rummy or cribbage games. Some lit cigarettes.

And some, while aimlessly staring out the right-side windows, over the wing and into the inky sky, noticed a different sort of smoke.

In the cockpit, a red flash on the instrument panel caught Murray's eye: fire in engine no. 3; inboard, right side.[4] The absence of an alarm bell puzzled him. Though fire warnings in general were quite common, silent ones were very rare.

From his workstation behind and to the right of Murray, flight engineer James Garrett confirmed the reported fire. Both men knew that most alarms weren't triggered by actual fires but by a high temperature that might lead to a fire, and that the most likely explanation was a simple electrical malfunction, given the Super Constellation's notoriously finicky fire detection system, with its miles of wiring and hundreds of electrical components stuffed into the 260 panels at the base of the bulkhead, at the rear of the cockpit. The two also took comfort in the belief that, had there been a serious technical issue, maintenance would have found it before the plane left New Jersey. They knew competing airlines and the U.S. Air Force often hired the airline to tackle their toughest assignments. Many an objective observer felt the Tiger pit crew was the best in the business.[5]

Still, Murray said: "Jim, feather number three and stand by to discharge."[6]

"Copy that." Garrett pulled the engine no. 3 throttle back to idle, pushed the feathering button in to streamline the propellor blades, then cut off the mixture control, which immediately disabled the engine; at which point an alarm bell began clanging riotously, amplified by the cabin's confined acoustics. Slumbering passengers were jolted awake by the "savage sound."[7]

Garrett raised his voice: "Ready to discharge, Captain."

"Fire one bottle," said Murray.

"Copy that," yelled Garrett. He pressed a button.

The alarm stopped ringing. The red FIRE light on the control panel went dark.

Murray would have liked to give his copilot more experience, given the fact that Parker only had 350 hours at the helm of a Super Constellation, versus Murray's 4,300.[8] But there was a time and a place for everything, and this was not the time for on-the-job training. So the pilot said, "My plane," and took control of the aircraft.

Meanwhile, Garrett still had one more task to complete. In many ways it was the most important: close the engine no. 3 firewall so as to cut off the flow of fuel, in order to prevent any flames from spreading to engine no. 4, or worse.

A rap on the door interrupted his train of thought. "It's Betty."

Flying had come a long way since 1903, when Orville Wright managed to stay airborne for 12 seconds and travel 120 feet. But aviation safety still had a long way to go: based on passenger miles flown, flying was 100 times more dangerous in 1962 than in 2020.[9]

Murray's plane seemed especially precarious. Lockheed Aircraft Corporation's highly profitable Constellation series was showing its age. Though the L-1049H Super Constellation that Murray was piloting had rolled off a Burbank assembly line on February 20, 1958, so she was only four and a half years old, "Connie" had actually been conceived in 1937. She still used the same basic piston technology first developed in 1844, as opposed to the jet turbine first used in 1939. Lockheed had stopped producing Constellations a few months after Murray's plane was manufactured.

But Connie wasn't just old. She was infirm. While her military ancestor's durability had helped win World War II, in her commercial incarnation nearly one of every five built since 1950 had experienced a catastrophic "hull-loss occurrence," aviation-speak for a total loss.[10]

The plane's problems extended beyond the hull, as evidenced by the November 30, 1961, flight that didn't even leave the tarmac in Richmond, Virginia. The departure was delayed due to an electrical glitch. Seventy-four Army recruits and 3 Imperial Airways crew members were told to stay seated and await the fire truck, which would arrive soon. It did arrive soon. But late: to the gruesome sight of 72 soldiers and 2 crew members dead of smoke inhalation.

On March 15, 1962, two Pentagon charters left California's Travis Air Force Base within minutes of one other. Hours later, one of the Flying Tiger Line Connies caught fire and crashed in Alaska, while the second Tiger flight disappeared without a trace, despite one of the largest sea searches in history, lasting eight days, canvassing more than 200,000 square miles, and involving all four branches of the armed forces.[11] Newspapers wrote of a "secret military cargo," while the airline speculated about sabotage, though admitting its conjecture was a "wild guess."[12]

As the wreckage and fatalities mounted, many wondered why Lockheed hadn't stopped making the plane in 1948, rather than 1958. Not Murray. He liked Connie's range, ruggedness, and versatility. Four powerful engines and five cavernous fuel tanks permitted coast-to-coast travel, while most other planes had to refuel. He loved her aesthetics, right down to her unique triple tailfins. Many considered her the apex of prop-and-piston design.[13] Connie was the first Air Force One, in 1953.[14]

Murray was loyal. He'd never forget how her early version had safely flown him to and from the Aleutian oil fields during WWII, despite some very harsh weather. He wasn't lured by the Douglas DC-8 or Boeing 707 jets or tempted by their bells and whistles.[15] He thought it was neat that Tiger headquarters were housed in the Lockheed Air Terminal in Burbank. For him the arrangement was a partnership.

True: Connie was prone to engine problems, but so were the Boeing and Douglas props. The Lockheed equipment had always performed when it was crunch time, even when Murray lost two out of four engines on back-to-back flights, piloting the same aircraft. Everything had turned out fine. "It's all part of flying," he'd said to a friend in Detroit.[16]

Few of the passengers who had boarded Tiger 923 at New Jersey's McGuire Air Force Base had had a choice in their mode of travel. Though technically a civilian flight, Flying Tiger Line's client was the Air Force's Military Air Transport Service. Apart from the airline's Atlantic region superintendent, who would disembark at the refueling stopover in Gander, Newfoundland, everyone else en route to Frankfurt was active duty or retired military, or a dependent.

The passengers included Army private first class Fred "Little Animal" Gazelle, 22, of Pasadena. As he walked past the Lockheed's weatherbeaten fuselage and four rattling engines, he said to his pal Samuel Vasquez: "Is that the plane we're leaving on?"[17]

"Yeah," said the 21-year-old paratrooper from Phoenix.

"That ain't gonna make it across."

Tiger 923[18] was a flying melting pot that included green recruits from big cities and small towns assigned to the Army's vaunted 82nd Airborne, the "All-American Division"; decorated veterans of WWII and the Korean War; a recent immigrant from Mexico; a Puerto Rican gynecologist; and elementary schoolchildren from Hawaii. The ages ranged from 9 to 54. Six couples were traveling together.

Bob Eldred, 48, of East Dennis, Massachusetts, was mixing business with pleasure. He'd made it across 18 years earlier on a different plane. Now he was just trying to get comfortable in his seat.

The retired Army captain hadn't been comfortable in many seats since mid-June 1944, when, in defiance of an explicit order that no one from his unit cross into German-held French territory, the artillery lieutenant "borrowed" a Jeep and drove it alone in a desperate attempt to resupply some paratroopers who were pinned down in a village outside Saint-Lô.[19] Before Eldred could reach the young soldiers, however, five Iron Cross–emblazoned Tiger tanks rumbled out of the hedgerows and unleashed their "monstrous ordnance." Eldred recalled:

> *My Jeep was thrown up in the air and 80 mm shell fragments went through my left knee destroying the knee joint, and another went*

under my right shoulder blade. That piece is still there. I found myself lying in the center of the roadway with my left foot on my stomach. The only thing holding my lower leg to the rest of my body was a narrow strip of flesh with no bone in between. That had all been blown out. Arterial blood was pouring out.

After a long stay in an Army hospital, his wife Edna nursed him back to health. After the war, when he flew alone on buying trips for his Cape Cod–based Windswept Antiques, he would compose and mail Edna sonnets, along with pen-and-ink drawings of the two of them in native garb. He missed her terribly, and the former high school commercial subjects teacher cherished the expressions of love.

Now that the 54-year-old Edna had retired, 18-year-old Bob Jr. was away at Middlebury College, and 17-year-old Karen was a high school senior boarding at Northfield School, Bob Sr. wanted to travel as a couple. Tiger 923 seemed like a perfect test run. Also, given the fact that the Bronze Star winner was, inconceivably, the lowest man on the totem pole when it came to free retiree travel (priority 14 of 14), it was rare for two seats to open up on a charter, so he felt he had better grab it. Finally, he could save a lot of money on the Jaguar he'd had his heart set on for years: buying it overseas saved money on tariffs, they'd forgo train fare, and Edna could help drive.

However, while on board and awaiting departure in New Jersey, Eldred read in *Time* magazine how charters operated by the likes of Flying Tiger Line were transporting America's soldiers despite serious safety concerns.[20] The unsettling exposé was consistent with what he had seen with his own two eyes on the tarmac: scratches and dents on the plane's aluminum exterior, and, inside, vinyl strips hanging from the ceiling, along with curls of yellowing tape. He wished he'd read the piece sooner. Maybe he would've sprung for a pair of Pan Am tickets. But all he could do now was stare wistfully at "the tarmac lined with beautiful gleaming Boeing 707s," compared to which his Lockheed Super Constellation looked "kind of . . . oh, second hand . . . crummy."[21]

Army major Carl Richard Elander, MD, 31, didn't need to read *Time* to be worried. All it took was for Dick to learn that his and his wife's flight to Germany was operated by "the Flying Tigers, which didn't please me because I'd heard much about their unreliability."[22]

As West Point's chief ophthalmologist, in close contact with Army brass, what Elander had heard about included the two mysterious disasters earlier in the year. No one knew why the Tiger charters had crashed within hours of one another, thousands of miles apart. All that was known for certain was that 107 had died, including 93 Army Rangers, and both of the doomed planes were Lockheed Super H Constellations. He'd wanted to fly a nonstop military jet to Madrid, their ultimate destination, but when he picked up his tickets he discovered that he, his wife Lois, 32, and the other West Point couple with whom they were vacationing were booked on a civilian prop that first had to stop in Gander for fuel and a new crew; then they'd have to collect their luggage and change planes in Frankfurt.

Notwithstanding the reservations of Eldred, Elander, and others, most spirits were high, in part because the soldiers were unchaperoned: their commanding officer was getting to Germany by some other means, though no one knew why or how. Banter was good-natured despite the racial strife roiling America. The Mason-Dixon Line didn't hold at 21,000 feet, at least not in the military, as an African-American Army private from Georgia enjoyed the not-separate-and-truly-equal seats, lavatories, and tray tables; beside a Yugoslavian-American private who enjoyed not being in an Austrian displaced persons camp; beside a newlywed from the State of Baden-Württemberg being served a Coke and pretzels by a newlywed from the State of Michigan.

Stuttgart native Helga Groves, 18, had married her U.S. Army sergeant husband at age 17. They were returning to John's base after her first visit to meet her in-laws in Cincinnati.

Newlywed Elizabeth Sims was flying in violation of the Flying Tiger Line policy that all stewardesses had to be single. When Betty tendered her resignation and informed the personnel department that Tiger 923 would be her last flight, the 10-year veteran failed to mention she'd gotten hitched five weeks earlier.

Captain Murray was more than twice as old as many of the young, eagle-eyed paratroopers in their spiffy new leather boots. His eyeglasses made him look more college professor than elite warrior. His uniform looked off: that's because, unlike the rest of the flight crew, his thrift had compelled him to buy an off-the-rack Sears suit instead of pay for the overpriced Tiger company store outfit.[23] Murray didn't look the least bit special to the Special Forces, but looks deceived.

In Gaelic, "Murray" means "seafarer" or "one who's settled by the sea." John Desmond Murray Jr. had fared well in the sea: as a sailor, swimmer, scuba diver, and seaplane pilot. The Chicago native even settled in a home on Oyster Bay.

He'd sought to carve out his own identity early. Known as the sort always to side with David versus Goliath, he'd survived typhoid fever at 16 and never backed down in the CYO boxing ring, no matter the foe or the scorecard. And according to his elder son, though his own father had been a pilot, "Dad hated the 'junior' designation with a passion. He dropped it when his father passed away and insisted I not repeat the offense on any son of mine."[24]

But the Tiger pilot felt his character was mainly forged in Detroit during the Depression. Between chemical engineering classes at the University of Detroit, he worked on the "fast line" at the Ford plant, where negligence could've cost him or someone else an arm or much worse. He was ethically and intellectually toughened by the University of Detroit's Jesuit teachers, physically tested on its gridiron as a linebacker, captained its top-notch flying club that beat Harvard and much better-financed schools, and as a 23-year-old flight instructor received some singular instruction of his own.

On a Sunday in 1941, an ice storm suddenly whited out the sky. His student panicked. Murray took control, flew semi-blind until he discerned an avenue of escape, then banked his two-seater Funk 90 "almost vertical" between some pine trees but into a web of high-voltage lines.

Thousands lost power, the plane was totaled, and a sheared-off wing bolt knocked him out and severed his right ear. Though an Ann Arbor hospital intern sewed it back on a bit clumsily and "it stuck out like a semaphore," his hearing wasn't impaired.[25]

His grit and improvisation served him well in the Army's Air Transport Command during WWII, where he flew many snowy, grueling sorties to and from Canada, delivering the oil to the Lockheed bombers that younger Army Air Corps pilots flew out of Newfoundland. After V-E and V-J Days, though armed with a degree in chemical engineering, Murray chose the wild blue yonder over the Bunsen burner. However, given the fact that Uncle Sam had taught 500,000 how to fly, Murray had a hard time finding work.

In late 1947, he began picking up WWII surplus German plane parts from Corsica and Slovakia and flying them into a desert airstrip in Palestine. Though a newspaper lists him as employed by American Airlines Murray also flew for a clandestine New York–DC syndicate formed to create some semblance of an Israeli Air Force in anticipation of the fury that would erupt when David Ben-Gurion declared Israeli statehood in May 1948; at least according to one scholar, American Airlines was also then involved in Israeli Defense Force–related black ops.[26] Whether or not he was moonlighting, it wasn't your typical American flight: Murray packed a sidearm, flew at night, and tried to avoid contact with the Egyptian Spitfires and antiaircraft batteries. He didn't always succeed. When confronted by U.S. State Department officials who said the holes on the underside of his plane told them Murray was running guns in violation of President Truman's executive order banning such shipments to Holocaust survivors, the 30-year-old said, "What, those? I just got hit by hailstones."[27] Murray also flew Yemeni Jews from pogroms triggered by Israel's founding, skirted East German MIGs so as to airlift food to blockaded Berliners, and braved snowstorms and T-55 tanks to fly anti-Soviet protestors out of Central Europe.

Thinking it made sense for a young husband and father of two to seek employment that was less hazardous and closer to home, he went to work for a small intra–New York State airline, making $360/month, logging 20-hour days. Aspiring for better pay and working conditions, he and a friend launched an airline. When it flopped in 1950, he joined Flying Tiger Line.

During the 1950s he had fathered two more children, worked hard, earned good money, and had a reputation as one of the most colorful characters in an outfit famous for its rainbow of personalities. He was especially famous for an adventure beneath the Hudson River and for his Melville, Long Island, farm. The New York papers wrote about how Murray bought a burro in New Jersey but, because Delores refused to sit in the back seat and munched the upholstery, the pilot entered Lincoln Tunnel with her in the front seat of his Ford Sunliner convertible, top down, braying at toll booth operators.[28] Delores the burro joined Joker the horse, goats Eva and Zsa Zsa, 10 pigs, the 15 sheep sheared by a Farmingdale Agricultural College student, and the 2,000 chickens that 15-year-old Kathleen fed, so 14-year-old John Patrick could collect the eggs, which 42-year-old Dorothy would then sell to a local co-op.

Pilots bid for flights based on seniority, and while there were often bidding wars for Paris or Rome, Murray (no. 51 out of 559 Tiger pilots) shied away from the glitter and run-of-the-mill. "There was no lack of excitement," John Patrick would later write to his daughter.[29] Murray flew out the Korean orphan babies no one but Americans seemed to want, flew relief supplies into and refugees out of bellicose Communist countries that tried to prevent him from landing, and often returned from Africa with "drums, masks, machetes and other exotic gifts."

He was a tough customer but he had a tender heart. At President Eisenhower's urging, and to avoid a provocative connection to the U.S. military, the Air Force contracted with Flying Tigers, and Murray bid to fly "refugees from the 1956 Hungarian revolution across the Atlantic to New York. One group gave Dad a small candle and candleholder with a ribbon in traditional Hungarian colors as a token of gratitude for flying them to the U.S. A small gesture from a people who had nothing, but immense in its simplicity and sincerity. He was deeply touched."

Murray hit his stride in the early 1960s starting with the arrival of his fifth child in 1961. When a newly built home on Oyster Bay came on the market, much as it pained the family to say goodbye to Delores, Joker, Zsa Zsa and Eva, neither Kathleen nor John Patrick would miss chasing after the pigs "that regularly escaped confinement and raided the local vegetable farms."[30] The chance to walk straight from their backyard and set off in a sailboat, go for a swim whenever they felt like it, and dig fresh clams for soup and pasta sauce made the decision an easy one for the entire family.

Come September 1962, Murray wrote: "Truly the good Lord must smile on the transport pilot."[31] He loved the fact that, unlike his attorney, doctor, and Wall Street friends and neighbors, "once on the ground there was no gnawing worry of what might happen tomorrow. There was no difficult law case, serious medical problem or office politics to provoke sleepless nights. An airline pilot has no problems to take home."

What the Tiger pilot had was a big mortgage, five high-spirited kids, and a wife who despite her strength of character and razor-sharp intellect often felt overwhelmed, especially when one or more of the clan had an ear infection or worse and John was halfway around the world. So the engineer had recently drawn up a new blueprint for life. While it included having another go at being both a farmer and an entrepreneur, he wasn't interested in trying to launch some new airline in competition with TWA founder Howard Hughes.

One of Murray's aspirations could hardly get any more down-to-earth: a Christmas tree farm. If he was successful, he could fly less and have more say over his schedule, and Dorothy would have some time to paint and pursue the journalism career she'd shelved, while he'd have more time to talk Irish history and politics with Kathleen; teach John Patrick how to drive; toss the football with Steven, 7; fish with Ellen, 3; and sail with 14-month-old Barbara, whom the pilot could already tell was a seafarer after his own heart.

The now-silenced and seemingly false fire alarm wasn't Tiger 923's initial setback. Though it had been fully refueled in Gander by 3:45 p.m., it was delayed because the ground crew hadn't drained the sumps, the plane couldn't leave until after a VIP had arrived, and the airport had but one runway long enough to accommodate the arrival and departure. The 76 passengers and crew members found various ways to bide their time in the largely vacant terminal at what had once been one of the world's busiest airports until the jet engine made stopovers in Newfoundland a thing of the past.

Many strolled around as if at the Guggenheim beneath the vividly colored 70-foot avant-garde mural *Bird of Flight*, one of the reasons the National Trust of Canada called the airport's lounge the country's "most important modernist room."[32] Others snoozed in the ritzy furniture "considered glamorous for its mid-20th century installation," or stared out through the plate-glass windows at the flat, forested land that abutted glacial-blue Gander Lake, up into what had been upon arrival an auspicious sky.

Running low on smokes, Army private first class Art Gilbreth, 22, from Big Bear Lake, California, went looking for a vending machine.[33] When he found one selling cigarettes beside another selling life insurance, he thought about making his mother, Opal, a beneficiary, but as both items cost a quarter and all he had on him was 25 cents, he bought a pack of Winstons.

Stewardess Carol Gould of Lyndhurst, New Jersey, liked Newfoundland because the "Goofy Newfies" were a bit like her: they didn't take themselves or life too seriously.[34] Also, the 22-year-old liked a guy in Gander who let her use his truck when she was on a long layover, but as he and his truck were gone this time, she couldn't give a tour to Jacqueline Brotman, 24, of Chicago, who, having been hired in July, had only logged 92 hours of flying time. "There's a lot of moose around here, Jackie," said Gould, standing in the airport cafeteria's buffet line, eyeing some desserts. Brotman didn't smile. Gould said: "I know . . . the selection's not the greatest."

"That's not it," said Brotman. "I just have a very bad feeling about this flight." Gould smiled. "Don't worry. Everything will be fine."[35]

PFC Fred Caruso, 21, of Spring Valley, New Jersey, shared Brotman's sentiment. The engines shook and spat fire pretty much the entire flight up the Eastern seaboard. Then the paratrooper witnessed an altercation.[36] He didn't know what it was about, but someone was mad. While the white shirt and dark tie told Caruso it was a man, the distance prevented him from discerning identities. (There were eight flight crew members, including the four who'd flown the McGuire-to-Gander leg, plus several guys pumping fuel and checking the engines.) Caruso saw yelling and finger-pointing but the guys were separated before it came to blows.

John Murray hated late departures because impatience was part of the Tiger DNA.[37] In 1941, after the U.S. Army Air Corps had refused to promote Texan Claire Chennault (because he kept telling his superiors they were lazy fools who preferred drinking gin-and-tonics in the officers mess to the exertion of progress and innovation), he quit the Corps and persuaded 111 other U.S. Marine, Navy, and Army pilots to join him and fly for a different country: China. President Chiang Kai-shek was offering $600/month plus $250 for every downed Japanese plane, versus the U.S. Army's $60/month and no bonus.[38] The Americans took to the skies two weeks after Pearl Harbor when U.S. morale was at low ebb.[39] Now it was Japan's turn to be surprised as the "Flying Tigers" emerged from their camouflaged bamboo hangars in the jungle to rout Tojo's pilots.

In 1943, the Pentagon, which had scoffed at the volunteers' prospects, insisted it assume control of the Tigers. They said negative, and disbanded.

In 1945, in LA, a dozen Tigers purchased an old plane, hangared it in an enlarged, converted two-car garage, and founded a cargo airline. Their vision was to ship California produce east and connect the U.S. with booming postwar Asia. Their first payload was some grapes to New Jersey.

When Murray joined in 1950, the airline was fighting to survive, battling with 300 other U.S. airlines. Competition was cutthroat. Pilots were paid a pittance.

By 1962 the scrappy outfit was the country's only fully transatlantic cargo airline, often among the top three passenger airlines, the Pentagon's no. 1 subcontractor, and did more humanitarian work than any other airline in the world, much of it pro bono. And while most pilots flew things like grapes to Newark, church groups to Rome, and soldiers to Seoul, others, including Murray, helped the company carve out a clandestine niche: off-the-books missions for the CIA.[40]

The airline's impressive roster of aviators included "Miss Flying Tiger" Diana Bixby, one of the first female commercial pilots, and Elgen Long, the first to fly solo around the world via both poles. Time and time again, in hot spots around the world, after the Postal Service and the Pentagon balked, Tigers would unhesitatingly say "Wheels up!" and do whatever necessary, be it flying 30 green Army paratroopers to Germany or perfumed letters to lonely leathernecks dug in along the 38th Parallel on the Korean peninsula. A comment often heard by grateful American GIs wherever stationed was: "Nobody brings in the mail like those Tiger birds."[41]

Though Murray lacked the fame of peers like Bixby or icons like Chuck Yeager, his logbooks were also replete with tales of derring-do. The airline's motto—"Anything, Anytime, Anywhere"—could have been his personal credo, emblazoned on his family crest.[42]

The slogan wasn't Madison Avenue hooey. It captured the honor-among-mercenaries ethos, like how one Tiger friend flew Spitfires for Egypt against his friend who flew Spitfires for Israel, and when Egypt's gun-for-hire noticed his adversary was also a veteran of Burma, rather than shoot him down, he gave him the thumbs-up and peeled away.[43] It's why the Pentagon relied on the Tigers to supply and maintain the vital and infamous nuclear defense "Dew Line" on the North Pole: no one else dared or had the skills or stubbornness. Perhaps most of all the motto captured the Tiger sense of duty, which Murray interpreted as: *If JFK feels it's important to rush some Army Airborne to the Berlin Wall, then I intend to do everything in my power to get those boys there, ASAP.*[44]

Sure, a drop or two of pride sometimes adulterated the Tiger virtues, but hubris rarely got in the way of duty, as Murray proved on a flight from San Antonio. "While comfortably seated in the men's room" at the rear of a C-46, he could tell that one of the plane's two engines had just failed and he could sense that the copilot had commenced to feather the wrong propellor.[45] "The sudden unearthly quiet was broken by my frantic 'gangway' as I charged up the aisle, with my trousers at ankle level, hurtled through the companionway door and with hands outstretched jammed every control on the pedestal to its full forward position," then feathered the correct prop. He had no problem making a spectacle of himself for safety's sake.

And he loved irony. So despite the aggravating delay at Gander Airport, he chuckled at the frilly bunting and long red carpet on which frenetic airport and city officials scurried about, hands on heads, trying to keep the wind from mussing their combed-over, Brylcreemed hair.

While he may have used a ballpoint pen to plumb the depth of a tire tread or run his fingers along some wing bolts to feel for any sign of oxidation, as opposed to relying on the absence of visible corrosion, for the most part he debriefed those whose job it was to make sure his plane was airworthy. It was mostly the flight engineer's responsibility. But he also checked the originating Tiger pilot's logbook, which had no entries of any significance, and talked with the airline's Atlantic Region superintendent, who said "the engines worked very smoothly on the flight."[46] After reviewing the weather forecast folder prepared by the Canadian Meteorological Service and the weight and balance figures prepared by his copilot, Murray signed the manifest.

Also, as this was his first trip with Bob Parker, Jim Garrett, and Samuel Nicholson, he used the time to acquaint himself with his 27-year-old copilot, 30-year-old flight engineer, and 32-year-old navigator. The four men talked about where they lived, their families, and the New York Yankees' pennant prospects.

Murray took an immediate liking to Hard Luck Sam.[47] Though the navigator was the only non–Long Islander in cockpit (he lived in tiny Dallas, Pennsylvania), like Murray, Sam was self-effacing, had a dry wit, loved motorcycles, and had cheated death many times.[48]

At 4:51 p.m., with the storm clouds darkening the dusk prematurely, the ground crew removed the chocks and signaled the cockpit. Murray shifted the brake pressure from parking (emergency) to normal and, once he'd gotten the all-clear signal from the marshaller, began to roll down the runway.

He didn't get far. A red light on the control panel flashed. Moments later Sims rapped on the cockpit door, entered, and reported "that the main passenger door seemed to have an air leak," which she'd tried but failed to rectify.[49] Murray stopped the plane in the middle of the runway by reapplying brake pressure, then told Garrett to accompany Sims and try to fix the problem.

Once beside the main entry-exit, Garrett grabbed a blanket from an overhead bin, wrapped it around the locking handle, and knotted it tightly. He then "yanked on it and sling shot the handle to the latched position."[50] But as Garrett could see the tarmac through a crack along the seam, he knew the door wasn't sealed. As he headed up to the cockpit to discuss the next step, paratrooper Sammy Vasquez, who was seated across from the door and had been watching the jerry-rigging, elbowed Little Animal, who was sitting beside him, and said: "They Mickey Moused it."[51]

Once Garrett was back in the cockpit and had debriefed his colleagues, the men discussed whether the issue was a "no-go" item or just a temporary glitch that was likely to self-correct.[52] While the cockpit warning light had gone out, Garrett could see and feel (from the wind snaking through the crack) that the main entry-exit door hadn't sealed. But he felt it would as soon as the plane pressurized. His colleagues agreed.

If Garrett was wrong, they'd all know soon, as once airborne the sound of an unsealed door was "deafening."[53] If it didn't seal, they'd simply return to Gander.

Murray released the brake pedals and resumed taxiing. The wheels were up at 5:09.

The main door warning light remained off through climb-out. No wind screamed through the crack. The door must have sealed properly, they inferred.

Three hours later, Art Gilbreth was sitting behind the Hawaiian mother and her two young daughters in row 17, along the aisle, on the right side of the cabin. It was his seventh plane trip. The six previous times he'd leapt out, yanked a ripcord, and floated to earth. When the Tiger 923 fire alarm rang, he wondered if he'd need to leap out again. But he thought more than worried: *Too bad my chute's in the cargo hold.*[54]

He'd been enjoying the well-behaved sisters' soft giggling and his more extroverted unit-mates' boasting. He laughed as Little Animal and the others in his unit tried to out-macho each other; trash-talked about ancestries, sports teams, and neighborhoods; and said they were looking forward to the "adventure" of crash-landing into a wild sea, then taking a raft "excursion" with stewardesses Gould, Sims, Brotman, or Ruth Mudd.[55]

The loud bell didn't put a damper on his trip because in his view Uncle Sam was just fulfilling his promise, and then some. The draw of the Army Airborne wasn't the $90/month wage but the adventure, which was priceless. "How many guys get to go through a fire alarm four miles up, a thousand from shore, at night?"

Though hailing from the forests of California, land of the lumberjack, prior to enlisting, he'd never felled a single tree. Instead he'd laid miles of oil pipeline connecting his home state and Oregon, doing some lifeguarding on the side. Lifting all that steel, concrete, and cable left him with a Paul Bunyan build, which enabled him to survive the Airborne's 85 percent washout rate and made him perfect for jumping out of planes, lugging 60 pounds of gear, fighting with tenacity and endurance, and doing all the other things the Army expected of its elite parachutists, whom the Nazis had called "devils in baggy pants."[56]

Gilbreth believed what the stewardesses were saying: that everything would be okay, the plane was rugged, and the pilot had been through this sort of thing many times. Recalling how the engines had flared up on the tarmac in New Jersey, then again in Gander, he thought: *It looks like fireworks. Nothing's gonna happen. We're just gonna have a great story to tell.*[57]

It didn't bother him that the plane wasn't exactly showroom new. It was still a lot better than he was used to. The old, creaky, drafty ones he leapt out of over Fort Bragg didn't even have seats (just web-strip benches), let alone tasty dinners and foxy flight attendants.

Plus, Gilbreth was looking forward to Germany because there wasn't much to look back to. He was so over sleeping through high school, telling kids not to run by the pool, tarring himself while laying down pipe, and the stifling North Carolina heat of Jump School, with his sadistic drill sergeant's yelling into his ear, disgusting cigar-spittle flying every which way.

And finally there was this: his girlfriend was so over him. But as he'd heard how hot the German girls were, and the Army sergeant's pretty 18-year-old wife was sitting right across the aisle, he was still looking forward to fishing in a different sea.

Another 18-year-old sat two rows ahead of Helga Groves, also by the window: Harold Lesane. Hal never faulted his parents for having moved the family from Jim Crow's South Carolina in the early '50s. But the

African-American from North Philly had experienced enough of cops like South Philly's Frank Rizzo to know the City of Brotherly Love was a false lure for brothers like him.

Hal's skin color wasn't the issue at Thomas Edison High School. Whites weren't barring him from entry, like the racist governor and others were James Meredith at Ole Miss. Hal wasn't a big talker but a classmate spoke for him: "When I went to Edison in 1962, I could not get in without fighting . . . I had to fight for 16 days straight to get into Edison and get through at least four different gangs."[58] The gangs didn't care about the color of Lesane's skin, just what "corner" he was from. It didn't help that Hal hailed from a backwoods corner in The Palmetto State. His drawl made him more of a punching bag. But having had to fight for attention, food at the table, and use of the shower with his 10 siblings, 7 of whom were boys, the quiet, smiling Baptist could take a punch. And throw one.

His skin pigmentation only mattered after school or sports practice, when he'd be stopped by the police and peppered with belligerent, belittling questions. If Lesane "mouthed off," he was lucky if he got thrown up against a squad car in front of his classmates and frisked; unlucky if he got thrown into a Red Ace, driven down a back alley, or dropped off at an Italian corner in Rizzo's neighborhood miles from home.

Given the gangs, police, and an unemployment rate three times as high as elsewhere in Philly, it's little wonder more than half of Edison's students dropped out. When they saw the slightest opportunity for a better life—a job in DC or the Army, they took it, as one of Lesane's brothers had done two years prior. Hal was really looking forward to reuniting with his 20-year-old brother in Germany, as well as teasing him in classic sibling rivalry fashion by noting how while Henry was just a "foot soldier" who'd been drafted into the infantry, Hal had enlisted in the storied Army Airborne, the heroes of The Battle of The Bulge, had made it through advanced infantry training and Jump School, and now had the brass lapel wings to show for it.

Lesane didn't know what lay in store. He just figured fighting overseas in a Cold War had to be better than fighting the many hot wars back home. Like the other 29 paratroopers, he didn't know much about his assignment, just that he'd be living at a place called Fort Lee in West Germany, thanks to the Marshall Plan, rather than Marshall Street in North Philly.

Raúl Acevedo was one of the few passengers aboard Tiger 923 who'd had a choice as to his mode of travel. The 22-year-old from Mexico now felt he'd made a really bad one.

He was all set to go by ship to a plum posting with a base quartermaster in Germany as a medic-in-training, but when an announcement came over the PA system at McGuire saying some seats were available on Tiger 923 and anybody interested could apply, Acevedo did and got the upgrade. *Some upgrade*, he now thought.[59]

He was the only Army PFC who wasn't a U.S. citizen and the only one not a paratrooper. The Airborne guys had received specialized survival training, he knew, and were headed off to be America's tip of the spear and, he supposed, parachute behind enemy lines (East German) in the event the Cold War turned hot, like they'd done in WWII, when they were the first combat troops to fight on German soil.

When his induction notice arrived, he wouldn't have broken the law had he returned to Mexico, only if he'd tried to stay and dodge the draft. He was staying with his older brother at the time in San Pedro, north of LA. "Raúl liked it here from the beginning," said Refugio. "He kept coming on a tourist visa and returning to Zacatecas to assure our parents he would enter medical school soon." When "the Army called . . . I advised him this was the time to keep his promise and return home and to school. But he was a man now and he chose the Army."[60]

Returning had never crossed Acevedo's mind. He wanted U.S. citizenship. "It's a fair price to pay. Plus, I'm not headed to the front or combat. I'll be a supply clerk working at a hospital, far out of harm's way."[61]

But now harm seemed a lot closer. Still, given how relaxed the stewardesses appeared to be, it didn't seem like the end of the world. At least big hunks of ice were no longer thumping against the exterior and he no longer heard the engines growl as the pilot tried to break free of the storm. So things weren't all bad.

Acevedo hadn't faced many storms in life. He was tall, trim, and very easy on the eyes. He'd lived a charmed existence. His father was the mayor of Zacatecas, a PRI party bigwig, and the proprietor of a successful general store. His mother had impeccable taste and was a fierce and flawless social gatekeeper.

Thanks to the surrounding area's vast network of once-fecund silver mines, the provincial capital of 44,000 (375 miles north of Mexico City) was once among the world's wealthiest cities, and thanks to its pink neoclassical mansions, quaint cobblestone streets, dazzling and ubiquitous bougainvillea, and whimsical spouting fountains, it still appealed to many. But Zacatecas didn't appeal to its mayor's sixth of seven children. It was too cloistered. Raúl much preferred the sexy bustle of Graumann's Chinese Theater in Hollywood to the cosseted processions to his hometown's famous baroque cathedral. So he defied his father and slipped across the border.

Like so many immigrants he took whatever jobs came his way, worked hard, and studied on the side. His first job was at a battery plant, where acid ruined his skin. He was drafted while packing tuna fish and taking international relations courses at UCLA.

He especially liked one of StarKist's benefits: he was the only unmarried male out of 48 as against "nearly a thousand young women employees who reported to me every day. Most were resident aliens like me but from Yugoslavia. Most were gorgeous. Many asked me to help them with their English!" He'd had girlfriends in Zacatecas and Monterrey, but in LA, "I really hit the jackpot."

Now, however, a thousand exotic women was a distant memory. Now a provincial life didn't sound so bad after all.

Rachel Hoopi's background was also provincial: a rural Hawaiian village. Before the fire alarm erupted, the trip to Germany had been a dream come true.

The 31-year-old was unique in several ways. Hoopi was the only one of the seven wives aboard not traveling with their husband, the only one traveling with children, and she was 2,500 miles farther from home than anyone else.

She'd boarded in a joyous mood, full of gratitude. Though it was open seating and the cabin was divided into two- and three-seat rows, she was able to grab an empty three-seat row for herself and her daughters, Luana, 9, and Uilani, 11.

Hoopi had been pleading with the Army for two years to allow her and her girls to join her husband, Bernard, who was stationed in Munich. She was on Tiger 923 because the brass finally relented. Now she wished she hadn't been such an effective pest.

Seven-year-old Tom Elander was home in West Point with his 5-year-old sister, Jill, and 3-year-old brother, Troy. Their parents, Dick and Lois Elander, were glad of that.

Dick was handsome, diffident, lanky, and laconic; Lois stunning, confident, and chipper, with a smile like a supernova. Before the alarm they'd spent most of their time catching up on sleep (they'd had all of 3 hours over the previous 24), playing gin rummy, or reading *Atlantic Monthly*. Major Elander removed the laminated "Ditching Drill" card from his seat-back pocket, read the instructions several times, but then, "irritated by its morbid message . . . leaned forward and turned it around."[62]

He now felt the scuttlebutt he'd heard about the unreliability of Flying Tiger Line wasn't idle gossip. He really regretted not springing for a jet, though doing so would've eaten up some leave and more money than a major's salary could comfortably afford. But two days and a few hundred bucks now seemed a cheap fare indeed.

The last thing the U.S. Military Academy's top eye doctor had wanted was another dose of stress. When the superintendent, dean of military instruction, or one of the generals who taught at the Academy or were always passing through called at 7:45 p.m. on a Sunday evening to ask if they could swing by his office for a routine exam in 15 minutes, Elander couldn't say: "As my wife and I just sat down to watch *The Ed Sullivan Show*, can we meet tomorrow?" He had to drop everything and obey.

Not that he complained. He felt honored to be part of such a noble institution, blessed to have a God-given talent, and humbled to be walking in the footsteps of all the great Army leaders who'd soared into outer space or otherwise served their nation by saving the world from tyranny, fascism, Nazism, and, now, communism. It was hard to be a good general, like Omar Bradley; a good astronaut, like Buzz Aldrin (he cross-commissioned in the Air Force); or a good president, like Dwight Eisenhower—West Pointers all—if you couldn't see. While maybe not to the moon or 1600 Pennsylvania Avenue, everyone knew Dick Elander was going places too.

Everyone also knew that the smartest place he'd gone thus far was down on one knee to propose to Lois, in 1954. The Phi Beta Kappa and former flutist with the Seattle Symphony had effortlessly transitioned to become the Academy's most sought-after dinner party hostess.

Though on account of her Hollywood beauty and Emily Post perfectionism some of the other Army wives were a bit conflicted, their husband-generals and -colonels put up a common front and seemed less concerned about what was going on in Southeast Asia than scoring an invite to Lois' next dinner party. They were a lot more fun and far less expensive than a trip to the City for a Broadway show and dinner. Fortunately, the Seattle transplants threw lots of parties: often twice a week, when they'd play host to four or five other couples.

Lois wasn't trying to impress anyone, hoping to advance her husband's career. She simply loved to cook and entertain and was masterful at both. After everyone had had their fill of her delicious beef stroganoff, millet bread, and blueberry-rhubarb cake, she'd regale them by playing Gershwin on the piano or Bach on her flute.[63] And while such feasting and festivities would've bankrupted other young couples with five mouths to feed on a major's salary, she knew how to stretch her S&H Green Stamps.

Lois and Dick looked more suited for a TV commercial aboard a Boeing 707 jet, zipping across the Atlantic, as opposed to aboard a banged-up Lockheed prop plane that needed to take a breather and swap out crews before reaching its final destination. They looked more the sort to have opted for white tablecloths, champagne, and prime rib, roasted and carved on board like in Pan Am's Clipper Class, as opposed to paper napkins, pretzels, and Cokes.

Their traveling companions were just as impressive. Naomi Devlin, 34, held a doctorate in psychology, as did her husband, John, 42. Like Major Elander, Major Devlin was part of the elite West Point medical staff: only his field was psychological research, including shell shock. Prior to attending Penn State (where he met Naomi), he'd not just flown B-17 bombers during WWII, for which he'd received the prestigious Air Medal for valor, but also survived a ditching in the Adriatic.

The four close friends had been very grateful the brass had granted them leave to travel, for the academic year had just begun and it was often the busiest time for West Point's medical staff. Now they wished the Army had been more typically bureaucratic.

Stewardess Carol Gould hadn't been helping her three colleagues hand out drinks and snacks because she'd snuck off to grab some sleep as soon as Tiger 923 cleared the storm. She was so exhausted, she slept right through the loud alarm.

She'd boarded in New Jersey half-asleep. "I'd just climbed into bed when the phone rang at four thirty in the morning."[64] It was Tiger crew scheduling calling to beg her to fill in for a colleague who'd taken ill. Had Gould not come to the rescue, Tiger 923 would've been scrubbed because the Federal Aviation Agency required four stewardesses even though just 68 occupied the 100-seat configuration.

At McGuire, chief stewardess Sims had assured Gould she could sleep the entire flight if she wanted. "The three of us girls can handle things fine."[65]

It's conceivable that Sims had eyed Gould with a bit of envy, but no jealousy, according to all who knew her. Gould was 22, Sims, 32: the mandatory retirement age. Though at one time all stewardesses had to be registered nurses, Hugh Hefner's criteria now prevailed over Florence Nightingale's. So the highly competent Sims had to quit for two reasons: she was too old, and she wasn't single.

Sims didn't have much recourse.[66] As for another airline: why bother? Though she was slender, pretty, and blond, the endless stream of 18-year-old Miss Tulsas and Miss Chattanoogas made the industry's stewardess acceptance rate lower than the Harvard student acceptance rate.

And while American Airlines began allowing stewardesses to marry in 1957, often to their own insistent pilots, the age and marriage prohibitions remained in force at most airlines until struck down by a federal court in 1968.[67]

So Tiger 923 would be Sims' final flight, at least professionally. Once back in the Big Apple, her commercial pilot husband would represent the family in the sky.

There was no bitterness. Though she'd had the flying bug really bad, though she'd quit Wayne State University with less than a year to go before getting her degree and returned to the skies, though she'd quit the two terrestrial jobs in which she'd dabbled to placate her Highland Park, Michigan, parents who'd begged her to settle down close to home, Sims had had a good run, and she was now looking forward to being a wife, homemaker, and, God willing, mother.

Gould also had the flying bug. She'd attended Rutherford Secretarial School but found her work with United Airlines, then Frontier, then Flying Tiger, more suited to her personality. She preferred Flying Tiger Line to her former gigs. First, while United and Frontier employed more than two stewardesses for every pilot, given the Tiger focus on freight, it employed three pilots for each stewardess. "Now those numbers are more like it."[68] Gould also liked the potluck adventure of not knowing where she was off to next, or whom the passengers might be. Rather than the same humdrum New York–to–Boston shuttle, she might be taking GIs to Seoul one day, seminarians to Rome the next, then Roy Rogers and Trigger from LA to Chicago.

Like Sims, Gould was also a catch. She was comely and ebullient, reminiscent of Mary Tyler Moore. Her olive skin and big brown eyes added a sultry mystique to the easygoing way she'd laugh along with the guys who, once they learned her mom was born in Syria, would say things like "Hey Carol, what's it like riding a camel to work?"[69]

Unlike secret newlywed Sims, however, Gould was still available. Unfortunately for the paratroopers, the competition was fierce. Even heartthrob-singer Johnny Cash had tried to pick her up, but she'd declined his invitation to rendezvous backstage after a concert in Phoenix.

The main reason Gould had agreed to sub was the double pay. She was saving up to buy a car. She hated having to rely on men to drive her hither and yon.

But Murray's being the captain was a plus. He was her favorite pilot. "He's such a gentleman!" she'd told Jackie Brotman when she'd asked what he was like.[70]

Gould and the pilot had a lot in common. They loved traveling to exotic destinations but also enjoyed spending quiet time at home with their families. They adored animals. They were thrifty. And their Catholic upbringing strongly influenced their lives.

Though he was twice her age, she found him attractive. Gould liked Murray's shy smile, short hair the color of Irish brown bread, and piercing blue eyes. His off-kilter right ear added a rakish appeal, she thought.

But both knew implicitly where to draw the line. Gould knew lots of pilots who spent more time fooling around than flying, but Murray wasn't one of them. (She knew most Tigers were great guys but also knew others whose loutish ways couldn't be compensated for by quintuple pay.[71] She liked to party, but she had no interest in joining the Mile-High Club.) Plus, Gould would never be what some Other Woman had been to her family: a home-wrecker who'd forced her mom and 5-year-old Carol to move from their beloved Carney home "into an abandoned shoe store across the street from a chemical plant that spewed foul-smelling, eye-itching smoke. And I had asthma."[72]

Gould's Tiger 923 sleeping arrangements weren't ideal: two vacant seats at the back of the plane, beside the Mickey Moused main cabin door. While two small Murphy bed–like bunks were curtained off in the cockpit against the port bulkhead, behind the navigator station and across from the galley, they could have strings attached. On a prior trip she'd been awakened by the shirr of curtains, then startled and repulsed by a male crew member who had slipped under the blanket beside her, uninvited. Gould wasn't taking any chances this time.

Brotman shook Gould's shoulders. "Wake up! There's a fire in one of the engines!"[73]

Gould didn't want to wake up. Domiciled in that hazy, not-quite-asleep-not-quite-awake borderland, her mind was playfully debating the morality and feasibility of dating two guys simultaneously and surreptitiously. But she yawned and got her bearings. "Huh?"

"A fire!"

"Oh," Gould began, her tone tolerant. "I'm sure they're just dumping fuel. Happens all the time." She was trying to be understanding because the rookie was a nice girl, an earnest girl, and now a really nervous girl. "Plus, I didn't hear any fire alarm. Did you?"

Brotman nodded. "But it went out."

"Well then, see? Relax." Gould tufted her pillow, lowered her head, and shut her eyes.

Seconds later someone yelled, "Fire!"[74] Brotman said, "See! It's no fuel dump!"

"I'll have a look." Gould headed down the aisle.

She had only made it two rows when a hand shot out and clamped onto her forearm. "We're falling down!" cried Helga Groves, her Upper Rhine accent thick with emotion.

"There, there . . . relax," said Gould, smiling at the newlywed, then at her American GI husband, who'd pulled the stewardess aside before departing from New Jersey to confide that his bride was terrified of flying. "We're not going anywhere, except back to your home country."

She compassionately pried off Groves' hand and made her way to row 9, where, after saying "Excuse me" to a paratrooper, she leaned across his lap and looked out into the nighttime sky. Though the engine farthest along the right wing (no. 4) was enveloped by a routine gaseous blue penumbra, the one closer in (no. 3) was spitting wild, red-orange flames. Gould trembled as she backed her way into the aisle. She glanced about for Sims. Spotting her near the galley, she made her way over to the chief stewardess.

Sims was smiling at the time, comparing hairdos with the two little Hawaiian girls who were on their way to see the daddy they'd not seen for over two years. But she stopped smiling the moment she saw Gould's ashen face. Sims went to have a look. After seeing the flames, she told her colleagues to reassure the passengers, to tell them that everything would be okay, that even if one engine was having difficulties the plane could easily fly on three; then she headed for the cockpit.

Fred Caruso wasn't buying the stewardess happy talk. He thought to himself: *An engine's on fire four miles up, and everything's okay? Please. I wasn't born yesterday!*[75]

He'd been daydreaming from his window seat behind the right wing when "in a flicker . . . my spell was broken . . . by the loudest shrieking godforsaken alarm I'd ever heard. First came orange sparks mixed among the blue glow of the exhaust. Then yellow and red sparks. Then the engine burst into flames. I could nearly touch it. Oh, my God . . . I hate fire."[76]

For him it was just another chapter in his Army Airborne nightmare. He felt gypped and trapped in a 30-month tour, bamboozled by a slick recruiter who'd lied to hit his quota of gullible college kids. "He knew a sucker when he saw one," Caruso said to some fellow suckers.[77]

He was missed back home: all the girls thought he was dreamy, what with his dirty-blond hair, brown eyes, and confident smile. He had a weightlifter's body: strong, slightly bowed legs, anvil-like torso, Popeye forearms, thick neck. The former lifeguard was one of the strongest men on board and one of the shortest, at 5'6".

He was likely the most obstreperous too, the product of a Sicilian-Neapolitan family whose ruling matriarch passed Old World Catholic judgment while moonlighting behind the parish priest's back to cast evil eyes and other hexes for a fee. Art Gilbreth, who'd trained with Caruso and was now seated five rows behind him, said: "You're trained to follow orders and stay alive but he wasn't very good at taking orders."[78]

Caruso had signed up for adventure but only after having been assured of a stateside posting so he could be near his girlfriend, pals from the neighborhood, the City. "Of course I only mean greater New York. No other place is worth jack."[79]

He'd quit Albany State Teachers College because his third dabbling in higher education had bored him as much as the first two, he realized he didn't have the patience to teach smart alecks like himself, and he felt it canny to volunteer for service in a unit barracked in the States rather than get drafted and shipped to a Korean hellhole. But the Army had outflanked him, sending him on a jinxed, defective plane to a German hellhole, along with more of the rubes he'd trained with in a sizzling summer Georgia hellhole.

Caruso didn't blame the stewardesses, however. He knew what it felt like being kept in the dark. As he told his folks when he phoned to say he'd not been granted leave to return home after all, as expected and per Standard Army Airborne Operating Procedure after Jump School graduation (September 18), for reasons that were never explained to him or any of his unit-mates: "As combat troopers, we're the first to go, the last to know."[80]

All he knew was that when he'd stepped on board at McGuire he felt like he'd stepped onto a plane more suited for the scrap heap than a long overwater journey. Just prior to takeoff, the massive propellor-engine combinations with blades more than twice his height shook, shot sparks, and spewed smoke. He wondered if he'd make it out of the Garden State, let alone all the way to Germany.

Then came Gander's inexplicable delays, foreboding weather, unsealed rear door, and crappy food. Even a fight almost.

Caruso was also angry over his seat assignment. Given that there were 32 empty seats spread amongst 68 passengers, he'd felt sure he'd have room to stretch out and grab some sleep. When it came time to reboard in Gander, he held off because, as they had in New Jersey, so many of the young "soldiers were likely to stampede to the front of the bus. They all wanted to sit up there."[81]

Nor was he greedy, trying to hog a two-seat row. He just wanted to share three seats with one other guy, preferably Airborne, from the greater NYC area. He grabbed a middle seat, thinking it was the best tactic.

When Caruso heard someone say the main cabin door had been shut, he felt it was safe to move to the window seat, so he slid over. Moments later a man in the aisle at the end of his row asked: "These two free?"[82]

The Army private turned to appraise Army major Elander and thought: *Not if it's up to me.* Dr. Elander clearly wasn't Airborne, given his squiggly medical insignia. Plus, he was likely married, given the woman beside him (his wife, Lois). *Friggin' great. A leg officer who steps outta jeeps, while I leap outta planes. We have nothing in common. Just when I thought this trip couldn't get any worse.*

Recently retired Air Force major Harry Benson was also unhappy with the current state of affairs, but he was mostly mad at himself. Having piloted Connie on many occasions, he knew her virtues and peccadillos. He was worried at how violently the engines were shaking on the tarmac in New Jersey, and so concerned again prior to the departure from Gander that he'd almost gone up into the cockpit to share his concerns with Captain Murray. But Benson let it slide because he knew the Wright 3350 turbo-compounded engines tended to idle rough and he didn't want the civilian pilot to feel a military pilot was questioning his chops.

When the engines stopped rattling and spitting fireballs shortly after climb-out over the eastern tip of Newfoundland, Benson concluded he'd done the right thing by not offering his two cents to Murray. But now, given the fire, he was having second thoughts as to the plane's airworthiness.

In the cockpit, before receiving news of the fire, Murray was sharing his reasoning that the fire alarm may have resulted from unexpected idling on the tarmac. Unplanned simmering accounted for the most common type of alarm: a false-positive triggered by the application of maximum takeoff power. When high-octane fuel flared into an insufficiently cooled engine, it often spat flames.

Or the thermal spike could have reprised what Murray had experienced two months prior, and recorded in his logbook: "I was flying a DC-Seven to Yugoslavia with a hundred and twenty nine refugees en route back home when an alarm sounded and the panel lit up. It was false, caused by a slight crack in the exhaust stack. Once the engineer confirmed the source we throttled back on the problematic engine and made it to Belgrade without further ado."[83]

Or the overheating could have been caused by the high-blowers. They were designed to give a turbo boost, but he'd needed sustained power to punch through the troublesome weather. He'd noted the whine and engine strain. It didn't sound right.[84]

Or it could have been something as simple as the dinner the stewardesses had just begun heating in the galley. The mouthwatering aroma of the mac-and-cheese rumbled his stomach.

Every potential fire implicated a different analytical protocol, and the delayed bell added another forensic wrinkle. Given the fact that the L-1049H was considered "a flight engineer's airplane," it was protocol for Jim Garrett to play a central role in the analytics.[85] Eastern Airlines having recently furloughed him didn't warrant a change in protocol. Though this was Murray's first flight with Garrett, given how he'd efficiently performed various system checks in Gander, the engineer impressed the pilot from the get-go.[86] Murray knew the industry well enough to know that being let go shouldn't necessarily be held against you. Given the engineering union's strict seniority system, coupled with the current economic downturn, lots of good young people were out of work. Garrett had racked up 2,450 flying hours on the Super Constellation, a very solid number.

Copilot Parker told Murray that in the 55 months since it had rolled off the assembly line, Lockheed Serial No. 4827 had logged 15,800 hours and 42 minutes in the air, or about 9.5 hours a day. As Murray knew from keeping up on his professional reading, this was lower than the industry's average daily utilization rate; it supported his belief that the plane's imperfections were cosmetic or otherwise minor, within the tolerances prescribed by the operating manual and common sense.

He also knew Tiger headquarters pushed the fleet. That's what had probably caused the rear door sealing problem. Fast turnarounds and reconfigurations from military cargo to civilian passenger to hybrid flights were often the key to the Pentagon awarding a contract to the Tigers as opposed to Riddle or Seaboard. "When the airplane was in freighter configuration, the passenger exit, being a door within a bigger door, got exposed to the elements during cargo loading and unloading and got banged around during freight ops," which, over time, "could cause problems when the plane was in passenger configuration."[87] While all the rough-and-tumble sometimes resulted in aircraft that, to the untrained eye, looked in need of a full-scale overhaul, all that was needed were some routine repairs and a soapy hose-down. Murray's eyes were highly trained. He also knew about cleaning and routine repairs, having started his aviation career in the late '30s as the one-man maintenance crew for the pilots who'd barnstorm and take families for sightseeing tours around Detroit.

As for all the smoke? Murray had often seen and heard Connie's four giant engines belch ominous-looking gray-black plumes, especially after extended layovers, and he knew the sound and fury typically signified nothing but the burning off of high-octane vapors.

And the sparks Major Benson and PFC Caruso had seen? Such minor showering was likewise no cause for concern: it was probably just the result of routine exhaust flames coming into contact with the aluminum cowl or cylinder fans.[88]

And the tarmac dustup? Just a smelly prank. Flying Tiger Line had contracted with rival Seaboard Airways to have its maintenance crew service the plane in Gander, and this included emptying the toilets. However, though its competitor had plenty of time, it never got around to pumping the sumps. While it would have been understandable to take offense at the prospect of flying 2,600 miles with a pile of poop deliberately gifted by a business rival, given the fact that Tiger 923 was already late, the weather was deteriorating, and the crapper couldn't have been too full after the short hop from New Jersey with 32 empty seats, it's understandable why Murray wouldn't have wanted to compound the delay by insisting his friends at Seaboard do what they'd contracted to do.

He had, however, made one allowance for potential problems. Though Hard Luck Sam suggested adding 2,200 pounds of reserve fuel, Murray added 3,000 pounds of "Grandma's gas."[89] He knew how crowded the skies over Europe could get and how the capricious autumnal weather lent itself to thick curtains of fog that materialized out of nowhere and hung in place for hours if not days, requiring holding patterns or diversions to far-off airports with better visibility and less congestion.

A sharp rap on the cockpit door interrupted the theorizing. The chief stewardess announced herself but didn't wait for an invitation before entering. Sims said she'd seen a fire.

Murray told Garrett to have a look. What he meant was: reach over, slide a panel in the cockpit, and look out through the prism; but as Garrett had been trained by Eastern on its fleet of all-passenger Super Constellations and they didn't have the up-front prisms necessitated by jam-packed cargo flights that prevented going aft, Garrett walked through the companionway door to eyeball the engine from amidship.

Murray hailed the U.S. Coast Guard's *Ocean Station Charlie* and informed them of the situation, and told Parker to inform Gander Airport and request clearance to 9,000 feet. Murray didn't like seesawing his passengers but there was nothing he could do about it. His flight-plan altitude of 11,000 feet had flown him into the teeth of a nasty storm. Climbing 2,000 feet didn't fix things; he'd needed to leapfrog up another 8,000. Now, after having just hit 21,000 feet, a mile above the tallest Rocky Mountain peak, he had to take them right back down into the miserable weather.

Tiger 923[90]: Gander ACC [Air Control Center], this is Flying Tiger Nine Two Three: We have a possible fire in the Number Three Engine. We are requesting clearance to descend to nine thousand feet.

Gander: Copy that. Tiger Nine Two Three approved for descent to level ninety. Are you requesting an escort?

Murray shook his head.

Tiger 923: Negative.

John D. Murray. Chicago, undated.
COURTESY JOHN P. MURRAY.

J. R. Rossi in cockpit of P-40 after flying from Kunming to Rangoon nonstop. 1942

(Top) A Chinese soldier guards the American planes that helped defeat Imperial Japan. COURTESY U.S. NATIONAL ARCHIVES. (Bottom left) Ace Dick Rossi played a key role in the search for Tiger 923. COURTESY LYDIA ROSSI. (Center right) Camouflaged plane under repair in Burmese jungle. COURTESY U.S. NATIONAL ARCHIVES. (Bottom right) "Flying Tiger" logo designed by Walt Disney. COURTESY ROBERT T. SMITH, ANOTHER TIGER ACE.

Wedding photo of John and Dorothy Murray, 1945. COURTESY JOHN P. MURRAY.

30

1948, 24. květen, Žatec. – Zpráva okresního velitele SNB v Žatci ministerstvu vnitra o provozu na letišti Žatec ve dnech 19.–25. května 1948.

Opis

Věc: Letiště Žatec, přistání letadla
Odpověď k ústnímu příkazu dr. Brože

Oznamuji, že dne 19. 5. 1948 o 8. hod. přistálo na Staňkovickém letišti okr. Žatec:

1. Dopravní letadlo „Northhern" – NC 58021 s následující posádkou:
   1. Moses Samuel ELKÁN, nar. 20.7.1921 v Gravenhage[a], holandský příslušník;
   2. Seymour LERNER, nar. 3.5.1920 v Rusku, čís. pasu 96020, vyhotovený dne 26.6.1946 ve Washingtonu, americký příslušník;
   3. James Henry WINSON, nar. 18.9.1919 v Tallahasee, č. pasu 161842, vyhotovený dne 10.12.1946 ve Washingtonu, americký příslušník;
   4. Paolo Antonio CAMPUS, nar. 26.1.1917 v Brooklynu, č. pasu 12010, vyhot. dne 13.2.1947 ve Washingtonu, příslušník USA;
   5. William Francis HALLEAN ml., nar. 14.4.1918 ve Flushing, čís. pasu 48833 ze dne 15.3.1946, vydaný ve Washingtonu, přísluš. USA;
   6. → John Desmon MURRAY, nar. 19.2.1918 v Chicagu, č. pasu 1156, vyhotovený de 13.2.1947 ve Washingtonu, příslušník USA;
   7. Robert HILL, nar. 5.5.1919 v Pittsfieldu, č. pasu 3238, vyhotovený dne 12.8.1947 ve Washingtonu, příslušník USA.

   Vpředu uvedené letadlo odstartovalo dne 20. května 1948 o 11.25 hod. s jmenovanou posádkou.
2. Dopravní panamské letadlo RX 138 – dne 20. 5. 1948 o 16.30 hod. s následující posádkou:
   1. Jack RASS, nar. dne 14.8.1923 v New Yorku, č. pasu 176554, vyhotovený ve Washingtonu, příslušník USA;
   2. Philip SCHILD, nar. 3.11.1919 v Brooklynu, č. pasu 197604, vydaný ve Washingtonu, příslušník USA;
   3. Lawrence PUL RAB, nar. 11.2.1924 v Millville, č. pasu 157272, vydaný ve [chybí zbytek řádky]
   4. Julius CUBURNEK, nar. 14.3.1918 v Pittsburgu, č. pasu 7196, vyhotovený ve Washingtonu, příslušník USA.
3. Dne 20.5.1948 o 16.35 hod. dopravní panamské letadlo zn. RX 135 s následující posádkou:

103

In: **Marie BULÍNOVÁ** (ed.): *ČESKOSLOVENSKO A IZRAEL 1945-1956* DOKUMENTY (Czechoslovakia and Israel 1945-1956 Documents) (p. 103) - *Ústav pro soudobé dějiny AV ČR* (Institute for Contemporary History of the Academy of Sciences of the Czech Republic), **Praha** 1993

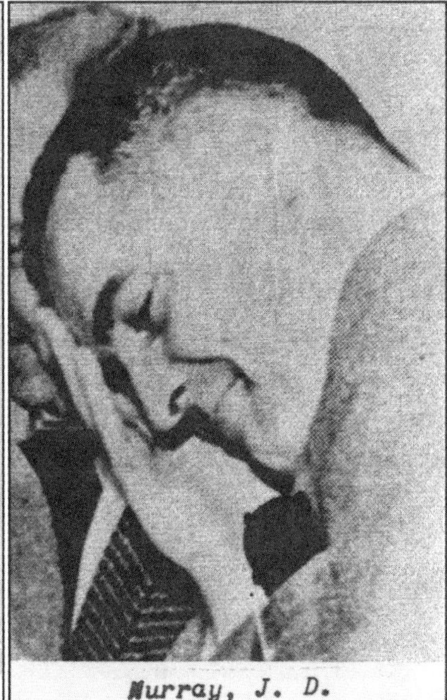

Murray, J. D.

(Top left) May 1948 manifest listing 30-year-old Murray as pilot of a clandestine and illegal DC-4 (per President Truman's executive order and the Neutrality Act) that flew Czech-built WWII German Messerschmitt Bf 109 plane parts per Operation Balak to help transform Irgun's Palestine Flying Service into the Israeli Air Force. COURTESY ZDENEK KLÍMA. (Top right) August 1950 photo of Murray in Tiger ground school class. COURTESY LARRY LEFEVER. (Bottom) August 1948 photo of Ruhama airfield. COURTESY ISRAELI AIR FORCE.

(Top) 1954 photo of Maj. Carl Richard Elander, MD, of Seattle, and Lois Gunderson, of Enumclaw. COURTESY ELANDER FAMILY. (Bottom) West Point's chief of ophthalmology and his wife attended President Kennedy's May 1962 speech to the graduating class, four months before Tiger 923. COURTESY JFK LIBRARY AND MUSEUM.

(Left) Tiger stewardess Carol Gould in her uniform, probably in Newark. COURTESY CAROL HANSEN. (Right) Army private first class Art Gilbreth holding his reserve "chute" at the Fort Bragg Jump School graduation photo, taken 10 days before boarding Tiger 923. COURTESY ART GILBRETH.

(Top) Raúl Acevedo in 1956 photo of Zacatecas State basketball team in Monterrey, at Mexico championship tournament (back row, second from right, he played forward) and (bottom) as a U.S. Army private first class in 1962, after basic training at Fort Ord, in California. COURTESY RAÚL ACEVEDO.

For the Chinese, 1962 was the Year of the Tiger. For Flying Tiger Line, it was the Year from Hell. It started the year with 12 Lockheed Super Constellations; by year's end, it had 8. The airline started the year without having suffered a single passenger fatality since its founding in 1945; by year's end, it had lost 121, plus crew members and bystanders. March 15, 1962: Soldiers boarding a Flying Tiger Lockheed Super H Constellation at the U.S. Air Force's Military Air Transport Service's western headquarters, at Travis AFB, California, for a trans-Pacific flight. This and another Tiger flight would leave within hours of each other: one would crash in Alaska; the other would disappear somewhere between Guam and Saigon, without a trace. COURTESY FLYING TIGERS CLUB ARCHIVES.

Chapter 2

Anything That Could Go Wrong

Captain Murray's declining an escort wasn't questioned. Though the junior officers had only known their captain a few hours, he didn't strike them as the reckless sort.

He was not. Also, if rescue control centers scrambled or diverted aircraft every time a Lockheed or Douglas engine caught fire, few flights would ever reach their destinations on time. Pilots used a triage system: Distress (aka Mayday), Alert, or Uncertainty. What Murray saw and sensed was still just uncertain. That's why he had instructed Parker to say a fire was "possible": it appeared *controllable.* Almost every prop engine ever manufactured had caught fire at some time or another, and most four-engine planes had safely made it to their destination.[1] Murray had twice flown with only two engines working.

If he couldn't salvage the no. 3, he wanted to squeeze every ounce of power from it, but such husbandry was tricky. Pushing a distressed engine too hard increased the risk of explosion. A single spark could bring a plane down were it to collide with fuel vapors.

While 62 passengers were U.S. Army or dependents, there was also a 6-passenger Air Force cohort: Master Sgt. Peter Foley, 45; Maj. Harry Benson (ret.), 46, who'd racked up 5,000 hours as pilot in command, including many at the helm of Super Constellations; intelligence officer Lt. Col. George Dent, 42, and his wife, Elizabeth, 41; and Capt. Juan Figueroa-Longo, 37, and his wife, Carmen, 35. While none was happy with the quality of service provided by their branch of the armed services (via its subcontractor), Dr. Figueroa-Longo was probably the most peeved.[2] The OB-GYN had put in beastly hours to earn leave, delivering squadrons of babies. Often his wife didn't know when her husband might have to be called away or when he might return home. They'd both earned lots of R&R, but there was no rest or relaxation for them now.

The crisis seemed over when Garrett returned to the cockpit at 8:11 p.m. Given he felt sure the fire was in the exhaust stack and told Murray it was already "diminishing in intensity," the pilot decided not to have him shoot the second bottle of suppressant.[3]

Right after sharing the good news, however, Garrett realized he'd forgotten the key fourth step in fire prevention: close the engine firewall. Maybe he wasn't used to the layout in the Tiger cockpit or maybe he was disoriented. No one knows why he did what he did, only that he pulled the wrong lever.

So, rather than hear Garrett say "Firewall number three closed," Murray heard "a shrill obscene snarl from the left side of the airplane, a near-deafening whine, ever increasing in pitch," followed by Parker yelling: "Runaway on number one!"[4]

Murray turned and saw how Garrett "had inadvertently pulled the No. 1 firewall shut-off valve."[5] "I'm sorry, John. I goofed."[6]

Murray said nothing.[7] He was now totally focused on interdicting a midair explosion.

Shutting the wrong firewall started a dangerous chain reaction: one of the good engine's hydraulic subsystems stopped pumping, the blast air stopped cooling its generator, and fuel and oil stopped flowing to the motor and governor. This caused the propellor to spin uncontrollably at close to the speed of sound. If the 13-foot metal blades were to break free, which sounded imminent, the resultant projectiles could down the plane.

Murray knew the no. 1 propellor needed to be feathered, fast. Yet he also knew doing so wouldn't be easy. He told Garrett to try.

"Copy that," said Garrett. But he said it'd take a few minutes.

Murray knew they might not have even one minute. He muscled all the throttles back. Once decelerated to 210 mph, he began easing Connie's nose up, improvising a makeshift brake from the air current.

Disaster was averted. The blades slowed just enough to allow Garrett to feather the left outboard engine (no. 1).

But Murray knew disaster might only have been delayed. Now he had two bad engines.

Engine no. 3 was in worse shape, especially if Murray's theory was right and it had a ruptured oil seal in its power recovery turbine. While Garrett could transfer fresh oil from the auxiliary tank to the no. 3, the pilot felt this was too risky. He felt that at best it'd only take a few minutes before the new oil leaked out; at worst, the transfer would directly result in another, more serious fire.

The prognosis for engine no. 1 was much better because while Garrett had interrupted the flow of cooling air, Murray neither saw on the instruments nor felt in the inscrutable way a pilot feels things any indication of a malfunction in the generator itself.[8] He said: "I have high hopes we'll re-start this engine."[9]

Wanting confirmation of his instinct that engine no. 1 was salvageable, he asked Garrett to consult the manual, but all the pilot got was semantic equivocation. The engineer read aloud how a propellor's peaking at 3,300 rpm required an "engine change."[10] The vagueness arose because while it wasn't clear if the prop hit 3,300 or just shy of it, it was clear that Murray had slowed it fast and the manual said anything "under thirty three hundred rpm" required only an "'engine inspection' at the next stopover."

Bottom line: it was impossible to know how badly no. 1 had been impaired. Only time would tell.

Murray concluded he should keep the no. 1 running but not push it too hard. He slowed to 160 mph, the speed required to un-feather a prop per the manual. Glancing to his left, he was enormously relieved to see the left outboard's propellor blades fully turn twice, suggesting the mistake hadn't ruined the apparatus. Murray told Garrett to try restarting the engine.

He tried. Nothing, other than *click . . . click . . .* When the prop blades slowed, then shuddered to a stop, he turned the feathering switch to the OFF position.

Murray felt the starter must be malfunctioning. Akin to how he'd push a stalled car downhill then pop the clutch, he dipped the nose and turned the yoke counter-clockwise. The plane banked sharply left.

Garrett switched the No. 1 feather switch to ON, hoping the wind would do the rest. It did.

Murray saw the prop un-feather in the full flat pitch position and start to inch around: 5 degrees . . . 10 . . . Then it stopped abruptly.

Many, especially those seated on the left side of the plane, felt a distinct shudder. There was some shrieking and a lot of agitated whispering.

Murray now knew engine no. 1 was out of commission for the rest of the flight. He'd lost two engines in seven minutes, 972 miles from land. Ditching was now a very real possibility.

He knew the implications of a "controlled water landing."[11] Every previous attempt to ditch a commercial airliner in a violent sea had failed, in part because most fatalities resulted not from the aircraft's impact but after evacuation.[12] If he managed by some miracle not to shatter or sink his plane before everyone got off, the reward would be a gauntlet of hazards ranging from hypothermia to hungry sharks, attracted by the blood and splashing.

Carmen Figueroa-Longo's first indication of trouble was "the boys across from us looking through the windows and whispering about something wrong."[13] She couldn't hear what they were saying. When she drew her window curtain, she was shocked: unlike the engine closest to her, the left outboard wasn't emitting the normal blue exhaust she'd seen thus far during the flight; and unlike the closer propellor, which was a blur, she could tell the far one had stopped turning. When she looked across the aisle at the whisperers and saw that the right inboard engine-propellor combo resembled the left outboard's, shock turned to terror.

Partly because Peter Foley was in one of the few seats without a window and partly because he'd been asleep, he wasn't aware that Tiger 923 had lost two engines until someone woke him. Yet Foley seemed unfazed.

By all accounts the *Stars and Stripes* reporter's ever-present smile and easygoing manner masked a tenacious can-do attitude, forged by having experienced at least as many close calls as Murray and Hard Luck Sam. When he was a teenage motorman hauling ore back and forth deep inside the belly of Montana's most dangerous copper mine, it had collapsed on top of him, yet he miraculously survived. A few years later, when he was an airplane mechanic aboard a cargo plane during WWII, Foley's plane got lost and ran out of fuel, yet he parachuted to safety, saying he "thoroughly enjoyed" free-falling through the clouds and birds.[14] A few years after that, while serving in Korea, he earned five commendations during his three-year tour, including the Bronze Star. Despite the engine problems, Foley was confident he'd see his pregnant-with-twins wife and three kids between the ages of 15 months and 10 years. He just felt he'd have himself another adventure story to add to his already rich library.

The other Bronze Star winner on board, Bob Eldred, wasn't as relaxed. He'd had great difficulty just ascending the steps and walking to his seat. To ease his chronic pain, he'd draped his left leg over the armrest of the empty seat in front of him. If the plane were to ditch, well, he preferred not thinking about it.

But he was told he must think about it. So he thought about how hard it'd be to squeeze his big, mangled body out through the small window, onto the wing, and down into a raft. The grandson of a Provincetown whaler thought about how he used to love to swim, but had hardly swum a stroke since five German tanks had crippled him in the summer of '44 in a field outside Saint-Lô, after which Army doctors told the former artillery captain he needed to find a "sedentary occupation."[15]

PFC Fred Caruso began writing a letter to his parents. "Thank you, Mom and Dad, and farewell," he began, before pausing to say to himself: *As if a letter would ever get there.*[16]

"Another engine . . . on the left side . . . went kaput. Then the plane's nose cone tipped up, like a whale'd just jumped on its tail. Oh, God, help me!"

Murray felt a pilot's main job wasn't flying a plane but "evaluating the performance of others," then deploying and directing them for optimal effectiveness.[17] He knew he wasn't supported by just 7 crew members but by 68 passengers, and they could help or hinder.

Passengers were often a pilot's eyes and ears. They could see objects not visible from the cockpit, hear things, smell fuel vapors; or incite panic.

Tiger 923's passengers all wanted to know what was happening, what might happen, and how to prepare. Many just wanted their hands held.

Engine no. 2's "severe vibration" on the tarmacs in New Jersey and Gander had worried veteran pilot Harry Benson.[18] Now, with no. 1 and no. 3 down, he felt he needed to tell the Tiger pilot about no. 2. Better late than never. So he rose from his seat and headed for the cockpit.

Stewardess Jackie Brotman stepped over and blocked his way. "Where are you going?"

"Up to the pilot compartment."

"I am sorry, they are too busy there, you have to go back to your seat."

"Okay, lady, if that's your orders." Benson returned to his seat.

Chief stewardess Betty Sims was consummately poised, seemingly everywhere at once, doing the job of three people. She was "almost constantly" on the PA system reassuring people; up in the cockpit conferring with the flight crew; in the galley or amidship overseeing and often correcting the work of her cabin crew.[19] Though she'd not heard Major Benson say he wanted to talk with Captain Murray, when she heard he'd been an Air Force pilot, she moved him by one of the exit windows and, as he told others, gave "an excellent briefing on ditching procedures."[20]

Lois and Dick Elander were playing cards when Sims headed their way down the aisle. In a soothing tone and via relaxed body language she was telling the passengers that despite the loss of two engines in seven minutes there was no cause for alarm because the plane was built with redundant engines and could easily fly on the two working ones. As if to prove her point, Sims said that she and her colleagues were about to begin serving dinner, and added in what sounded like an aside: "As a routine precaution, please check to see that you've got a life vest in the seat back in front of you."

Elander said: "Once we took our life vest out of the plastic pouch, it became much more real. I didn't feel like playing gin rummy any longer. Besides, I was losing."[21]

He asked Sims: "How long does one of these things stay afloat?" His gesture made it clear he was referring to the plane, in the event of a ditching.

Sims smiled and waved nonchalantly: "Oh, plenty of time. Ten minutes, at least."

Elander exclaimed: "My goodness! Ten minutes!"

"Oh, that's plenty of time. You just walk out on the wing, hop in your raft, and cruise away."

Turning around and eyeing Major Devlin, who'd survived ditching in the Adriatic during WWII, the doctor asked his West Point colleague: "What's it like, ditching?"

"Well, I'm here to tell about it."[22]

The cockpit was a busy place. Bob Parker was on the radio nonstop in an attempt to keep the various rescue control centers apprised of Tiger 923's coordinates and altitude, but he was struggling to communicate over the narrow, mid-oceanic frequency because it was often drowned out by the HAM-operating soccer fans ranting about the European championship test matches.[23] Jim Garrett and Hard Luck Sam were just as busy attending to their duties and dials.

Even if engine no. 3 was salvaged and came back online, Murray knew he shouldn't try to make it all the way to his original destination. He laid out the three alternatives: pull up short at Shannon Airport, which was about 1,000 miles closer than Frankfurt; divert north to Keflavik Airport; or, if absolutely necessary, ditch. Ireland and Iceland both seemed feasible. While losing one engine would've been a heckuva lot better than losing two, clearly, at least each side of the plane had a power source. Tiger 923 couldn't have stayed in the air more than a few minutes absent a working engine on each wing.[24]

Beyond some semblance of balanced aerodynamics, however, there were loads of issues to consider and decisions to make. But one question dominated Murray's deliberations: *Is this it? Are we out of the woods? Or are more problems lying in wait?*[25]

The pilot didn't know. No one could prophesy. Every crisis was unique, as he once wrote: "There are no textbooks on transport flying. There is no reference literature on the subject. The single biggest source of information is 'hangar flying'—like when a fellow airman explained his action when on take-off from LaGuardia both engines on his 220 iced up so fast that he was forced to fly under the Bronx Whitestone Bridge."[26]

Every decision was hamstrung by the possibility of some future mishap or malfunction, whether affected by equipment failure, human error, or an act of God.[27] Yet Murray knew this was no time for paralysis of analysis. He knew he had to think about variables like winds aloft and waves below while monitoring Connie's suspect power systems, avionics, and hydraulics. But he also knew he had to act.

Murray asked Garrett to check the performance charts and run the numbers to determine the cruising altitude that would cause the least strain per the current two-engine configuration and weight. A few minutes later he reported back: 5,000 feet, assuming Murray intended to continue with maximum except takeoff power (METO) on the good engine.

Hard Luck Sam said they had plenty of fuel to reach Keflavik or Shannon. He said it'd take between five and six hours to reach Ireland and 40 minutes less to reach Iceland, depending on head- or tailwinds.[28]

After Murray mentioned how he'd once before diverted to Iceland in a dicey situation and that everything turned out fine, Parker asked Iceland for the latest weather report.

> Keflavik Airport Air Traffic Control: Prevailing wind two hundred forty degrees . . . Forty-two knots . . . Gusting to fifty-nine knots . . . Rain . . . Scattered . . . Thick cloud-cover . . . Starting eighteen hundred feet . . .
>
> Tiger 923: Roger.

Iceland was out, said Murray. He hadn't diverted to Keflavik into the teeth of gale-force winds. So it was Ireland or the sea.

The pilot asked Sam to plot the revised course for Shannon. The navigator estimated an ETA of 2:00 a.m., Monday morning.

Murray put a positive spin on needing to travel an additional 115 miles (Ireland lay 950 miles west; Iceland, 835 north): they'd be closer to more potential escort planes and above more heavily trafficked shipping lanes. He instructed Parker to inform Gander and, this time, request an escort.

> Tiger 923: We now have Number One and Number Three Engines feathered and are requesting five thousand feet.
>
> Gander: Roger . . . Are you requesting an escort?
>
> Tiger 923: Affirmative.

An escort could guide Murray's struggling Lockheed to a safe diversionary landing or auspicious ditching site by illuminating the area and relay messages back and forth between air bases, oceanic weather stations, ships, and planes. What's more, taillights and tipped wings would reassure the besieged captain and crew that they weren't lost or alone. Morale is often the most potent weapon, no matter the adversary.

But there were no escorts near Tiger 923. The sky was empty. The sea too.

Though the land-based transmission towers were far away and the babble of frequencies and languages made comprehension of the spotty reception very difficult, Parker managed to cobble together enough scraps of information to discern that five aircraft were headed their way. An Alitalia jet was the closest, followed by an Air Force prop plane and a Riddle Air prop. What he couldn't discern, however, was how far away the planes were, or their ETAs.

Murray grabbed the intercom mic off the left side of the cockpit and called Betty Sims. He informed her of the situation and instructed her to mobilize Carol Gould, Ruth Mudd, and Jackie Brotman. She said she'd do so at once.

Sims beckoned her team to the forward galley, where, beside big bags of pretzels and individually wrapped slices of cake, she said they had to make sure that any passengers evacuating via the four over-wing windows (instead of the main cabin door at the rear of the plane) did so one at a time so they didn't block the hatches. She reminded them that though the windows looked narrow the specially constructed emergency exits were plenty wide for most people to fit through.

"How 'bout the normal windows?" Gould asked. "Can we go out them? And could any of the windows break, I mean on impact?"[29]

Unlikely they'd break, Sims said, since they were double-paned plexiglass. But sure, if one did break, then it could be used as an exit.

The four stewardesses then divided the cabin into groups, each with approximately 17 passengers. Sims announced over the PA that a ditching drill was about to begin.

When Gould told her group that they should either fold over onto their pillowed laps and lock their hands behind their legs or lay their pillowed heads and arms against the seat back in front of them, Fred Caruso (row 11, right side, window seat) couldn't understand why anyone would do the latter, as it seemed like that would result in a broken neck. But when he glanced around, he saw that for the bigger passengers it was impossible to fold over. They were already squished. The only option they had was to use the seat backs. He felt very fortunate being 5'6".

Lois Elander, who was two seats to Caruso's left, along the aisle, turned around and asked her good friend John Devlin how he'd braced when he'd ditched in WWII. When he folded over and locked his hands behind his calves, she and Dick followed suit.

On the left side, Raúl Acevedo (row 7, aisle) made a mental note of the number of rows between his seat and the nearest over-wing exit: four. As he felt sure it'd be a dark madhouse after a sea crash, he wanted to be prepared. As Gould passed him in the aisle, she said he'd most likely not even get his feet wet, as he'd only have to walk about ten feet to the nearest exit, two feet out onto the wing, ten more along to the wing's edge, then step a few more feet down into the waiting raft. Such specifics comforted the prospective supply clerk, at least a little.

At 8:28, after Gander control center okayed his request to descend from 9,000 to 5,000 feet, Murray added:

> Request Air Force Two Four Six intercept ETA, over.
>
> Gander: Standby . . . Will check with Airway Traffic Control. Stop. Control request to know if you think you will have to ditch.
>
> Tiger 923: At this time negative.
>
> Gander: Roger . . . Working on intercept now.

Everything had happened so fast: the thumping hail, insistent red blinking fire warning, riotous alarm bell, unexplained smoke, yellow-orange flames and purple-black carbonized fuel, a mistaken firewall shutoff, a correct shutoff, a screaming runaway prop, more alarms, more fires, the earsplitting runaway propellor no. 1 shuddering to a stop just minutes before engine no. 3 decelerated from a roar to a whimper to windmilling silence. The last 15 minutes especially had been a blur.

But with the plan set, the escorts hailed, the revised destination locked in, and, at present, no fiery engines or clanging bells, Murray felt it prudent to circle back to review the engine shutdown procedures contained in the Tiger operating manual. Earlier, given the crises, there had been no time. The captain wanted to make sure nothing was missed that might compound the flight engineer's mistake.

As the plane pierced the clouds and Murray gripped the yoke, his flight crew consulted the "Abbreviated Emergency Procedures" to make sure, for instance, that the cowl and oil cooler flaps had been faired, the emergency lever was back at the full OFF position at the third detent, and the fire extinguisher selector switches were set properly. They all agreed that, apart from pulling the wrong firewall lever to catalyze the crisis, they had followed the punch list as well as could be expected in light of the pressure-cooker situation.

> Prestwick [Scotland]: Air Force Two Four Six . . . Request listen out One Twenty-One Point Five for Flying Tiger Nine Two Three Super Connie . . . Presently on two engines . . . Estimating

Fifty-Five North Thirty West . . . Request intercept ETA . . . Nine Two Three proceeding to Shannon.

Air Force 246: Copy that. Will advise, over.

Prestwick: Tiger Nine Two Three . . . Escort being scrambled.

Tiger 923: Copy that.

It was 1st Lt. Joseph Lewis' first time in the left seat, as pilot in command. The native of Tuscaloosa, Alabama, had been told to expect a routine flight from the U.S. Air Force's Military Air Transport Service base at Prestwick to Newfoundland's Harmon AFB (for fuel), then New Jersey's McGuire AFB, where he was stationed with the 30th Air Transport Squadron. But as the Air Force magazine *MATS Flyer* would later recount: "It is doubtful whether any aircraft commander will recall a more dramatic initial line check episode."[30]

Lewis hailed Murray on the 121.5 frequency: "This is Air Force Two Four Six. Can we be of any assistance?"

"Yes," Murray replied, "we would like you to escort us to Shannon, if you are able."

"Give me your position and we'll attempt intercept."

"We're about three hundred miles south, twenty degrees west, at sixty five hundred feet."

"Copy." Lewis began descending from 10,000 feet, told Murray his estimated intercept time was 10:00 p.m., then asked: "Do you have UHF/DF?"[31]

"Negative."

Without the military's ultra-high-frequency channel and especially in the absence of any direction-finding capability, given the clouds and darkness, both pilots, along with everyone else monitoring the situation, knew the likelihood of a successful intercept was greatly diminished.

But at 9:00 p.m. some good news arrived: Tiger 918 hailed Gander. The Lockheed Super Constellation had departed the same airport three hours after Tiger 923, also eastbound but on a different vector toward Europe. At the helm was the legendary WWII ace Dick Rossi, one of the original Flying Tigers, who was famous for having survived innumerable harrowing crises in Burma and China.[32]

Tiger 918: Request information on emergency Flying Tiger Nine Two Three.

Gander: He has Number One and Number Three Engines feathered . . . He is Fifty-Four Zero Five North Thirty-Thirty West at Twenty Forty-Eight Zulu.

Tiger 918: Roger.

News of Rossi's involvement lifted Murray's spirits. Though at least three hours away, Tiger 918 could help relay messages among and between the shore stations, ships, and aircraft; those that happened to be in the vicinity of Tiger 923 as well as the specialized maritime rescue aircraft that were now en route.

The good news didn't last long, however. Twelve minutes later a red light flashed in the Tiger 923 cockpit: fire in engine no. 2. Once again the bell clanged loudly and insistently. Perhaps because there hadn't been an alarm for 20 minutes was why this one seemed so unnerving. "Some people lost it," said Gould.[33]

Murray had doubts as to the alarm's validity. After all, at least some circuitry was faulty because the first fire alarm hadn't rung, just flashed, and the likelihood of three engines on the same plane catching fire was minuscule. He suspected the problem was haywire electronics, not another bad engine.

Still, he wasn't about to take any chances, so in order to buy some time for forensics he reduced power and told Garrett to feather no. 2. As soon as the flight engineer did, the warning light went out and the unsettling alarm fell silent.

But now the plane was flying on just one engine. It couldn't do so for long.

Garrett was told to reverse the feather. The flight engineer did and the props realigned themselves without incident. Tiger 923 was now back on two of its four engines. As the pilot throttled up to just below METO, the no. 2 appeared to be operating normally.

Yet Murray was concerned. Engines no. 2 and no. 4 were clearly being stretched to the max. While he'd twice before lost two engines on an L-1049H and made it safely back to land, in both of those instances he was but a few miles and minutes away. Here he was more than 800 miles and five hours away.

If either engine no. 2 or no. 4 failed, Ireland was out of the question because Murray couldn't fly Connie for five minutes let alone five hours on just one engine. So while he still harbored doubts about the validity of the fire detection system, he felt that the latest alarm, coupled with the strain on engine no. 2, warranted ratcheting up the ditching drills.

Murray summoned Sims. Once she'd joined the four men and shut the door behind her, the pilot turned to the two pressing questions of what to tell the passengers and how to deploy the eight-member crew in the event of a ditching.

As for what to tell the passengers, Murray left it up to Sims. He trusted her and knew she had a far better sense of the cabin personalities and dynamics. But, he added, of course he'd be the one to inform the passengers if a ditching were required.

As for crew deployment, Murray asked Parker to brief everyone. The copilot turned to the "Ditching Stations and Raft Assignments" section of the manual and walked everyone through the stipulations:

- The captain evacuates via the aft port-side window-exit, steps onto the wing and into the inboard raft once it is jettisoned from the left wing-bay and automatically inflates, and is joined by a stewardess;
- The copilot exits via the aft starboard window-exit and occupies the inboard raft after it automatically inflates, and is joined by a stewardess;
- The engineer exits via the forward right-side window-exit, occupies the outboard raft after it automatically inflates, and is joined by a stewardess;
- While none of the stewardesses is assigned a specific raft, three are supposed to sit in the window seats in rows 9 and 11 (port/left side) and 10 (right/starboard), while the fourth sits in either row 12 or row 20, beside the navigator; and

- The navigator exits via the main cabin door just aft of the captain's raft (left side), manually inflates the emergency raft, and occupies it.

Murray saw no reason to change the recommended deployment, but he clarified the pre-ditching seating arrangement. He told Parker and Garrett he wanted them to sit near their exits in row 9, not in the cockpit with him. The copilot and flight engineer protested. Murray said his decision was final. As Super Connie pilot Larry LeFever would later say, "All four men knew the nose was the worst place to be. They knew anyone seated there would hit hard, probably be knocked out and might not be able to evacuate. John was essentially saying, 'I'm expendable but you need to help people off the plane.' It was the definition what being a captain is all about: going down with your ship."[34]

Sims suggested she sit on the left side of the plane, two rows behind Gould and across from Brotman, and that Mudd sit on the right side, across from Gould. Murray assented.

The discussion turned to the emergency raft affixed to the back of the cockpit door in the manner of the spare tire mounted on the back of a Jeep. As opposed to how the four main outboard rafts inflated and were jettisoned once a lever was pulled inside the cabin, the emergency raft had to be inflated manually outside; i.e., Hard Luck Sam would have to dive out after the raft in the dark, find the two tabs amidst the folds of rubber, and pull them to release the canisters of CO_2.

Sam assured his colleagues that he knew the raft had to stay tethered to the D-ring that was anchored to the floor before pushing it out into the sea, lest it shoot off into the night before anyone had a chance to board. He also knew that if the raft were to inflate inside the cabin it would block the main exit.

Sims went over the procedure regarding the main rafts. As soon as possible after the plane hit the water, Mudd and Gould would pull the T-bars on the port and starboard sides of the plane, over the wings. Each bar controlled two rafts. Pulling the bars would fire the rafts from the wing-bays out into the sea and inflate them automatically.

Sims stressed the need to avoid one of the main evacuation hazards: people inflating their life vests too soon. While the prospect of contending with an intimidating sea led many, quite naturally, to want to inflate their vests while still inside the plane or on the exit's transom, premature inflation could clog the exits.

Murray asked if there were any questions. There were none. He thanked Sims and she returned to the cabin.

He revisited the issue of engine No. 2. Given the recent fire alarm and its suggestion of strain and overheating, with about five hours of flight time remaining he knew there was a real possibility that the no. 2 might not make it to Ireland.

Murray led a discussion into the possibility of deviating from Tiger 923's current route to Ireland so as to overfly Britain's *Ocean Station Juliett* or America's *Ocean Station Charlie.* If ditching proved to be necessary it would be much better to do so near one of the floating, well-provisioned outposts rather than in the middle of the open, frigid sea.

Deviating wasn't a straightforward proposition, however. First, while the British weather station was 100 miles closer (250 versus 350), the U.S. Coast Guard cutter *Owasco* was presently moored beside *Charlie*, and it could travel much faster than either sluggish outpost in the event people were injured. Second, overflying the British or American base could add another 175 miles and 60 minutes of engine strain. To keep his options open as long as possible, Murray directed Parker to reestablish contact with the *Owasco.*

Onboard the plane, the absence of panic was surreal.[35] Most of the 76 souls were calm and stoical, despite the fires, alarms, ditching drills and seesawing altitudes. Many felt Fate was toying with them or God was torturing them. But what could they do about it other than try to make peace with it and settle their affairs as much as possible?

Strangers swapped intimate details about loved ones, missed opportunities, whatever crossed their mind.[36] "If I had it to do over . . .?" "Have any pets?" "Think the Yankees have a strong enough bullpen?" Many reread the Tiger emergency pamphlet, "Always Prepared," which jutted out from the seat-back pockets, though by outward appearances they did so in a resigned or casually curious way, like they might be reading a *Reader's Digest* article on how to make gingerbread men rather than a to-do list summarizing how to survive what appeared to be unsurvivable: crashing headlong at race-track speeds into a violent sea at night, some 900 miles from land.

Not everyone was so poised, however. Some whispered nervously. Others hoarded food. The rookie German wife Helga Groves spoke for the rookie American stewardess Jackie Brotman by repeatedly muttering, "I know we will fall from the sky."[37]

The panic was often checked by unexpected sources of moxie, like Edna Eldred, who was knitting some socks when a soldier asked her "Aren't you scared?" She looked up, smiled, and said, "Why should I be? My husband is sitting right here."[38]

But her Bronze Star–winning husband, who'd survived a tank barrage in France and a hurricane in Mexico, was scared.[39] Given his agitation, though he'd quit smoking decades earlier, Edna suggested Bob light up. "It might do you some good. What do you have to lose?"

After he'd bummed a cigarette and smoked it, Edna suggested they play cards. He said: "How could anyone play gin rummy at a time like this!"

Sims was the glue that held the cabin together and contained the panic. She felt certain Captain Murray would win this fight, and her confidence was contagious.

But she continued preparing for the worst. Recognizing the need for privacy and candor, again she assembled her colleagues in the forward galley. The women huddled close, surrounded by stowed serving trolleys, coffee makers, and Murphy beds. Sims flipped through her dog-eared ditching manual, annotated with insights gleaned during her 10-year career, most notably how important it was to comprehend the state of mind and morale of each member of her team, and on whom she could rely.

Brotman worried her the most. Her fear was obvious, which meant it could go viral, which led Sims to omit sharing what Murray had told her about the cold water, wind chill, and wave height. She'd cross that bridge later.

On the other hand, Gould didn't worry Sims at all. Despite all the crises, she'd kept it together. Her tone was controlled, her instructions pragmatic. She was chipper. In a trip full of bad breaks, Gould's last-minute substitution was some recompense.

Sims said: "My most recent wet ditching drill was last month. Ruth joined me. Carol, what about you?"[40]

"The month before that. In July. In Brooklyn, at the Coast Guard facility."

"Great. And Jackie, how 'bout you?"

Brotman bit her lip. She explained how she'd only completed Ground School a little over two months ago, on July 19 (two days after being hired), and that had only included a dry drill.

While the novice's not having received any in-water training (just classroom) concerned the chief stewardess, she knew it wouldn't help to pour gasoline on the smoldering fear. Sims smiled, said not to worry and that that was partly why she'd stationed Brotman across from her, so she could lend a hand or answer any questions. Sims added that a ditching remained an unlikely *if* as opposed to a *when*.

Sims then held up her manual, opened to the cabin layout and the emergency exits, and showed everyone their seat assignments on the plane and the rafts, as well as where the guys in the cockpit would be stationed. It was all there in black and white. She reminded them that as each of the five rafts could hold up to 25 people, though 20 was recommended, if Murray did have to ditch there'd be plenty of room. She went over the distances to the respective exits with each of the three stewardesses, one by one.

Her granular precision eased the tension. Even Brotman felt she could manage 12 to 17 feet, even in the dark.

After fielding and answering a few final questions and knowing Gould was probably the most religious of the group, Sims asked her if she'd like to say a prayer.

"Yes, thanks."

"But quietly?" whispered Sims. "No need for the passengers to take it the wrong way."

The Christian and Jewish stewardesses held hands and bowed heads as Gould began in a hushed voice: "The Lord is my shepherd. He leadeth me beside still waters. Yea, though I walk through the valley of the shadow of death, I will fear no evil . . . Amen."[41]

Gould arrived at row 8 on the left side of the plane, counted off the 18 passengers she'd been assigned on both port and starboard sides of the cabin, placed a life vest around her neck, removed the "Always Prepared" ditching pamphlet from a seat back, and introduced herself. "For those I've not met, I'm Carol. Carol Gould. I'm a Jersey girl, from Lyndhurst."[42]

"Can I have your number?" said a paratrooper.

Gould smiled. "Sorry, I've got a fella already." (*Two, actually,* her conscience nagged.)

The suitor snapped his fingers. "Rats."

She held up the pamphlet, almost touching the cabin ceiling. "The captain's asked us all to prepare. I guess most of you know by now we've had problems with two motors, but we've got four. You've probably felt us descend. We're heading down to five thousand feet. But as of now we're *not* ditching. This," she said, while tugging on the vest straps, "is just a drill. Just in case. We're headed to Shannon Airport, on the west coast of Ireland. An escort plane's on the way. It'll be by our side the whole way."

A different soldier asked: "Has our pilot ever dealt with anything like this before?"

"You mean like . . . ?"

"I mean like a plane losing power four miles up in the middle of the ocean. That's what I mean."

Others nodded, murmured. "Yeah."

Gould shrugged. "I honestly don't know. The best thing we can all do is prepare. So you'll find these instructions in your seat back. Please look them over carefully."

She tapped a soldier's shoulder, pointed at two blankets on an empty seat, and asked him to help her use them to gather up all sharp objects, shoes, or other clothing that "might restrict your ability to swim."

Geez Louise! Gould realized she'd probably unnecessarily amped up the anxiety level by conjuring the thought of swimming in really cold, really rough water.

"Not that you'll have to *do* any swimming . . . We'll exit from this window right here," which she tapped, "then simply step out onto the wing and into the raft without ever having to set foot in the water.

"Please hand over any pocketknives, pens, anything else that could potentially injure you on impact or puncture the raft. Including reading glasses, dentures, belts, buckles and boots. A few of the knives," she added, "will be given back, but Betty wants them all collected, first."

Paratroopers contorted themselves in their cramped seats in order to unlace and remove their leather boots. They stood, rummaged around, and pulled knives and other items from the rucksacks in the open overhead bins. They unpinned their brass Army Airborne lapel wings.

Lois Elander handed Dick her pierced pearl earrings but kept her wedding ring on and tucked a gold bracelet under her shirt cuff. She didn't see how these items could hurt anyone and she didn't want to lose them. They meant too much. She also gave her husband the $50 she'd squirreled away to buy something special in Paris. After stuffing the cash into his pants pocket, Dr. Elander removed his reading glasses, rolled them up in a sock, and dropped them in the second blanket, along with his wife's earings.

Gould nodded at the clattering blankets. "This'll all be kept in the blue room . . . er, I mean, lavatory.

"Now . . . if the captain is forced to ditch you'll be alerted ahead of time. . . . Remember to bend over and tuck yourself either between your knees or snug between your seat back and tray table, using a pillow or a blanket to protect your head."

"I don't have a pillow," a soldier said. As Gould turned around to look at the young man, another said, "Me, neither." A third said, "Can I share a pillow with you, Carol?"

Gould ignored the flirtation. "We're flying light, so we've got plenty of spare pillows. I'll bring one to anyone that needs one, once I'm through with this practice drill.

"Here's another important tip: make a mental note where this exit is"—again she tapped the window—"bearing in mind you might have to make your way to it in the dark. So it's a good idea to count the number of seat backs from your aisle to this spot right here.

"Another thing: if the captain is forced to ditch, be prepared for two or three skips across the water. Don't unbuckle your seatbelt until the plane comes to its final resting place."

Geez Louise! Did I really just say final resting place? Gould shook her head. *I can be such a nincompoop!*

"Everyone has their own life vest . . . located in the seat back in front of you, in a pouch. Please double-check to make sure one's there by unzipping the pouch. But don't pull it out, just leave the zipper open. If you've no pouch or it's empty, let me know, I'll bring you one. We've got plenty." People began rummaging for, unzipping, and inspecting vests.

"This is also really important: inflate your vest only after touch-down, when *outside* the plane, while standing on the ledge or wing, about to jump into the raft. You'll follow me to the exit, and out. Again: to this spot, right here." She tapped the window again. "Row eight. Our raft'll be right outside . . . there." She pointed out into the dark night.

"How do you know it'll be there?" someone asked.

Gould reached for the T-bar lever and drummed her fingers on its protective plastic cover. "See this?"

People nodded.

"All I've gotta do is pull this, and two rafts pop out from inside the wing-bay. Pulling the T-bar also pops the C-O-two cartridges that fill the rafts, automatically."

"Just two rafts? For all of us?"

"Just two on this side of the plane." Gould turned and pointed out the window across the aisle. "Ruth'll do the same from her station. She'll also release two rafts by pulling her T-bar. Plus, the navigator will launch a fifth from the back of the plane."

When a paratrooper asked if the rafts might be swept out to sea by the wind or waves, she told him not to worry "because each is tethered by a rope. The rafts aren't going anywhere, until we want them to."

Raúl Acevedo was queasy with fear. He tried to pay attention to Gould's ditching drill. But it was hard focusing on what to do if and when the plane hit the water, given the whining (thus to him evidently struggling) engines, lurching altitude, sobbing German girl, and his own hammering heart. His dad had a weak heart and now he wondered if his own heart would hold out, even if they didn't ditch.

Being attentive to detail had served the Mexican citizen/American GI well throughout his life. It had helped him assemble the documentation needed to enter the U.S. legally (behind his disapproving father's back, who didn't want him to leave Mexico); locate two great places to live; find two great jobs; perform so well in the most recent one that his boss had recommended him to be the manager of the new StarKist Tuna packing plant being planned for sunny, Spanish-speaking Puerto Rico, which, as if preordained for Acevedo, was set to come online just as he'd finish his tour in Germany; enroll in the courses he'd wanted at UCLA; land a plum medical corps posting with the base quartermaster; and nab a coveted ticket on Tiger 923.

He'd once coveted it, anyway. Now he self-recriminated.[43] But mostly he was fixated on how far he was from the nearest exit window: maybe 10 feet. He shut his eyes and imagined counting each seat back as he grabbed it in the dark.

Fred Caruso didn't know what the real deal was. Gould seemed pretty relaxed. But that was part of her job, he knew: contain panic.

He felt the new girl from Chicago was probably a better indicator of what lay in store. His eyes drifted across the aisle as Jackie Brotman drilled her group. He thought: *She's got a bad poker face.*[44]

His lifeguarding in New Jersey hadn't prepared him for this, nor had his Advanced Infantry training in Georgia, nor had his Jump School in North Carolina. He'd been trained to fight Commies by leaping out of planes with a chute on, not fight huge waves in a Mae West, in water so cold it'd likely shrink his balls to the size of marbles.

His ire made it hard to think rationally. He'd scoffed aloud when Gould said "This is just a drill," as he had when, over the PA system, Sims referred to the preparations as "routine." He fumed as he recollected the Army Airborne motto: "Death from Above." *That's not supposed to mean this!* His chute was in the hold, his knife and boots in the crapper. All he had by way of survival gear was a ballpoint pen and some chewing gum.

A few minutes into Gould's spiel, however, terror eclipsed anger. His mind's eye saw vivid wreckage, flailing survivors, excruciating pain, and the futility of the ditching drills. *Why even bother with these bullshit drills?*

But Caruso pushed back against the emotion. Airborne alphas weren't supposed to be afraid of anything. Fear was for the elite forces washouts, not him.

If he let on how he really felt, then everything panned out? *I'll never hear the end of it. I'd be razzed every second of my three-year tour.* So he maintained his warrior mask, same as all the other real or pretend tough guys, nodding and smirking as they joked about looking forward to a picnic on the water with Gould and the other stewardesses.

The cockpit was a warm, busy place. While the big plane was experiencing only minor turbulence as its controlled descent neared the new cruising altitude of 5,000 feet, down from 21,000, and settled into its new cruising speed of 168 mph, down from 330, Captain Murray could feel and see on the control panel's jumpy gauges the drag, yaw, and other signs of aerodynamic strain occasioned by the brisk winds, coupled with the uneven thrust from the left inboard (no. 2) at reduced power and the right outboard (no. 4) at full METO.

Hard Luck Sam and Jim Garrett sat at their workstations, one headphone on, one off, so they could hear Murray and copilot Bob Parker. The navigator was calculating Tiger 923's ETA at Shannon Airport and various longitude-latitude markers en route, while the flight engineer was busy monitoring fuel consumption and other metrics.

When Parker heard some staticky chatter, he put on the second headphone, closed his eyes, and tried to concentrate. While he couldn't establish contact with anyone and the communiqué from an unidentifiable source didn't last long, he reported that, so far as he could make out, the weather ahead was much worse. The winds were stronger, with squalls and even less visibility than at their current position, which was poor.

Dick Rossi couldn't help his colleague John Murray by relaying the latter's sitrep because no one knew Tiger 923's whereabouts. The last reported position translated into a search area of more than a thousand square miles.

Rossi wasn't the only one in the dark as to Murray's whereabouts. None of the rescue control centers, air traffic controllers, military or civilian planes and ships could locate Tiger 923 given the conspiracy of archaic communication devices, incompatible transmission frequencies, national security protocols, inclement weather, and darkness.

On paper, a Canadian battle group was an impressive first responder, especially given its aircraft carrier, equipped with planes and helicopters. But the 4,000 Canadian Navy sailors and aviators were much farther away than the 33 merchant seamen on a Swiss grain freighter, which was at least 10 hours away from Tiger 923's anticipated ditching coordinates, if it came to that.

Meanwhile, Murray was deciding whether he should dump fuel. On one hand, the 3,000 pounds of insurance fuel he'd added in Gander proved to have been prescient, and the logic of a cushion still held. On the other hand, the more fuel, the more engine strain.

The discussion was brief, as they had little time for debate. Murray explained that the benefit of reducing the plane's weight by 5 percent (the excess fuel beyond what was needed to reach Shannon) and the added buoyancy of an empty tank wasn't worth the cost of losing the cushion. So no fuel was dumped.

The next question involved whether to overfly either of the two oceanic stations. Parker told Murray that, in his opinion, changing course to ditch near *Ocean Station Charlie* no longer made sense, given it would require a 175-mile deviation. Murray concurred, then asked Sam to post a long-range radar fix on *Ocean Station Juliett*, which wasn't as far out of the way.

After quickly running some numbers, Sam said that Tiger 923 could be over the floating British Navy weather station in about half the time it'd take to reach the Coast Guard's oceanic outpost: 40 minutes. Plus, doing so would only divert them 10 miles off their Shannon track, instead of 175. As Murray considered diverting . . .

Another alarm bell rang out, destroying the fragile composure in the cabin.

Lois Elander about jumped out of her seat. She squeezed her husband's hand and peered into his eyes. Dr. Elander stroked her hand and returned a moist glance. "Dick, it's been a great marriage, whatever happens." He said, "Heavens! Don't talk like that! We're going to make it through this."[45]

In the cockpit, the control panel flashed red: fire in engine no. 2. Jim Garrett rushed aft to get a closer look. He was back in less than a minute. He confirmed the fire.

Murray could see the left inboard engine spitting orange flames back toward the triple tailfins and coughing purple-black comets into the inky sky. He thought: *Things are beginning to look pretty grim.*[46] But he didn't tell Garrett to shut down no. 2 or feather its prop because that would have severely compromised the plane's aerodynamics, making it akin to a one-winged (really heavy) bird trying to fly. Nor did Murray tell Garrett to shoot a bottle of fire extinguisher, because he wanted to hold this precious commodity in reserve in the event all other corrective measures failed. Instead, the pilot throttled back and the "ruthless clamor" ceased.[47] The four men all breathed a sigh of relief.

Though Murray had never gotten to the bottom of engine no. 2's problems, he'd never written it off. He asked Garrett to use his synchroscope's rotating magnetic fields to ascertain whether the alternator voltage frequencies were in sync. The device usually gave a more precise reading as to whether there was really something wrong with an engine.

Garrett rummaged around in his black leather flight bag, removed and peered through the scope: the arrow was pointing where it should be. He tapped the glass with two fingers to ensure the feathery aluminum prong wasn't stuck and conveying a false-positive. It was not. Nothing was amiss. Garrett said the reading supported Murray's theory that a cracked exhaust stack had triggered the alarm by permitting routine exhaust flames or the heat emitted therefrom to get too close to one of the plane's fire detection units, setting off a false warning.

It made sense to Murray. He'd experienced many such exhaust cracks over the course of his long career. It was the most plausible explanation.

Engine no. 2's flames weren't "false." It was just that Connie's thermal combustion was supposed to work behind the scenes, not leap out and lick the wings and frighten the passengers.

The intercom buzzed. It was Sims. Because Murray had asked her to do everything she could think of to create an air of optimism and normalcy, she had disappeared inside the crew's curtained-off sleeping area (beside the two fold-down bunks), slipped out of her standard uniform, and emerged wearing her spiffy blue pinafore dinner service attire. Sims felt actions spoke louder than words: what better way to persuade the passengers they would make it to Ireland as now planned than by feeding them as planned?

However, when Sims said she and the other stewardesses were about to start the dinner service, Murray asked her not to use the ovens and coffee makers, as every ounce of power had to be conserved. Sims said that wouldn't be a problem as "most of the passengers had lost their appetite."[48]

By 9:17 p.m., 70 minutes after the first engine alarm and fire, the fear in the cabin was much more palpable. Most of the passengers who were seated on the left side of the plane could hear the inboard engine "running wild."[49] It sounded like it might explode any second.

People began to entertain dark thoughts.[50] How long have I got? Minutes? Seconds? Enough time for a final cigarette, kiss, or prayer? If the engine explodes, will I pass out right away? Or will I feel the impact of the plane hitting the water? Will I soil myself?

Sims tried to combat the crescendoing anxiety, but her credibility had suffered over the past hour and a half of pep talks. In passing she told Gould how important it was to appear calm before the passengers in the event Murray did have to ditch.[51]

Despite having been told to wait until a ditching was a certainty before removing the life vests from the seat backs, some took them out and unzipped the cellophane bags enclosing them, but the stewardesses weren't about to stop them, much less scold them, provided they didn't try to inflate them. When Carmen Figueroa-Longo put her vest on backwards, Gould helped her reverse it. Noticing the doctor's wife hadn't removed her stockings, Gould asked her to do so.

"Why?"[52]

"They're really slippery," said Gould, "but they'll knot really good around your waist so people can grab hold and help you if they need to."

Figueroa-Longo did as she was told.

Gould asked her group to listen up: she said that while a ditching was unlikely, it was still a good idea to go over the emergency procedures once more. So she put on another show-and-tell regarding how to inflate the life vests, pry off the emergency exits, step out onto the wings, and board the rafts.

Most of the Airborne guys gave Gould their undivided attention. Not always for the right reasons. "Hey, doll, what say just you and me we borrow one of the rafts and set out on our own private cruise, hmm?"[53]

They're making a game of it, Gould said to herself.[54] *Like they haven't got a care in the world. Is that good or bad?*

People were using the cellophane bags that had held the life vests as makeshift rucksacks, including PFC Michael Murray, who'd fibbed to three stewardesses to score five slices of cake. Bartering broke out. "I'll trade a pack of cigarettes for some cake. Got any matches?"[55]

When Peter Foley slipped on his vest, the WWII and Korean War hero who'd once before had to jump from a disabled plane noticed right away that the Tiger life vest was lighter than the military issue and had no supporting leg straps. It was disconcerting.[56]

But Foley tried to stay positive. Negativity had played no role in his having survived a supposedly unsurvivable copper mine collapse, ferocious North Korean offensive, and previous midair disaster.

Instead, he broke it down: what he should and should not do, listen for, feel for, and look out for. Like everyone else, he had been told the vests would inflate automatically after he pulled the two little strings (one for each bladder), which would pop the seals and release CO_2. He was also told that, as a backup, the vests could be blown up like two small beach balls through the two little plastic tubes (each the size of his pinkie) attached at chest level.

Overhearing the paratroopers bemoaning having to remove their jump badges (a brass insignia depicting a parachute with wings, attached to their tunics with pins that would puncture a life vest), he suggested to rowmate PFC Peter Koltac, of Wierton, West Virginia, that if he wanted to keep his badge he should tuck it inside his field jacket. Koltac did so.

At 9:20, Murray was optimistic about being able to nurse engines no. 2 and no. 4 and make it the remaining 715 miles to Ireland. There had not been a fire alarm for 20 minutes, nor any further indication of engine trouble. That he was now cruising at half-speed translated into much less engine strain. As for engine no. 2, which seemed weaker, a check of the maintenance logs revealed that it had been completely overhauled 20 days prior. It had flown just 244 hours before departing from Gander, versus engine no. 1's 939 hours.

Yet Murray knew he wasn't out of the woods. So he asked Hard Luck Sam to remove the emergency raft affixed to the back of the flight deck door and carry it to the rear of the plane as a backup raft to be launched manually, to supplement the four stowed under the wings that would inflate automatically.

"Copy that."[57] But Sam couldn't get the embryonic raft to budge. It seemed welded to the back of the companionway door. As he couldn't find the onboard axe, Sam jimmied the lightweight door back and forth, ripped it off its hinges, opened the lavatory door, stuffed the other door inside beside all the boots and badges, and shut the door; then he and the two soldiers he had enlisted to help lugged the unwieldy rubber clump aft to the main cabin door.

On his way back to the cockpit Sam ran into Carol Gould. As he squeezed past her in the aisle, he asked her to double-check and make sure the paratroopers had secured the rope lanyard to the floor-mounted D-ring so the raft wouldn't be carried off. Gould said she would.

In the cockpit, over the intercom, Murray asked Sims to review the passenger seating one final time so as to optimize the plane's weight and balance. Given depleted, asymmetric engine power, the aircraft needed all the aerodynamic help it could get.

"Excuse me, Private," Gould said to Raúl Acevedo, "would you please follow me?"[58]

"Why? Where're we going?"

"The captain's asked me to move a few people to improve the weight and balance."

"Where do you want to put me?"

"Row eighteen."

Acevedo glanced back 11 rows from his current seat in row 7. He looked dubious.

Gould leaned down and whispered: "It's the safest part of the plane in the event of a ditching . . . not that the captain expects to, but just in case. You'll be sitting across from the navigator."

Reasoning that being by the navigator probably wasn't the worst place to be if he might soon be on a raft in the middle of the ocean, Acevedo quickly unbuckled his seatbelt, stepped into the aisle, pulled his rucksack down from the overhead bin, and walked to his new seat.

Unfortunately, Gould hadn't whispered softly enough. Several people overheard and the news traveled fast. "The back's the safest place to be!"

Suddenly the aisle was jammed as a couple dozen passengers all wanted to move to the rear of the plane at the same time. People were getting elbowed in the ribs: "Ouch!"; or hit in the face by gear being slung over shoulders: "Hey, watch it, pal!"

"Guys!" Gould yelled, "you can't all move! Please stay in your existing seat unless a stewardess directs you to change seats."

Juan Figueroa-Longo removed his eyeglasses and as Gould passed by his row carrying a blanket he dropped them in, along with his ballpoint pen. She thanked him and then, glancing about the cabin and feeling more weight-and-balance fine-tuning was in order, she ushered the Air Force OB/GYN and his wife, Carmen, to row 16, behind John Groves and his wife, Helga, and in front of George Dent and his wife, Elizabeth.

Dr. Figueroa-Longo struck up a conversation with Bob Eldred, who sat catty-corner across the aisle in row 15. When the men discovered they were both picking up new cars from factories overseas, discussing Eldred's Jaguar, Figueroa-Longo's VW, and their respective travel itineraries became a most welcome diversion.

Until another earsplitting alarm rang out.

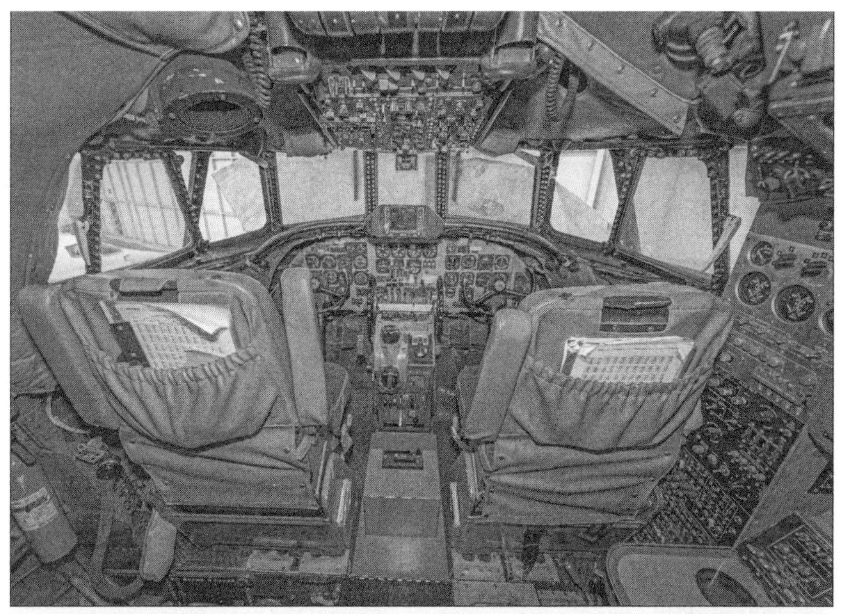

Circa 1962 Super H Constellation cockpit: pre-computer, pre–Black Box, pre-GPS (visible device retrofitted in 1980s). COURTESY URS MATTLE AND ERNST FREI.

Circa 1962 Super H Constellation fuel dumping and firewall junction box (located at flight engineer's workstation). COURTESY PETER W. FREY.

(Top) Circa 1962 Super H Constellation cabin with Flying Tiger Line's "Always Prepared" ditching pamphlet and life vests in seat backs. COURTESY FLYING TIGERS CLUB ARCHIVES. (Bottom) U.S. Coast Guard "wet ditching" training at Brooklyn motel swimming pool, circa 1970 but using the same raft as on Tiger 923. COURTESY DAWN SEYMOUR-ADAMS.

Chapter 3

Fixin' to Die

At 9:25, Murray throttled back the No. 2 engine. The plane slowed as its nose lifted. The bell stopped ringing and the FIRE light went out.

But the pilot knew that if he kept throttling back he'd never reach Ireland. He would not be able to sustain the minimum thrust necessary to counter gravity and stay aloft.

As an aviator who'd flown this route over a hundred times and as a student of history, he knew what was implicated by the prospect of ditching in the 15 million square miles of Atlantic bounded by Ireland and Newfoundland. It was very disconcerting.

Murray knew the North Atlantic seabed was a mausoleum, home to the remains of countless aircraft, Britain's supposedly unsinkable *Titanic*, and dozens of Spain's supposedly invincible galleons.[1] He knew hitting the water would feel like crashing onto a serrated cement runway, foul weather and darkness were a lethal mix, and no seaplane attempting rescue could operate in such surging swells and crashing waves.[2] He knew that by far the likeliest two outcomes were that his big plane would either break apart on impact or sink in seconds.

According to the U.S. Coast Guard and common sense, the three main determinants of a successful ditching were the weather, the aircraft, and the pilot. Weather-related factors included conditions in the sky and on the water. Aircraft issues encompassed the condition of the engines, propellors, elevators, ailerons, fuel tanks, hydraulics, and innumerable other components and systems. The pilot-related issues included how many hours he'd flown the type of plane to be ditched, how much sleep he'd had since his last flight, what limitations existed at the time of the ditching (e.g., on account of illness, prescription glasses), and how long it had been since his most recent wet ditching drill.

According to the Coast Guard criteria, Tiger 923 had two big strikes against it. First, the plane: two of four engines were down, with a third on its last legs. Second, the weather: winds were gusting to 65 mph, just 9 below hurricane strength; and, according to the cutter *Owasco*, some of the waves topped 25 feet.

Yet according to the same criteria, Tiger 923 had a big advantage: Murray. His experience navigating around Michigan lakes, piloting Connies to safe landings despite dead or sputtering engines, and flying in seaplanes and amphibians, for which a "controlled water landing" was the norm, made him uniquely qualified for his current predicament.

However, he felt his chief job qualification was tenacity. Murray often thanked God for being "lucky" enough to possess a "fanatic determination."[3] He channeled and focused his impassioned grit on the fulcrum of his predicament.

Hard Luck Sam handed Bob Parker and Jim Garrett their life vests, donned his own, then tugged and tightened the straps. Then Sam held out the pilot's.

Murray ignored it. Sam understood: given the fierce, capricious winds, the pilot didn't want to be distracted or remove either hand from the jittery yoke, even for a second. He was struggling to keep the plane on a semi-even keel while processing the metrics on the gauges before him: winds aloft speed, altitude, aircraft speed, engine rpm, rate of fuel consumption.

Sam edged closer and opened the vest wide. Murray poked his right arm through one opening, his left through the other. As Sam tightened the vest as gingerly as a bomb-squad technician, leaving the straps hanging, turbulence rocked the plane, reminding the flight crew why they had ascended 15,000 feet above their current altitude two hours earlier.

At 9:40, as there'd been no warnings, alarms, or fires for 15 minutes, Murray wondered if he should dim the cabin lights so everyone's eyes could get accustomed to the dark. But he worried that by doing so people would infer that ditching was imminent when it was not. Also, given the rocky air, passengers wouldn't be able to read the "Always Prepared" emergency pamphlet or as easily use the bathroom. However, knowing being prepared for the worst was the top priority, he told Parker to switch off all the cabin lights other than the parallel rows that ran along the joint where the walls met the ceiling. The tiny bulbs glowed a soft cobalt blue.

Carol Gould was trying to project an air of calm. She didn't think she was pulling it off.

As she was sweeping some individual cake slices into a brown paper bag, her thoughts drifted back home. She thought about her New Jersey State Trooper friend who'd recently been killed by a hit-and-run driver on the Turnpike when he was standing on the shoulder helping a motorist fix a flat tire. She thought about the horse that had thrown her and nearly killed her. She wondered: *Has my luck finally run out?*[4]

The clouds dissipated somewhat as the plane continued its descent. Though the moon remained mostly hidden, Rachel Hoopi could now see some stars above and, below, the erratic tracing of whitecaps. The sea looked angry.

Based on what she'd overheard, the cold worried her most. Hawaii was famous for its rough-water surfing, and Rachel, like her two girls, swam before she walked. But while the water back home was typically in the 70s or 80s, the sea she might soon find herself in was in the 40s or 50s.

From across the aisle Sgt. Alfred Bodung saw the fear in Hoopi's eyes. The native of Indianapolis wanted to buck her up. But when Gould passed by asking if everyone had turned over everything that could be a hazard in the event of a ditching, and false teeth qualified, he remembered he had forgotten his, so he removed them, put them in the seatback pouch, and gummed: "Don't worry, lady, everything will be okay."[5]

Up in the cockpit, as the altimeter arrow fluttered down, communications with the outside world grew spottier. While Bob Parker had just moments ago been in contact with several planes on emergency and standard frequencies, and they'd relayed helpful and to some extent reassuring information, there was now impenetrable interference.

Moreover, Tiger 923 had just flown into an oceanic seam separating two rescue control center jurisdictions. Given the darkness and awful weather, coordinating the complexities of such an extensive search-and-rescue operation was already problematic, but now, with Canadian and British centers both laying legitimate claim to being in charge, more confusion arose.

Yet some good news slipped through the static. Parker received word that USAF 246 and Riddle 18 were both closing in.

However, more bad news followed at 9:42 p.m., when another alarm bell rang out and the left inboard engine, no. 2, began shooting fiery blue-black carbonized fuel globules "the size of a lady's fist" past the passengers' windows.[6]

Jim Garrett was on it: he flipped two switches in quick succession. The first silenced the alarm while the second opened a valve at the base of the exhaust stack to purge it of any trapped, combustible gas.

But Murray knew he couldn't purge his way out of trouble. He no longer felt an engine exhaust stack was the cause of the fire alarms, given the persistent behavior. It didn't add up. "Ditching seems probable now," he said.[7]

Garrett focused on the engine readouts, Parker reviewed the ditching instructions, and Sam eyed the altimeter. Though the manual advised starting a descent at 3,000 feet and they were above 4,200, none of the crew felt the 40 percent steeper slope presented a problem.

Precisely how the plane should approach and make impact with the sea was the problem they needed to solve, said Murray. And they didn't have much time.

His crewmates were confused. They likely exchanged puzzled glances. After all, Parker had just read from the manual, which stipulated: "Never land into the *face* of a swell (or within 45 degrees of it)."[8] These same instructions were found in all the other specifications Murray and Parker kept up on: Navy tip sheets, Flight Safety Foundation accident bulletins, Air Line Pilots Association newsletters, Civil Aeronautics Board accident investigation reports.

Yet Murray refused to fall prey to the crutch of convention or "the fallacy of decisive action."[9] To his way of thinking, when it seemed like there was no time to think was just when pausing to think was most essential. It was counterintuitive, like steering into a skid.[10]

He explained he wasn't ignoring the manual, just overriding it. "In almost every ditching training session," he reasoned, "after a discussion of why it's better to land parallel to the swells, there'd always be an old-time flying boat captain who landed his Sikorsky or Boeing *into* the swells."[11] Plus, "while the Coast Guard's ditching tests sound sensible in theory, none was conducted with the conditions we're dealing with." Because Murray felt the stiff winds on the surface would reduce his speed and minimize sideways drift, he said that, absent "a significant change in their direction or velocity, or the primary swell direction or height," he'd do what the flying boat captains did: fly into the wind and facing the swells, touching down between two of them.[12]

With the ditching maneuver settled, timing was the next variable. When to ditch was primarily a function of the speed and nature of the winds aloft and near the surface. That both winds were so brisk and unpredictable made it really hard for Murray to time his touchdown.

The airspeed indicator read 138 mph versus the manual's advised 110. Murray needed to decelerate but if he slowed too much he ran the risk of aerodynamic stall, allied with the wind, taking control of the glide slope.[13] He throttled back cautiously.

Where to touch down was the next question, visibility the next problem. Murray's eyes weren't the issue. (His FAA license required him to wear glasses.) And by now he was beneath the cloud cover, so visibility was a lot better.

The issue was unique to ditching: the "height perception illusion." For the human eye to process the countless inputs that bombard it constantly, it needs a canvas of crisp, discrete focal points on which to paint a comprehensible picture. Seldom is this a problem when landing at an airport, since the three-dimensional topography comprising trees, telephone poles, air traffic control towers, and myriad other fixed objects blends into a concrete referential pointillism, easily processed by the eye.

A ditching is totally different, especially where the water is so violently active. The sky merges into the sea, bleeds into the horizon, and plays tricks on a pilot's eyes, wreaking havoc with depth perception. Illusions led pilots to hit the water at the wrong spot or wrong angle; too soon or too late; too slow or too fast.

As he dipped below 2,000 feet, Murray could clearly discern the direction of the swells. He estimated their height at between 15 and 20 feet and the interval separating them at around 150 to 175 feet. The numbers were intimidating. Murray had at best 12 feet of wiggle room to lay down his 163-foot plane without it cracking against a swell. It didn't help that the wind kept blowing his plane 15 to 25 feet in every direction. He was also concerned that secondary swells might be lurking beneath the whitecaps, upending his calculations.[14] If he was going to avoid disaster, Murray would have to almost perfectly calibrate and orchestrate his big wobbly plane's wings, timing, speed, and point of impact, yet the height-perception illusion made such precision nearly impossible.

Though there had been no announcement that ditching was definite or imminent, most of the passengers were resigned to both prospects. An air of inevitability pervaded the cabin.

Betty Sims seemed to be everywhere, her demeanor calm and earnest. She'd be heard over the PA system speaking from the flight deck, asking everyone to make sure their overhead bins were empty of all potentially hazardous objects, then seen amidship, telling Carol Gould there was no need to search for the first-aid kits because she had already distributed them, along with pocketknives and lots of flashlights.[15]

Sims oversaw a superb ditching drill according to Harry Benson, who had ordered and participated in many during his 20-year career in the Air Force. Though he'd flown the Super Constellation many times over this same stretch of the North Atlantic, he'd never faced anything this intimidating, yet to him Murray was handling the situation as if it were routine.[16] "Occasionally the pilot would turn because I could see the stars, and he was making a slow turn to the left or right."[17]

The chief stewardess huddled with Gould, Ruth Mudd and Jackie Brotman in the galley behind the cockpit where, according to Gould, after taping "everything down that was loose . . . Betty got out her manual and started going through most of the things that we learned in class, and she started drawing diagrams and showing the exact positions of the levers to pull a window out and how it worked, and the raft compartment.[18] She drew little pictures of the raft compartments and where the handle was, and the T-bar and explained how that worked. . . . And then she would go over the key points again, and . . . place . . . us in certain positions. All the while she kept saying not to panic and if we did panic, there would be no chance."

As soon as Sims left, however, her colleagues began to lose their composure. Rookie stewardess Jackie Brotman said to rookie paratrooper Paul Stewart: "This is my last flight, Muscles. I've already quit."[19] Gould moved a passenger aft near a window; moments later, Ruth Mudd moved the same person forward into an aisle seat.[20] One stewardess told people to use a window-exit; another told the same person to use the main door at the rear of the plane.

Sims proceeded to row 13, and while helping 9-year-old Luana Hoopi and her 11-year-old sister Uilani don their life vests, she asked for a volunteer to escort the girls off the plane and into a raft.[21] There being no takers, Sims tapped Sgt. Ernest Wilson on the shoulder and locked eyes: *Please?* He nodded. "Sure. I'll do it."[22]

"I thanked God for that bit of kindness," said PFC Fred Caruso. "I wouldn't have been able to say yes if she asked me to take one of the girls—I was worried sick over the prospects of saving myself—but at the same time, just like the others, I would have had a hard time saying no. How could an airborne trooper say no?"[23]

At the time, Caruso was busy scribbling a letter to his folks. He glanced around furtively to make sure Gould couldn't see his contraband pen. He'd already removed his boss jump badge, lest it poke out his eye or puncture a life raft, and his beloved Army Airborne boots, lest they weigh him down or knock out someone's teeth. *She's not getting this. Got too much to say. And even if what I gotta say never makes it to Mom and Dad, at least God'll know I tried. If He's even there, paying attention. If He even cares.*[24]

The three-time college dropout was simultaneously cramming for a ditching: repeating in his head how to brace his body and inflate his life vest, and looking toward the nearest exit. The practical stuff led to writer's block. There was so much to remember and say, yet so little time. *Crap, crap, crap!*

Caruso knew he'd better wrap things up. "I'm looking at the water raging right out my window . . . churning and foaming and rising into enormous swells. Mom, you're the best! Pop, you too, for taking the night shift at the bakery, so we could move . . ."[25] He addressed the envelope, stuffed it into the cellophane sleeve that'd held the ditching instructions, and slid it inside his jacket pocket.

Six seats back from Caruso, also on the right side of the plane, Art Gilbreth stared out the window and watched the wind shear the tops off waves, exposing whitecaps. *It'd be so beautiful . . . if not so scary-looking.*[26] It sent a chill up his spine.

When he looked across the aisle, he saw Carmen Figueroa-Longo staring back at him, crying softly. He smiled and formed an OK sign with his thumb and index finger. The doctor's wife brushed away a tear, smiled, and nodded.

Then, seeing as how just about everyone else was already braced, he shut his eyes and lay his head down on his pillow.

Six seats up from Gilbreth, Lois Elander squeezed her husband's hand, which prompted the response: "Just think positive. Just remember: as soon as we hit, swim as hard and as fast as you can—away from the plane. Get away from the plane."[27]

Three rows back, Edna Eldred wondered if she'd ever see her family again. Thinking of her 17-year-old daughter and 18-year-old son led her to think she and Bob needed to split up so as to spread the risk.[28] Edna laid her hand on her husband's forearm and peered into his eyes. "Bob . . ."

"What? What is it?"

"What about Karen and Bob Jr.? If we separate, there's a better chance one of us might live."

The retired Army captain didn't want to separate. First, so far as he could tell, he and Edna were seated in a really safe spot: three-quarters of the way back and near a window-exit. Second, not only were their new friends Juan and Carmen Figueroa-Longo not separating, but also he could see another Army captain and his wife (the Devlins), and they were locked in a tight embrace. Bob shook his head. "I'd like to stay with you."

Edna persisted. "I'll go up a bit, you stay here." She unbuckled her seatbelt and rose.

"No!" He grabbed her forearm.

Edna pried his hand off and kissed it. She said, "I love you, God bless you," then started to walk toward the front of the plane.

But she only made it a few steps before Gould shouted: "Sit down!"[29]

Edna stepped into the aisle seat directly in front of her husband and buckled up.

Bob was really relieved. Now he'd be able to watch over her.

As Sims approached Gould, who was standing by her window-exit studying the T-bar release, she could tell Gould was confused and worried. Sims smiled as she said, "Don't worry, I'll be there to help if you run into trouble."[30]

Hard Luck Sam butted the rubber clump on the floor beside his foot with a closed pocketknife and handed it to Gordon Thornsberry, who was seated across the aisle in the middle seat. Sam said, "Here: take it. But cut the rope lanyard only after the raft's outside, and I've inflated it. Got it?" "Got it," said Thornsberry.[31]

Raúl Acevedo left Mexico hoping for a better life in the U.S. "Do some good" is how the kindly power-broker in Ciudad Juárez responded when Acevedo asked, "How can I ever thank you?" after the man had helped him secure a tourist visa and cross into Texas behind his father's back.[32] Now Acevedo doubted he'd be able to do any good, to clear his debt and his conscience.

His conscience was really loud because the cabin was eerily quiet . . . but for the straining engine, sobbing German newlywed, and praying Hawaiians. The soft glow of the cobalt-blue ceiling lights made it seem like he was inside a horrible tunnel, aboard an out-of-control train, hurtling toward only God knew what.[33]

His new seat assignment troubled him. *When I was seated in the middle of the plane, I could just step out onto the wing and down into an already inflated raft. Here I must wait for these guys to blow this up, then jump straight into the ocean? I thought the stewardess told me this was a better spot?*

He'd by now grown dismissive of the pep talks. He didn't see how the plane could skip like a pebble across a tranquil lake, then bob on the water like astronaut John Glenn's *Friendship 7* space capsule had off the Florida coast seven months prior. Nor could he imagine 76 terrified people calmly exiting the plane, walking out onto the wings, and stepping into the life rafts. Plus, he'd overheard someone say there weren't any ships nearby.

Acevedo made the sign of the cross, leaned his head into the blanket he'd bunched up against the seat back, locked his arms under his legs, knotted his fingers, and prayed: "*Madre de Dios, por favor . . .*"

In the "hideous moments before impact" he reconsidered his decision to emigrate.[34] Was home really so bad? Now the idea of working alongside his father, Roque, at his general store in downtown Zacatecas seemed like a dream job.

Five rows up from Acevedo, Hal Lesane stared out from his window seat, likewise wondering if he'd made a really foolish decision. Was working alongside his father, Thaddeus, at the Whitman candy store in downtown Philly really so bad?[35]

But Lesane had craved adventure. "The flight was the climax of a lifetime dream," said his 25-year-old brother, James. "He always wanted to be a paratrooper." To complete the transformation that had begun in tiny Germantown, South Carolina, Hal had even changed his name from "Le Sane."[36]

Murray joined the other 75 souls on board in a moment of mortal reflection. Though his hands gripped the yoke and his eyes scanned the sea for some quiescence amidst the violent chop, his mind drifted to his family.[37] He knew he'd failed to appreciate Dorothy's 18 years of managing their three girls and two boys between the ages of 14 months and 15 years: rousting them up each morning, dressing them, and getting some breakfast into them while making their finicky lunches; shuttling them to bus stops and three different schools, attending PTA meetings, school plays, baseball practices, ballet recitals, and Mass; doing load after load of laundry while filling Green Stamp booklets, clipping coupons and haggling over decent cuts of meat at the A&P. He so wanted to see his wife again, to thank her and seek forgiveness for his extended absences and other errant prioritizing; and to hug each of his children.

But he knew the odds. He knew that most likely the last thing he'd experience of earth would be hard, wet, cold and unforgiving, and the last he'd see his clan was now, in his head.

Sam interrupted his introspection: "The aircraft is ready."[38]

But he spoke too soon. Just as Murray began turning the yoke to angle the plane for his final approach, in order to use the stiff wind as a brake . . .

The controls locked up.[39]

As Murray reached over to disengage the hydraulic boost so as to reset and divert some pressure to restore controls, Jim Garrett yelled: "Not that!! The hydra-crossover switch!"[40]

Murray's hand balked over the boost switch. His glance Garrett's way said it all: *Good catch, Jim.* The pilot flipped the crossover switch and felt the return of hydraulic pressure to the boost system. The yoke reactivated. He resumed his turn into the wind, reducing the speed at which the aircraft would impact the sea.

As the moon emerged from hiding and lightened the sky, the height-perception illusion dissipated. But then it started to "rain like mad."[41]

Still, Murray could now more clearly make out the distance between swells: they looked to be about 200 feet, crest to crest. In other words, given his 163-foot-long plane, he had a 37-foot margin of error rather than 12; still not much, given the fact that his 120-mph speed translated into Tiger 923 traveling at 176 feet per second. The waves seemed to be every bit of 20 feet, high and powerful enough to snap both wings off and send the rafts stowed in their bays to the bottom of the sea.

Murray told Sam that once seated at the rear of the plane he should commence counting down loudly until impact so the passengers could brace. But before Sam headed to his vital post, Murray asked him to use the radio altimeter to determine how high the plane actually was above the surface, as the absence of a current barometric pressure setting could result in a calamitous miscalculation.

Here, now, being even a few feet off could make all the difference in the world, especially given the reach of the propellors. The 13-foot-long blades further complicated an already exceedingly complex maneuver.

Before Sam could take a reading, however, a new crisis arose: the elevators were losing power. Murray had lost elevator power before. It had been serious. Here, it could be fatal. He needed them to raise Connie's wings and nose just before impact. Figuring the problem was ice accumulation, Murray toggled the trim tabs once, twice. Nothing. Betty Sims entered the cockpit as he tried a third time. She was a charm: The elevators worked.

Murray switched on the plane's landing lights, then asked Sims if she'd stationed two men at each window-exit to help her and the other three stewardesses usher the 68 passengers out onto the wings. She nodded, then reminded Sam to be sure to grab the flare pistol, a box of spare cartridges, and some extra flashlight batteries. He nodded, then expressed his concern that Connie was still descending 35 percent faster than the advised 1,500 feet per minute for a normal runway landing. The engines should pull the plane, yet here gravity was pulling the aircraft. Sam told Murray that unless he could elevate fast they'd hit the water in less than a minute at a catastrophic rate of descent.

Murray wrestled with the winds and gravity. The lone non-problematic engine on the far right (no. 4) struggled to sustain 73 tons with only a minor assist from the faltering no. 2 engine; both billowed blue flames. Meanwhile, the feathered, locked-in-place no. 1 and no. 3 propellors resembled stick bugs trapped in a dark indigo-amber sky.

On board Air Force 246: Maj. Edward Guthrie had been observing his student's every move for nearly an hour. As of 9:45 p.m., Lt. Joe Lewis had acquitted himself very admirably. The pilot had responded immediately to Captain Murray's alert, changed course adroitly, and instinctively enlisted his 8 crew members and 19 passengers (all soldiers) to assist in the search and intercept. Lewis acted more like a 20-year veteran than a first-timer in the left seat. Problem was, in 15 minutes Lewis was supposed to intercept Tiger 923, but he had no idea where it was.[42]

"However, just after breaking out of a cloud deck, Lewis spotted lights ahead. Simultaneously the navigators reported a radar target 40 miles away. For identification the Connie was asked to turn off its lights momentarily. The Air Force crewmen peered forward in suspenseful anticipation."

When Tiger 923 copilot Robert Parker flashed his lights and USAF 246 copilot Michael Burnett responded in kind, both crews were greatly relieved that a "lonely, distressed aircraft had been pinpointed amidst the vast blackness over the North Atlantic Ocean."[43] Burnett and Parker turned on their exterior lights to improve sighting, turned off most of their interior lights so the combined 87 passengers and 15 crew members could search the sky better, and Major Guthrie prepared to shoot flares.

At 10:00, "Lewis flew past the Flying Tiger, then maneuvered into position above and behind. He barely had the wings leveled and airspeed reduced when Murray reported serious difficulty with a third engine. The Connie then disappeared into the cloud layer below.

"What's your altitude?" Lewis asked.

"We're trying to restart number three," Murray said.

"A few moments later an unintelligible transmission was heard. The [Air Force] navigators lost the target on radar, and all further attempts at radio contact were unsuccessful. Lewis pursued the radar blip into the clouds, to the right of Murray's point of penetration." When USAF 246 "broke out beneath the clouds at 2,000 feet, it was engulfed by the pitch darkness of the Mid-Atlantic night. The crew searched frantically for any sign of the Flying Tiger."

On board Tiger 923: the blaring alarm bell was redundant. Almost everyone had felt the muffled thump on the left side of the plane, heard the tray tables rattle, and glasses tinkle. People knew what it meant: the third of four engines had failed (no. 2). The situation was dire.

Yet apart from Helga Groves telling her husband "We're dropping out of the sky," there were few other exclamations of distress or outward signs of panic. Most aboard had by this time turned inward, praying quietly, silently clutching their spouse's hand. Or they were being practical: rereading the emergency pamphlet, scrutinizing the life vest inflation tabs, counting the rows to their nearest exit.[44]

While Sims had done a stellar job informing everyone of many essentials over the PA system and in person, one piece of information could not be delegated, Murray knew. Bringing the mic close to his lips, he said: "Ladies and gentlemen, this is your captain speaking. We're going to have to ditch."[45]

Once the mic was back in its cradle, Murray eyed Parker and said, "Let people know," which prompted the copilot to issue his final communication:

> *Mayday! Mayday! We've lost Engine Number Two. Only Engine Four now operating. Getting reading to ditch.*

At an altitude of about 750 feet, Murray nodded toward the water and said: "There. That spot looks ideal."[46]

Though his plan was to clear four or five 20-foot waves and "land just past the top" of the last crest, into the longest trough feasible, just beyond the second approaching swell he saw an unexpected gift: a long, relatively flat stretch of water. "Guys," he said to Parker and Garrett, "my curiosity isn't strong enough to investigate conditions beyond that next swell. Time to head to your ditching stations. That's an order." The copilot and engineer left the cockpit and made haste.

As the landing lights illuminated his intended point of impact, Murray called out over the 121.5 frequency:

> *Mayday. About to ditch. Position at 2212 Zulu Fifty-Four North, Twenty-Four West. One engine serviceable. Souls on board seventy-six. Request shipping in area prepare to search. Over.*

Being within range and having access to both the FM frequency favored by planes and the AM used by ships, Britain's *Ocean Station Juliett* immediately relayed the message:

Merchant Vessel Celerina, this is Ocean Station Juliett.

M/V Celerina: This is the Celerina.

OS Juliett: As you are closest to Tiger Nine Two Three . . . Request you proceed to ditching site Fifty-Four North, Twenty-Four West.

M/V Celerina: Copy that. We have come around, and are en route.

Murray reached to his right, "chopped Engine Number Four and eased Tiger Nine Two Three down to the waiting sea."[47]

In the aisle of row 19, Carol Gould and Ruth Mudd were kneeling, arms braced against the seats for balance, still trying to figure out how to anchor the raft to the cabin floor via a rope and a D-ring so when Hard Luck Sam threw it out the rear door it would stay beside the plane so people could easily and safely board. After the two stewardesses had "secured the emergency raft as best they could with what seemed like, it looked like, a large seatbelt, with other parts to it," someone yelled, "Sit down, girls! We're just about to hit the water!"[48] Gould raced back up to her seat in row 8, and Mudd raced to hers in row 10.

When Betty Sims ran by her going the other way, heading aft, Gould got really worried. Sims had said she'd be by Gould's side amidship to help her remove the exit window, launch the two rafts stowed in the left wing, and evacuate. However, at the last minute, Sims decided it was more important to seat herself beside the navigator so as to help him launch the emergency raft, inflate it, and oversee the evacuation from the rear door.

From his seat in row 20, and in accordance with Murray's instructions, Sam got ready to start his countdown to impact. Staring out the left window, he could see the water clearly enough owing to the landing lights. It looked formidable. Though Murray had somehow managed to find a comparatively flat patch of ocean, Sam could see big swells and wild whitecaps bearing down on Tiger 923. "Ten . . . nine . . . eight . . ."[49]

Most everyone heard the countdown. To Raúl Acevedo, "the moments seemed like an eternity."[50] When an acute cramp seized his neck, he popped out of his brace position.

"Seven . . . six . . ."

Across the aisle, an instant before tucking her head, Sims said something unintelligible to Gordon Thornsberry about the rope that was supposed to anchor the emergency raft to the cabin floor.[51] But the Army private couldn't comprehend her over the countdown and "on account I was fixin' to die."[52]

"Five . . . four . . ."

In the cockpit, Murray ignored his aching forearms, the squawking radio, the howling winds. It was just him and the sea.

He wasn't braced. It was too confining. He needed the freedom of motion to react to any last-second exigencies.

"Three . . . two . . ."

As a wind shear slammed into the plane's right flank, Murray yelled: "I'm ditching!"[53]

Before being named chairman of the Joint Chiefs of Staff, Army general Henry H. Shelton commanded the 1st Brigade of the 82nd Airborne at Fort Bragg, where Fred Caruso, Harold Le Sane, and others had trained. During the chairman's remarks commemorating the 60th anniversary of the creation of the airborne, he commented on the iconic photograph of "a dirty, scrappy, tough paratrooper . . . you simply know from the look: he's Airborne." COURTESY U.S. ARMY.

Sometime between late October 1961 and October 1962, a U.S. Army soldier (possibly an Airborne paratrooper) leans against a U.S. tank and eyes through his binoculars the Soviet tanks facing him across Friedrichstrasse, the only one of six Berlin checkpoints that allowed non-Germans to enter and exit. The tanks squared off right after the East Germans began constructing their infamous Berlin Wall in August 1961. (They would continue to enlarge and fortify the Wall until it was torn down in 1989.) COURTESY CIA.

Pvt. Harold Gene Le Sane

The father of 21-year-old Fred Caruso (top left) baked bread in Spring Hill, New Jersey; the father of 18-year-old Harold Le Sane (top right) made candy in Philadelphia. They were both headed to U.S. Army base Robert E. Lee (center), just outside Mainz, West Germany, headquarters of the 505th Infantry, and the Airborne's main base in Europe. Only one of the two volunteers would make it. (Bottom) An 82nd Airborne honor guard drilling at Lee. COURTESY FRED CARUSO, U.S. ARMY.

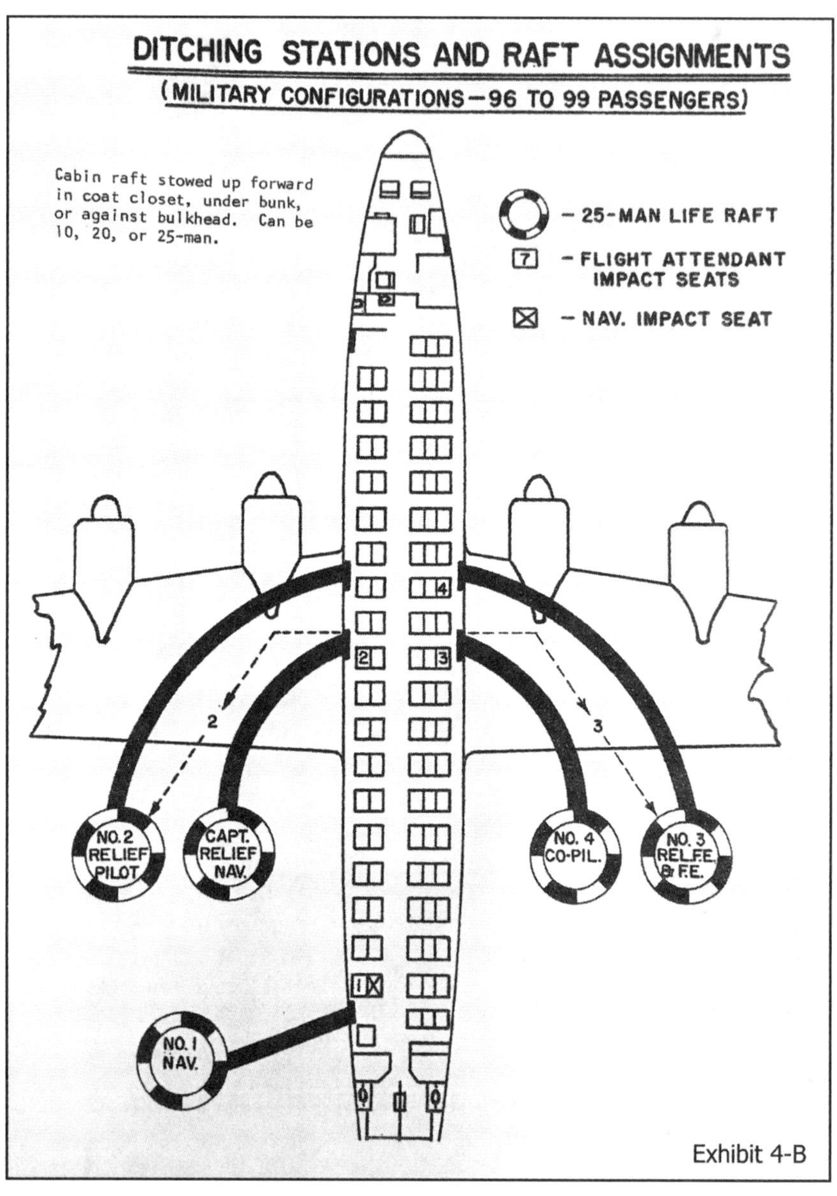

One of the thousands of exhibit pages entered into evidence during the U.S. Civil Aeronautics Board's hearing into Tiger 923, November 14–16, 1962. However, this configuration is contradicted by sworn testimony and other forensics. Though Tiger 923's cabin layout remains unclear, most key details are clear. For instance, while the forward left-side window-exit may have been closer to row 11 than row 8, it was definitely Gould's point of egress. COURTESY U.S. DEPARTMENT OF TRANSPORTATION.

SEATING AT TIME OF IMPACT

Cockpit		Flight Deck
	J. Murray	Forward Galley

Row		< Rows 1-6 Empty >				
07	M. Murray					
08	C. Gould					
09	R. Parker			D. Tumminello	L. Pierce	J. Garrett
10		R. Mudd		J. Brotman	E. Apanel	H. Benson
11	G. Brown			L. Elander	C. Elander	F. Caruso
12				J. Devlin	N. Devlin	
13	H. Lesane		AISLE			J. MacDonald
14				E. Eldred		
15	H. Groves	J. Groves		R. Eldred		
16	J. Figueroa-Longo	C. Figueroa-Longo		R. Hoopi	L. Hoopi	U. Hoopi
17	E. Dent	G. Dent		A. Gilbreth		
18	A. Bates	R. Acevedo				
19		W. MacGlothren			F. Gazelle	R. Mendez
20		S. Nicholson		E. Sims	G. Thornsberry	

Estimated seating at 10:13 p.m., September 23, 1962. Based on a sometimes conflicting composite of official (e.g., U.S. Department of Commerce hearing transcripts) and unofficial (e.g., interviews) sources, the above is the best available reconstruction. Many survivors couldn't recall where they or others were sitting, both at the November 1962 CAB Board of Inquiry hearing and half a century later in their living room.

Lockheed Super H Constellation, circa 1962. Though these are not the actual soldiers who were on Tiger 923, this is the actual plane (tail number N6923C), the same disembarkation process used in Gander, and the actual door out of which Hard Luck Sam was supposed to launch the emergency raft.

PART II

MISSING LIFE RAFTS

Since I'm utterly doomed in any case, I might as well put some effort into it.

—*Capt. John Murray*[1]

Chapter 4
Trouble in the North Atlantic

There was a flash of blue. The right outboard engine clipped a wave. The first rebound snapped off the left wing; the second tore most of the three-seat rows off the right-side cabin floor. The right tailfin hit the water, then the nose. An internal fuel tank ruptured, and fuel gushed up through the carpet. A dozen windows imploded: *Phoom-phoom-phoom-phoom.* The pilot's head hit the glare shield. The landing lights shorted out and the plane began to take on water. It all happened in seconds.

To Bob Eldred (right side aisle seat, row 15), it felt and sounded like "just one crashing smash . . . like all the nails in Christendom being pulled out of boards at once."[1] He went "flying through space, strapped to the seat, as though it had never been bolted to the floor."

Copilot Bob Parker was unhurt. He unbuckled his seatbelt, rushed up from amidship, and laid his left hand on Murray's right epaulette. It was sticky with blood. "John?"[2]

The pilot stirred, said he was okay, and told Parker to return to his station. Murray said he'd follow soon.

At the back of the plane, Hard Luck Sam, also uninjured, unfastened his seatbelt, grabbed the raft with his left hand and with his right opened the main cabin door. The ocean roared in: pinning him against the opposite wall. "It seemed like he'd opened the doors of hell."[3]

Sam dropped the raft, ducked his head, and raised his arms until the onslaught ebbed, then spat out seawater, again reached for the raft, and tugged at it. But given the deluge, he couldn't budge the heavy hunk of rubber.

Sam's assistants were gone: the impact catapulted PFC Thornsberry two rows forward; Betty Sims had also disappeared. But Sgt. Ralph Bates rushed back from row 18. He and Sam muscled the uninflated rubber mass out the door and into the water.

But as the raft wasn't tethered to the cabin floor, the wild waves and fast current shot it out to sea. As Bates stared in horror, Sam dove after it.

Eldred landed in the middle of aisle 13, three rows up from his wife. He was face down, underwater. Though knocked out on impact he regained consciousness, lifted his head, and shouted, "Edna! Edna!" but soon realized he "was [being] pretty silly. No one could have heard an individual voice in that noise. It was bedlam, voices, a 30 mph wind, the wrenching of the plane."[4] He unbuckled his belt, rose to his knees, then feet, and limped over to the right-side window-exit in row 10, where he "reached for the hatch and, with another officer, got it open. The sea poured in immediately."

Four rows back, by the window, Fred Caruso unbraced, his only apparent injury a sore ankle. He didn't know what had become of his row-mates, Major and Mrs. Elander, just that as there was now no one between him and the nearest window-exit, he intended to make the most of the clearing. Though he'd been told to wait for a stewardess to lead the way, he didn't see one and as the voice inside his head was yelling, *We're sinking!* he unbuckled his seat belt and stood.[5] Recalling the evacuation demonstration, he pawed about until he located the window, flipped a latch, grabbed the sides of the frame, jerked it off the wall and dropped it onto what had been a carpet but was now a North Atlantic tributary. It splashed.

Caruso climbed out, stepped onto the wing, and slid more than jumped into the water. While fumbling for his life vest's two inflation tabs, he looked about for the two life rafts he'd been told would be waiting for him, fully inflated. There was no sign of them.

Most of Dr. Elander had been propelled forward into the aisle of row 9, but his ankle was caught on a strut in his original row, 11, on the right side of the cabin. Mostly underwater, the ophthalmologist lifted his chin in an effort to keep his eyes and mouth above the torrent.

He was frantic about what had become of his wife. Craning his neck back toward Lois' seat, in the dim light, he could just barely make out a soldier assisting her out onto the wing.

Across the aisle, on the left side of the plane, stewardess Ruth Mudd was standing on a seat, yelling at PFCs Edward Apanel and Paul Stewart, who were struggling with the hatch in row 8. "Somebody pull the window out, pull the window out!"[6]

Apanel succeeded. He handed the window to Stewart, who, looking confused, heaved it in the direction of the cockpit.

Four rows back, Dr. Figueroa-Longo opened the other left-side exit-window and started climbing out headfirst. When his wife yelled that he was doing it the wrong way, he reversed himself and went out feetfirst.

As Rachel Hoopi stood in the aisle to Carmen's right, struggling to unbuckle one of her daughters' seat belts, the Air Force doctor's wife heard her husband "calling me from the outside to jump. So I put my legs out and sat on the edge of the window and . . . I said I just can't, and then he grabbed my legs and pulled me down."[7]

Sgt. John Groves helped his teenage bride up onto the sill of the same exit. Helga "held his hand as they jumped from the aircraft into the black spray."[8]

Stewardess Carol Gould was amazed that her only injury was a bruised thumb. She watched from the aisle as a third paratrooper yelled at George Brown and Michael Murray, "Get on with it!" as the pair struggled to remove another exit-window.[9] Murray finally wrenched it off and dropped it onto an empty seat nearby.

As she stepped over toward her assigned and now open window in row 8 and reached for the lever that would jettison the two rafts stored in the left wing-bay, several soldiers barreled into her and began pushing her toward the exit. She yelled: "No, wait, no, wait! I have to pull this red lever!"

Harry Benson regained consciousness in time to see Gould being forced out the exit through "a steady wall of water flowing over the window."[10] He shouted: "Stop pushing her!

"I pulled one man away, and as I was pulling him, one man got out, the second man got out, and the third got out. Just a matter of seconds. It was one, two, three and they were out."

Now it was Gould's turn. She clutched the frame with her hands and dug her feet into the sill. The howling wind scared her and the cold water drenched her. Just before stepping through the window and onto the wing, she looked out and realized: *There is no wing!*[11]

Another batch of soldiers pressed against her. "Jump, Carol, for Crissakes!"

She replied: "I have to pull the lever!"

As the scrum kept pushing her inexorably out the exit, she couldn't reach the raft-release lever. She thought: *Someone else will have to do it.*

"Jump, Carol—dammit!"

She jumped.

After likewise balking at and fretting over the absence of a wing to step out onto, Benson and several others followed Gould out the left side. None pulled the raft-release lever.

Others, hearing the shouts about the missing left wing, crossed the aisle to crowd around the right-side exits in rows 8 and 10. They understandably preferred stepping onto a hard metal surface as opposed to jumping out into the wild waves, especially since, as instructed, few had inflated their life vest. Their logic was misplaced.

At the back of the plane, Gordon Thornsberry regained consciousness and opened his eyes underwater in his overturned seat in aisle 18. He held his breath, unbuckled his seat belt, extricated himself, stepped over other uprooted seats, and waded his way back to the main cabin door. Once there he felt about for the knife Hard Luck Sam had given him, but it was gone.

However, when he saw that the emergency raft was also gone, he was relieved because there was no longer any need to cut the rope that had anchored the raft to the floor of the cabin. The Arkansan stepped up onto the sill and dove out.

To Raúl Acevedo, whom a brutal cramp had unbraced seconds before the plane hit, the impact felt "like twenty cars smashing together, at race-track speeds."[12] Though conscious at impact, he lost consciousness soon thereafter.

Awakened by the sound of windows exploding all around him and the sensation of ice water creeping up his pants' inseams, he tried to get up, but a stabbing pain in his lower back checked him. Fuel trickled down his throat, triggering a semi-puke that brought the gasoline right back up, now flavored with stomach acid.

Though the cabin was dark and he was three rows back, he could still make out a soldier helping the little Hawaiian girls out through a left-side over-wing window-exit, one sister after the other. That's when Acevedo realized: *Dios mio! If I don't get out, I'm gonna sink to death!*

He flipped his seat belt latch and rose unsteadily, his vest draped around his neck. As he began to make his way back to the rear exit 10 feet away, pushing past floating candy wrappers, cigarette butts, and air sickness bags, Acevedo heard some muffled voices but couldn't pinpoint their origin. He saw no one until he was standing by the exit, peering out into the dark. Now he knew where the voices were coming from: the sea.

"I can't inflate my vest! I don't know how to swim!"

"Where are the rafts?"

"Help!"

Acevedo paused. The scene was terrifying, every option awful. He could feel the plane sinking, the water rising up his legs. But he could also see the endless "mountains of water" outside and hear the cries of those who'd jumped. It sounded like they wished they hadn't.

Despite terrible pain he managed to get both stockinged feet up onto the sill. He patted his chest pocket for his Our Lady of Guadalupe prayer card, made the sign of the cross, pulled the upper life vest string and then the lower one, and, once he felt the bladders billowing, jumped out the main exit.

Art Gilbreth was in a textbook brace position at the moment of impact. That just made him more aerodynamic. He flew forward about 25 feet from his right-side aisle seat in row 17. The paratrooper landed upside down, his head under more than a foot of bitter-cold water, still buckled into his seat, the nylon belt slicing into his ribs. As he tried to lift his head and gasp for air, his shattered vertebrae brought tears to his eyes . . . as the North Atlantic poured in through a nearby window and washed him back to row 19, where he passed out.

Something or someone jarred him conscious. *I gotta get the hell out of here!* But the latch wouldn't budge, and his seat was entangled with several others. *Why bother?*[13]

He winced as he pulled at the latch one last time. The buckle popped open. Rising into an enfeebled crouch and assessing the situation as best he could in the darkness, he could tell it was bleak. The plane was clearly sinking. There were no signs of anyone, no voices, just a sense of total disorientation.

However, mystifyingly, his pain was gone. He felt energized. His eyes having sufficiently adjusted he was able to make out a blurry white line a few rows down: ocean foam whipped up as the sea crashed against the top of the fuselage and poured into the cabin through the open exit. It was a terrifying sight but also maybe the only way out.

Gilbreth clawed his way over to the froth. Once by the window-exit he gripped its sides, took a deep breath, and prepared to plunge, but was greeted by another oceanic blast and tumbled backwards.

Staggering to his feet, in his peripheral vision he saw a different flash of white: a male crew member's shirt sleeve. The guy grabbed Gilbreth by the shoulder and elbow and pushed him through the exit-window.

But another thunderous wave met him and sent him reeling back in. A ricocheting eddy threw him against the cabin wall, then swept him aft.

This time he resurfaced beside the main cabin door at the rear of the aircraft. It was half underwater. Gilbreth stood, took a deep breath, and "shot out of the plane like a torpedo."

In the cockpit, Captain Murray tried to think straight, but a split-open skull made it hard. Muddled though his cognition was he knew he needed to evacuate fast. He could see the rising waterline through the wraparound windshield.

With the flight deck door gone he listened for voices. He didn't hear any, suggesting that most of the other 75 souls had evacuated and perhaps were safely aboard the five life rafts. He felt thankful for that, as well as for being alive and ambulatory.

Though the captain was as eager as anyone to get off the rapidly sinking plane, he knew his first priority was accounting for every man, woman, and child and, if necessary, helping them evacuate and get clear of the plane's inevitable undertow. Given the rate at which she was taking on water, it was clear to him that Connie wouldn't stay afloat much longer. He just wasn't sure if he had five minutes or five seconds.

Unbuckling his seat belt and standing made him dizzy. While leaning into his seat for stability, he paused to feel about for any additional injuries apart from his head, which hurt like hell.

He waded aft. Though it was dark, the small blue ceiling lights hadn't zapped out yet and some moonlight refracted off the water through the windows. Murray could see well enough.

It was slow going. The pilot fought his way past the icy sea shooting through the windows and the noisome fuel seeping up through the floor, past the workstations, crew bunks, and galley; then headed down the aisle, glancing left and right, flipping over the occasional seat. There was no sign of anyone. It was heartening.

It took him about two minutes to make it to the rear of the plane and the main cabin door, which was almost entirely underwater. After stepping up onto the sill and bending his knees, an instant before diving out, an idea seized him: *Maybe I should go back for a torch?*[14]

While it may have seemed insane to pause, even briefly, doing so comported with his philosophy of avoiding the fallacy of decisiveness. Though Betty Sims had assured him she'd collected a lot of flashlights, who knew how many had made it off the plane? Or how many had sunk? Or how depleted the batteries were?

As he stood in the doorway mulling things over, a white-shirted silhouette framed by the dark exit, had anyone been looking his way they might have thought the pilot was in shock. Or that he'd suffered a concussion. Or both.

First, there was the matter of his even being able to make it back into the cockpit before the plane sank. He'd have to make his way 150 feet in really cold, waist-high water, obstructed by 76 sets of personal belongings and other flotsam.[15]

Second, the sputtering cabin lights seemed ready to give out. He'd lost his prescription eyeglasses. One eye was obscured by blood. Even if he made it to the flight deck and there was a flashlight there, would Murray be able to find it in time?

Concluding that not attempting was the fallacy, the pilot turned around, gulped some air, shut his lips, and dove under the water. He powered his way past 100 seats, many overturned and piled high in the aisle; entered the flight deck; swept aside mushy dinner rolls in the galley and waterlogged manuals in the cockpit; and there it was, wedged at the base of the very same glare shield that had knocked him out and split his head open. Murray grabbed the flashlight, turned around, and headed aft.

By now a lot more seawater and fuel had flooded the cabin. Still, he made it back to row 8's starboard-side wing exit. He tried to catch his breath. He was more winded than he'd ever been in his life. He was ruing his love of Pall Malls. His life vest was on but unclipped. After pulling the raft-release lever for good measure, he gripped the sides of the exit, tilted his head up, and gulped some oxygen from one of the few remaining pockets of air. Just as he stepped up onto the sill, a wave crashed through the open window behind him—knocking him overboard.

Murray surfaced beside the hull at 10:20 p.m., immersed as much in aviation fuel and hydraulic fluid as seawater. With his unfastened, uninflated life vest more impediment than aid, he gagged as he fought to keep his head above the nauseating brew. Unlike everyone else, he'd been unable to remove his shoes; now, waterlogged, they felt like lead anchors. Though he saw no sign of the five rafts, he saw lots of soldiers nearby, dog-paddling, clinging to various parts of the plane, helping other passengers.

As the right wing was sinking, PFC Willie Smith "was standing on it . . . grabbing people . . . and helping them into the water."[16]

Nearby, according to Edward Apanel, some guy was "just hanging on my back, and then he pulled me into the water. We both came back up and a wave hit us. We both went under . . . and he never came back up."[17]

After George Brown helped a woman off the plane, "she grabbed onto my life vest and my shirt and pulled me under. I couldn't get ahold of the releases on my life vest. When we come up again I grabbed her arm and hollered, and I told her to take it easy before she drowned us both and she released her hand from my shoulder and then pulled her releases and I pulled mine. The life vest didn't hold me up too well, though."[18]

Leaning against the hull, Sammy Vasquez knew he should get as far away from the plane as possible, as fast as possible, because he thought *The first thing it's going to do is suck you down.*[19] But "being young, dumb and stupid," he also "wanted to see it sink," so he dog-paddled in place, "maybe ten feet from the aircraft."

Beside him, his buddy Little Animal was "with a stewardess, and she said to him, 'Are we gonna make it?'—then a wave hit her, and she was gone. I tried to find her, but it was dark, and I couldn't locate her."

Gordon Thornsberry

> *tried swimming but my legs were rather heavy because of the wool pants, so I pulled them off and I swam through a small cluster of people toward the wing looking for the raft. I heard the people asking where the raft was at and I swam up there and it wasn't there, with the understanding that there were two rafts on each wing, and the waves were going up over the plane and one carried me up almost to the top and I grabbed ahold of the two antennas there and stood up and looked on the other side of the plane . . . but there wasn't any life rafts over there, and a wave washed me towards the rear of the plane and one of the antennas broke off and I fell off.*[20]

Ex–Air Force pilot Harry Benson

> *could see the plane was sinking. I hadn't taken half a dozen strokes when somebody . . . got ahold of my hair and threw an arm around my neck and shoulder and they started climbing up on me. They actually tried to get up on my shoulder and I went under at that time, and I*

> *remember as I went under I swallowed two or three mouthfuls of salt water, and I could taste the gasoline and it was vivid.*[21]

George and Naomi Devlin vanished. The other five couples got separated.

Bob Eldred last saw his wife just before impact. He was desperate to find Edna but also desperate not to drown. His Normandy invasion wounds severely hindered both objectives.

> *It was a black night, a little lighter than inside the plane. There was no moon. I inflated my life jacket and there I was in the North Atlantic . . . not feeling cold, in my shirt, pants and socks.*
>
> *There were huge billows, a strong wind, but no scud. The reason for the absence of the blowing sea . . . was there was a sea of aviation gasoline all around me. The water tasted lousy.*
>
> *I could hear people screaming, but more as though to attract attention than in panic. I never did see any general panic, or hear any.*
>
> *Then the water began to feel cold, the shrieking wind and the shouting people sounded a long way off, and I knew I was going to die. I had a moment of wondering why I didn't just take a good swallow and go under.*
>
> *I wasn't afraid of dying. There were a few thoughts of pain, and of hopelessness, but not of dying. It was strange. A sort of resignation.*
>
> *Then I felt something bump into me. I grabbed it, felt all over until my fingers came to a padlock, and I knew I was hanging onto a soldier's duffel bag. It floated and it held me up. I began thinking of living again.*[22]

Nearby, Helga Groves dog-paddled beside the plane, screaming: "John! John!"[23] The 18-year-old hadn't seen her husband since they'd jumped overboard, hand in hand.

Dr. Elander's initial reaction to being in the sea? "It was the most wonderful thing to be out there."[24]

His opinion changed quickly, however, as he lost track of his spouse and worried about the sinking plane's suction. Hoping Lois had already managed to break free, the major kicked off the wing and started swimming as fast as he could.

He hadn't gotten far when a voice carried above the wind and water, stopping him mid-stroke: "Dick? Dick?"

It was Lois. He thought: *It's an absolute miracle!* He yelled: "I'm right behind you!"

Carmen Figueroa-Longo also found her husband, Juan. "We were separated and I heard him calling me. So I swam toward him and he asked if I had my life vest inflated, and I said no, and then he inflated it for me. And then I grab him and we were sinking. So we came up and he pushed me aside because I was just holding him down, and then a wave separated us."[25]

Air Force lieutenant colonel George Dent said it

> *seemed like Elizabeth and I had been in the water for some period of time and my wife called to me and said that we should swim away, that it appeared that a wing looked like it was going to hit us. We floated past the tail and this was coming down. We moved away from the aircraft probably ten, fifteen yards, and I found a piece of wood . . . a foot and a half square by about two inches thick. I passed it to her and told her to hold onto this and we were alternating together and separated by a couple or three yards because of the rolling action of the sea.*[26]

Only a few of the evacuees could make out the dark yellow clump skipping away from the plane. Fewer could make out the navigator in pursuit. Hard Luck Sam was a good swimmer but he'd never faced water this rough. The waves fought his every stroke but in less than 10 minutes he'd pulled up beside the raft. As he rested his hand on its side and caught his breath . . . a wave swept the raft off into the night.

He swam after it and grabbed it but couldn't keep the thing still, let alone inflate it. It was too cumbersome, too slick with aviation fluids, and too elusive in the swift current. It seemed hopeless, a lost cause.

Sergeant Ralph Bates and Private Michael Murray showed up and blocked the raft with their bodies, which allowed the navigator to paw about in search of the CO_2 releases. But they were hidden by darkness, waves, and folds of rubber.

More paratroopers arrived, attracted by splashes and voices. The added ballast enabled Sam to locate a tab and pull it. The CO_2 canister popped and hissed. He found a second tab and pulled it.

It took maybe three minutes for the raft fully to inflate. The men weren't in the mood to wait, however. They began trying to climb aboard.

But there were no handles or rope-braids. The sides were three feet high and really slick. Every time someone managed to hook a leg or an arm over the gunwale, a wave would sweep it back into the water. Soldier after soldier was repulsed.

That is, until a billowing crest lifted PFC Murray 15 feet up into the air and dropped him down in the center of the raft. He got his bearings, pulled in Sammy Vasquez; the two pulled in Bates and Hard Luck Sam; and the four began yelling over the wind and waves, trying to alert others to the fact that they'd found, inflated, and boarded one raft at least.

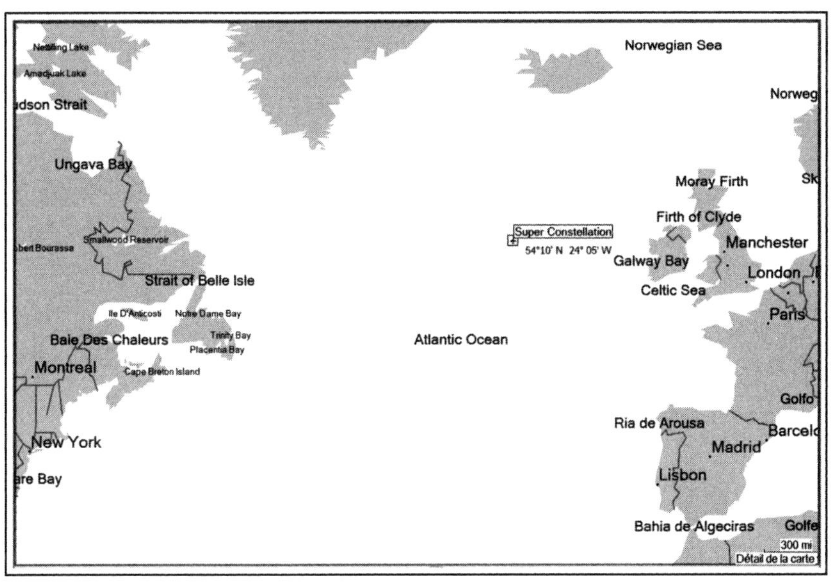

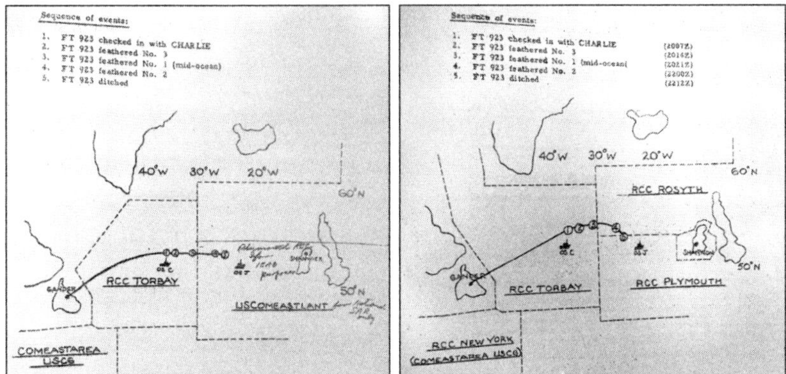

(Top) *Celerina* deckhand (and, later, marine architect) Pierre-André Reymond drew this map showing the precise ditching coordinates. COURTESY REYMOND. (Bottom) U.S. Coast Guard maps show how hard it was to track Tiger 923's path and search-and-rescue jurisdiction given the "pitch-black night" and incompatible communications. COURTESY COAST GUARD.

Chapter 5

Invisible

While the navigator had done a remarkable job estimating the ditching longitude and latitude, Hard Luck Sam's figures were disseminated at 10:04 p.m.[1] In the 24 minutes that had elapsed since then, the current had carried the raft about two miles from the ditching site.

An Alitalia jet was the closest. The next closest was a prop plane flown by Riddle Air, Flying Tiger Line's chief rival for Pentagon business. But as USAF 246 was just five minutes behind Riddle 18H and it had much better communication capabilities, the U.K.'s rescue center designated the U.S. Air Force prop as the lead aircraft in the far-flung search-and-rescue operation.

Lt. Joe Lewis didn't know how responsive he could be, however. Neither he nor any of the other 27 aboard his C-118 troop transport had seen any signs of wreckage, rafts, or survivors. Lewis was especially puzzled that nobody had seen any shooting red or floating (via tiny parachutes) purple flares, yellow raft sideboard lights, or white flashlight beams.

He knew that any survivors fending in the open water probably couldn't last more than 20 to 30 minutes and that, even aboard a raft, they'd last "a maximum of six hours in water of that temperature."[2]

An hour earlier, at 9:30, though 13 hours from Tiger 923's ditching coordinates, a Swiss freighter was the closest ship. The *Celerina*—which means "fast" in the native Romansh—was still the survivors' best hope for rescue.

Just prior to the Mayday, the youngest member of the *Celerina* crew, 19-year-old Pierre-André Reymond, was writing a letter to his parents in Lausanne.

> *We are experiencing gale-force winds. The Celerina tosses and rolls. The deck of the ship is swept by waves over 10 meters high. The porthole of my cabin is covered with a flap, a kind of inside metal shutter designed to protect us from the cannon-ball force waves that crash along the side of the ship. When we sleep we have to arrange our berths in a V position and stuff pillows and life vests under the mattress, so there is less chance of our being ejected by the rolling motion of the freighter. Waves on such a day can roll the ship up to 30 degrees. I must admit that the sea looks pretty awesome.*[3]

Apart from Reymond, everyone else not on the bridge, in the boiler room, or otherwise on duty was gathered in the warm mess, including Walter Wunderlin. Amidst plumes of smoke and the smell of coffee, Wunderlin was winning at cards, a rare outcome for the guileless 28-year-old country carpenter on a ship full of crafty, cosmopolitan merchant seamen.

As the carpenter gathered up his cigarettes, Capt. Domenico Lugli interrupted the game with a PA announcement, informing his multinational crew of 33 that an American aircraft with 76 souls on board was expected to ditch soon and, as the closest ship, the *Celerina* would be changing course to search for survivors. Lugli ordered his crew to stop whatever they were doing. Antwerp would have to wait to receive its 3,000 tons of Manitoba wheat.

Wunderlin thought: *Naturally, when I'm winning.*[4] After stowing his cigarettes beneath his bunk, he headed off to help the boatswain ready the painter's ladders, Jacob's ladders, ropes, and nets.

Reymond thought it was a lost cause. "The engineers told us that the sea temperature is only 7 degrees Celsius [45 degrees F]. This, combined with the wind, must have been horrible for the survivors, even if they could shelter inside inflatable life rafts."

Lugli didn't need to ask his wife and 15-year-old daughter to help. Though he felt guilty their quasi-vacation was being interrupted, they wanted to help, and immediately set about collecting surplus clothes and blankets and inventorying the coffee and hot chocolate.

While Lugli wasn't sanguine about the chances of finding survivors given how violently the North Atlantic was pitching his 12,000-ton ship, he nonetheless instructed the engineer to begin switching from heavy cruising oil back to a lighter viscosity (the first step to changing course, as its better flow enhanced maneuverability and engine reliability, especially in cold weather). Meanwhile, the radioman struggled to stay in contact with the rescue control center, as the donkeyman began inspecting lifebuoys and removing searchlight covers, the motorman began checking the lifeboat's engine, and the kitchen staff stopped preparing the regular dinner and started making soup, coffee, and tea. While there was no doctor on board, Reymond helped the second mate ready the ship's "hospital," which was little more than a small room with a single bunk where the crew could lie down and get some aspirin and a Band-Aid.

By 10:25 Captain Lugli had slashed his ETA. He'd more than doubled his speed, which was a minor miracle given the heavy chop. He now felt he might reach the ditching site in five hours. That was the good news.

But there was also bad news. First, the ship's engine might not hold out five hours at such a rigorous pace, in such rough conditions. The top speed of 17 mph was supposed to be reserved for calm water and fair winds, not 25-foot waves and gale-force headwinds. Second, the rescue lifeboat's engine wouldn't start. While the motorman said maybe he could fix it, he felt it highly unlikely because he didn't have the parts or the time. Third, when Lugli instructed the radioman immediately to notify other responders and the supervising British rescue control center of the predicament, he was reminded that such notification wouldn't be easy. As the neutral Swiss had no access to NATO's 1962 frequencies and most ships used FM rather than the AM preferred by most aircraft, the *Celerina* would have to do much of its communicating via a slow, cumbersome 1838 invention: Morse code.

Sixty miles east of the *Celerina*, another dozen or so survivors had found, swum to, and boarded the emergency raft. Despite the loud wind and waves, most could hear the rumble of aircraft engines in the sky above, even though Lieutenant Lewis' USAF 246 was hidden by the clouds. Someone yelled: "Who's got a flashlight? Let's send up a flare!"[5]

Hard Luck Sam was supposed to have brought a flashlight, a flare pistol, and extra flares. But all he'd managed to bring were some flare cartridges, which, absent the pistol, were useless.

But then he realized the raft was equipped with a flashlight and a flare pistol. *Phew!* He told everyone to look around and feel about for the storage compartment.

After a few fruitless minutes, an observant soldier noticed the raft's oddly sloping interior contours; how, rather than forming a crisp right angle, the sides and floor merged together, more a slope than a perpendicular. "It's upside down!"[6]

"What?" Sam strained to hear above the din.

"The raft's upside down! The flares . . . everything else, too . . . are underwater!"

As more people arrived and were pulled up and in, a furious debate ensued as to whether it made sense for everyone to jump back into the water, flip the raft over, then reboard. Sammy Vasquez spoke for many when he yelled: "It's still really slippery. I'm not sure I could get on a second time."[7]

There was no consensus but as those opposed to returning to the water were sufficient in number to prevent a flipping, it was settled: the raft would remain upside down. There'd be no access to flares, flashlights, potable water, or medical supplies.

More evacuees were closer to the plane than to the raft. Most didn't even know a raft had been located and boarded.

As the Lockheed's carcass sunk, rivet by rivet, dialing up a whirlpool, the mental quicksand that's symptomatic of hypothermia prevented many from realizing they needed to get clear of the hull, lest they get pulled under with it. Others, realizing the danger, set off feverishly . . . in every direction . . . not knowing if they were headed toward a raft or not.

Willie Smith "could see heads bobbing in the waves by the stars."[8] The paratrooper leapt off the wing and swam over to join six others who were in a circle, holding hands, "using the buddy system to stay afloat," fighting to keep their heads above water. Some had been able to inflate their life vests; others hadn't.

It didn't seem to matter. Even inflated, the vests seemed no match for the sea. "I thought I was going to die," said Smith. Then he saw a hazy image that gave him hope. "I asked God to give me the strength to make the raft. We started for it but only four of us could swim and only three made it."

Like most Hawaiians, 9-year-old Luana Hoopi and her 11-year-old sister, Uilani, had learned to swim before they'd learned to walk. But they'd never swum in water this rough and cold. After having been passed out the exit window, their uninflated life vests flat around their necks, they stepped onto the right wing . . . and disappeared.

Their mother searched frantically for her daughters, calling after them, but heard nothing, saw nothing. However, when Rachel saw a trail of people swimming toward a blotch off in the distance, and heard accompanying voices, she put two and two together: the blotch was a raft. Had the man who'd said he'd help already gotten his girls there? She set off after it and them.

Though Fred Caruso was the first to get off the plane, he'd not gotten very far. Though he'd been working his arms and legs like crazy for six or seven minutes, he'd just been churning water. "The water was filled with people, baggage, gasoline. There were people screaming for help, including me. Help me! Help me! I became very religious. I was praying."[9]

"The North Atlantic is cold. Terribly cold and choppy too. It seemed like eternity before I could find my inflate string. It was dark, the water so choppy, finally I got it. In one hiss I was floating in my life vest."[10]

He couldn't see any of the other 75 people who'd been aboard, just hear some voices. He couldn't see any of the five rafts. And he couldn't see any searchlights from the plane he'd heard someone say was escorting Tiger 923. All Caruso saw were the "cascading mountains of water hitting me like I was sitting in a chair and someone was throwing buckets of ice-water at me." The petroleum-infused water shot into his mouth, up his nose. He spat it out then yelled: "Where the hell are the rafts!"

"I tried to keep it together, reminding myself of all my Advanced Infantry lessons, about survival being mostly mind over matter."[11] He recalled how, just two months prior, while down in Georgia during its inferno of a summer, suffering from excruciating, popping heat blisters, the highlight of every day was the cold showers the Airborne trainees were allowed to take every 10 minutes in the middle of the woods, fully dressed. But his mind alone wouldn't save him, he knew. This wasn't a Georgia forest in July.

It got to him: the loneliness, darkness, disorientation, wetness, cold, and fear. He began screaming at the top of his lungs. "Oh, God—help me!"

He swam the length of the fuselage until he reached the outermost starboard tailfin, which protruded about 15 feet above the sea. He was clueless as to what his next move should be or where any of the rafts might be. As he watched the red taillights rotate and green-tipped right wing submerge, he thought: *This is it.*

A figure emerged out of the darkness within reach, startling him. He couldn't make out a face, just a male torso and flailing arms, saying nothing but gasping for air, struggling to keep his head above the high, churning water.

Then the opaque whirligig lunged, clamping onto Caruso's neck, cutting off his air, and pushing him beneath the surface. The two men grappled underwater. Every time Caruso tried to shake himself loose, the silent assailant's grip tightened. Feeling the guy's flat, uninflated vest told Caruso the intention was buoyancy, yet "I knew from my days lifeguarding that panicky people got really irrational and dangerous, and I couldn't help this guy survive unless I made sure I did, first. But that's not how the guy was thinking."[12]

Caruso finally pried the guy off, looked up through three feet of water, saw the taillights, and made his way toward them. Resurfacing near the starboard tailfin, he gulped air, twirled in the water, and tried to find the guy, but there was no sign of him, just the mostly submerged plane. "I was still way too close to it, in danger of being sucked down with it."[13]

On the other side of the plane, the waves that had engulfed stewardess Carol Gould and her group of evacuees coughed them back up.

Well, not everyone. Her group had shrunk in size from 17 to 8.

Gould should have been focused on inflating her vest, she knew, but human nature being what it is, especially under extreme duress, her top priority wasn't buoyancy but retribution. So when the sea pushed a paratrooper into her, she threw a sharp elbow.

The guy looked at her like she was nuts. "Hey?! What was that for?"[14]

It was for the way the Airborne guys had pushed her out before she was ready, before she had had a chance to pull the raft-releasing T-bar. It was for the way they'd not respected Gould's authority, though she was the one who'd recently had a ditching refresher course, training her for just this sort of eventuality.

Seeing no rafts, just seeing and feeling the cold, violent sea, her natural optimism yielded to despair. She looked up while thinking of her New Jersey State Trooper friend, who'd recently died in the line of duty. "I hope I'll be seeing you soon, Joe. I've missed you."

A soldier brought her back to the present: "What now, Carol? Other side . . . The other side of the plane. Check for that wing's rafts?"

Another soldier was accusatory: "Where are the rafts? You said they'd be right here!"

"I don't know where they are." She tried to puzzle it out but was having a hard enough time just staying afloat in her uninflated vest and not ingesting the foul sea. Then her thoughts leapfrogged back two months to her Coast Guard ditching drill in July. She recalled how when she'd jumped into the Brooklyn motel swimming pool the impact shot her life vest's rope-pulls up and over her shoulder, so she reached back for them and there they were.

One tug released half of the CO_2; a second released the balance. The upper and lower bladders filled rapidly, easily raising her svelte body above the surface. She bobbed, stopped dog-paddling, and closed her eyes. *Thank you, God.*

Despite the loud conditions, some voices on the raft carried across the water. Though when she first turned toward them "all I could see was black," a small section of moon emerged from behind the clouds, lighting the bright yellow, shiny-with-oil raft.[15] Seeing "glimpses of it between the waves," she yelled, "Follow me!" Gould started swimming. Her group followed.

It was rough going. The roiling water made the journey almost as vertical as horizontal. Plus, as the moon had retreated back behind the clouds, she wasn't sure she was still headed the right way. But after six minutes she was beside the raft.

She wasn't welcome. A man yelled: "This one's already full! You'll tip us over."[16]

Gould was speechless.

"Find another raft!"

She yelled: "There *are* no other rafts!"

George Brown shoved his way past the soldiers "and pulled me up and my life—the hook on my life vest got caught on the rope. I was half on and half off and had to wait there until he pulled the other people on and then came back and unhooked me."[17]

She gripped his forearm. "Thank you, so much!"[18]

"Sure."

Though it was really dark out, there was enough refracted moonlight for her to see his injury: "Why, your head's wide open!" Gould thought: *I've gotta try to bandage that! But with what?*

Then she remembered her half-slip.[19] (She'd started to remove it before the plane hit the water, but when she looked up and saw a bunch of guys ogling her she stopped.) She rolled it down, wrapped it around Brown's head as he continued pulling people aboard, and knotted it into a makeshift tourniquet. The waves kept sweeping it off. Eventually, Gould gave up trying to reapply it.

Thinking there had to be a better place for her to sit, she crawled about on her hands and knees in the wildly bucking raft, landing on the feet and fingers, groins and necks of 40 others, in space designed for half as many. "Big bodies were sprawled over every inch, several hanging over the rim. People were moaning, praying, crying. The water was so cold! It stunk of fuel and tasted of blood, whenever the waves crashed over the sides. I considered myself lucky to find a spot that was only two people deep, and collapsed in the yucky fluid, two feet deep."[20]

Elizabeth Dent said, "George, I think I see a life raft behind us."[21]

The Air Force officer turned and, though he saw no lights, "made out a shape which was possibly fifteen to twenty yards away." He said: "Well, go, because I am coming."

Elizabeth "swam to it and the raft washed in to her." She was pulled in.

But the current swept her husband past the raft, back out to sea.

Though Dick Elander arrived at the raft right behind his wife, upon boarding, Lois stumbled and fell to the left and he splashed to the right. The doctor lost sight of his wife.

The Army major knew she was there, however, because he could stretch his arm and, just barely, by the tips of his fingers, lift her head above the waterline. But he didn't know how long he could keep at it with the raft rocking so, knocking bodies into one another.

He was distraught. He knew Lois couldn't fend for herself. He didn't know she had a badly sprained back and dislocated shoulder, just that she was pinned underwater and couldn't move.

A terrified and helpless Bob Eldred rode the swift current off into the night, his attention divided between looking for his wife and the raft. Though there was no sign of Edna, "I heard voices saying 'Over here. Over here.' And there was the raft, loaded with people."

"It seemed . . . about one hundred yards away. I knew I couldn't swim that far in a safety jacket and with a stiff knee. But the next thing I know I was alongside, and a soldier had taken hold of an arm and the seat of my britches and was muscling me into the raft."[22]

Captain Murray was still beside the plane. He was also about 100 yards from the raft. The raft he didn't know existed.

Still, he felt incredibly fortunate to be alive. He knew how lucky he'd been for that long trough to appear between the big swells just before his plane hit the sea.

Yet the pilot wondered if his luck had finally run out. He wasn't a young man any more. Though a good swimmer, this was brutal chop and he was still winded from having semi-swum 100 yards inside the plane through spigots of seawater, fuel, and flotsam. His head really hurt. He figured he had a concussion, he'd pass out any second, and the plane would sink any moment. He couldn't see much and saw no sign of any of the five rafts.

Murray at least had the presence of mind to realize his top priority: buoyancy. But like so many others he couldn't find the pull-strings to open the CO_2 cartridges and fill his vest with air. He'd been fumbling for the inflation tabs since hitting the water.

Crabbing his way out of the sea and back up onto the right wing, he planted his feet near the fuselage hinge, gripped the side of the door he'd just exited with one hand, and, with his other, again felt about for the damnably designed lanyards. The engineer in him fumed.

His footing gave way and he started slipping down the wing toward the sea. Falling to his knees to add traction and lower the center of gravity worked, just barely: he came to a stop at the wing's edge. After pausing for a moment to catch his breath, he tried to crawl back up but the fuel-slick metal and cascading seawater wouldn't allow it.

But there was some recompense: a wave breaking over the wing flipped the inflation tabs into his hands. Murray pulled them one after the other, careful not to yank them lest they snap. The hissing was one of the sweetest sounds he'd ever heard.

However, the bladders' sudden filling upset his delicate balance, and his feet gave way. Murray slipped off the sill, down the wing, and into the sea.

Raúl Acevedo was pinned beside the mostly submerged Lockheed, 20 feet from the triple tailfins. He saw no one and heard nothing but the wind and waves. As the plane continued to sink, sliding down the palm of his hand, the soldier knew he needed to get clear of the suction but didn't know how. Though fit and athletic before the crash, cracked vertebrae made swimming impossible. Just trying to kick himself free from the hull brought tears to his eyes. The pain was otherworldly. His head below water more than above it, he gagged on the filmy, stinking ocean. *These life-vests are useless!*[23]

Before boarding Tiger 923, he'd lapsed as a Catholic. "I didn't even confess."[24] He made the sign of the cross. *Okay God, if it's my time to go, it's my time to go.*

Suddenly his pain was gone, or at least suspended in a surreal parallel universe, as he was transported back to Zacatecas . . .

Acevedo saw himself sitting on a bench with his girlfriend across from the city's main hotel, awaiting his bus to Texas, but two cops were threatening to lock the teenagers up unless he paid them a bribe. They didn't know he was the mayor's son, and he didn't want to tell them because his father didn't know he was off to the U.S. and would've put a stop to it. . . .

Next, he was zipping around town on his fancy French racing bike, not just the first kid in town to own one but maybe the first in all of Mexico. . . .

Next, he was repaying his father's bountiful love and support by defying, disappointing, and lying to him . . . saying he was calling from Monterrey, not Los Angeles. . . .

Next thing he knew, he was free and clear of the plane: moving fast, riding the current, hands over his thumping chest, eyes shut, praying to Our Lady of Guadalupe. "The waves were in command. I was totally at the mercy of the water."[25]

A few minutes later, as an enormous wave approached, he stuck his arm out to blunt the impact . . . and his fingertips touched rubber.

He felt sure he was delusional: that it was just his imagination, a tactile mirage. Still, he twisted his mangled body around, wincing as he did so, and had a look. *The raft!*

But bumping against it and boarding it were two entirely different things. The sides were impossibly high and slick. There were no ropes to grab onto. It looked like there was no room, what with several people hanging over the sides, half on, half off.

A soldier yelled: "This one is full! You'll tip us over!"

George Brown hoisted him up and in.

"Thank you!" said Acevedo, moments before passing out.

A wave hurled Art Gilbreth against the hull. Though he felt the unmistakable internal snap of fracture, he was still in no pain, and the cold water upped the anesthetic.

But it also upped the risk of hypothermia. He was having trouble keeping his eyes open and his mind felt like hardening cement. In response to people yelling "Where's the raft?" he thought: *Stop yelling—and look!*[26]

A woman's cry pierced the cacophony: "Help!" She was reaching for him as he turned around to look for her in the dark, but she was too far. "Please . . . I can't swim."

He swam over to her, spun her around, felt about, and pulled the cords on her uninflated vest. As it billowed and she got buoyant, she gripped his forearm and said, "Thank you!" He nodded. "We need to find a—"

A wave buried him. When Gilbreth resurfaced, the woman was gone. He looked about and listened, but there was no sign or sound of her. There was something, however: a splotch on the horizon. *Is that a raft?* He made his way toward it.

After a few strokes, out of the corner of his eye, three out-of-focus yet distinct geometric shapes emerged. *Sharks!* He stopped swimming abruptly, knowing movement attracted sharks. Terror gripped him like a vise.

A memory from his lifeguarding days relieved him: *Isn't this water too cold for sharks?* As the current bore him past the ominous-looking shapes, Gilbreth realized he was staring not at sharks' fins but at the plane's triple tailfins, half submerged. Unbeknownst to him, he'd been swimming over the top of the plane. *Phew!*

The plane lurched further underwater. As he tried to kick himself free, his right leg got wedged in the base of the port-side fin, just as a swell pushed the plane completely underwater, him along with it. He held his breath as he hacked and twisted, to no avail.

As he drifted down into the bone-chilling murk, his mind bifurcated. "One me was floating high above and could see everything: the sinking plane, the raft, people swimming. The other me was underwater. The above-me knew the below-me didn't know the above-me existed. The above-me was giving instructions to the below-me in the form of a low voice in my head, saying: 'Kick the silver thing below you. Hard! Harder!'"

So he kicked and kicked and kicked with his untrapped foot, each percussion threatening to pop open his oxygen-filled cheeks and battering his already shattered vertebrae. He finally freed himself with a desperate corkscrew twist, but the maneuver gouged out a hunk of his calf, unleashing the pain. It was hellish.

As the aluminum specter sunk, a powerful whorl somersaulted him underwater. Losing his bearings, he didn't know which way was up. He was almost out of air and his cheeks felt like they were about to burst. *Relax*, said the voice in his head as tiny bubbles streamed down his cheek through the plume of his blood. Looking up, he knew the surface was above him, as the sky was lighter than the sea. He swam toward the sky.

The cloud-mottled moon didn't throw off much light, but Gilbreth breached the surface at just the right instant and angle to see something yellowish in the distance. He took a deep breath and swam as fast as his searing pain would permit. He soon passed out. "I woke up in the raft."

Fred Caruso had been stuck by the right wing for what seemed like eternity. "I was getting hammered from all sides. I felt sure I was a goner. There was nothing I could do."[27]

To his left, barely visible over the top of the nearly submerged hull, he'd caught a glimpse of something. *Is that a raft?* It "seemed like miles from the sunken Tiger."[28] When there was a slight break in the waves, the former lifeguard took off.

Caruso arrived beside the raft physically and emotionally spent. Given the high, slippery sides and absence of ropes or other hoists, he knew he'd not get on board without assistance, so he raised his right hand expecting the paratrooper by the edge to help him up and in. Instead, the guy stared down and said: "Ya gotta find another one!"

Caruso yelled: "What? Let me on!"

While a second paratrooper echoed the first and called out, "Don't take any more or we'll swamp," George Brown started pulling Caruso aboard the packed 15-by-15-foot raft.[29]

The sea swept Rachel Hoopi into Caruso, interrupting his boarding process. When she reached up for assistance, Little Animal grabbed her hand and started lifting her aboard.

Though Caruso got aboard, Hoopi was only half on, half off when all hell broke loose. People were "coming in from all sides, in a matter of seconds."[30] As "waves were breaking over me about fifty feet into the air," those in the water grabbed onto overhanging feet, hair, wrists, anything offering purchase.[31] Those on board fought back, prying off fingers, pushing people off the raft, back into the water.

When Corporal John McDonald heard his buddy John Brown shouting for help, he managed to hoist him up and in, but "he had swallowed too much water. He moaned and moaned and died soon after getting aboard."[32]

As Hoopi cried, "Please let me up!" a soldier boarded, stumbled, and fell into Little Animal.[33] He lost his grip. Hoopi slid down the side of the raft and disappeared into the darkness.

Back by the plane, Carmen Figueroa-Longo had lost sight of her husband. She couldn't break free from the combined force of the current and submerging suction. Her big, ill-fitting life vest kept riding high up over her chin; she kept having to push it down to breathe and see, even if only a few feet given the darkness. She was terrified and shivering.

"I was swimming very close to the wing and someone came from there and I asked him to help me, and he came toward me and we hold hands. I told him, 'I think there is a raft, let's swim towards it.' So we swam towards the raft, towards—it was like a silhouette."[34]

The Good Samaritan tried to buddy-swim her to the raft, but "I just couldn't make it, and he started yelling for help. So a man came towards the side and started pulling me up and then this boy in the water was pushing me up until they finally pulled me in." Then "they just throw me in the raft and I fell kneeling and it was very crowded and right after me they pull another person in—Major Benson.

"And he was laying down and he kept telling me that the water was on his face because he was laying down and there were people on top of him. So he told me to 'Hold my head up,' so I tried to hold his head up, but I had something on my throat, and I told him, Well, I can not hold you unless someone takes this off from my throat, and he touched it and said it was a foot, and then—I don't know—the raft moved a little bit and he pulled it off."[35]

Carmen held Benson's head up "a long time," by his hair. After swallowing "a lot of water" and "vomiting a few times," she called out in the dark, more in hope than expectation: "Juan?"

Dr. Figueroa-Longo answered: "Where are you? I am in the raft."

"I am in another raft," she said.

Neither knew: they were in the same raft.[36]

Captain Murray had resurfaced near a nebulous cluster of survivors. His inflated vest easily held his head above water. Though he was still stuck beside the plane his "immediate reaction was an overwhelming sense of relief. That cockpit had been a mighty warm spot for the last two hours."[37]

He wasn't sure what he should do, other than remove his sodden shoes. It wasn't easy but he reached down, loosened the laces and heeled them off, one after the other. He watched them slip beneath the surface. When he looked back up, all the nearby survivors were gone. Once the plane's third tailfin had sunk, Murray was alone in the sea. He had no idea where to go. There were no sights, sounds, or other clues, apart from the direction of the current and speed.

He started swimming with it, while running some quick numbers regarding how long he may have lain unconscious, taken to evacuate, fumbled on the wing, and flailed in the water. His conclusion: the rafts could be up to a mile away, maybe more. It was a frightening thought.

Another thought hit him, in a cutting moment of clarity: returning to the cockpit for the flashlight may have been a fatal mistake. The sound of voices cut short his introspection. He stopped swimming and listened. Following the current had been the smart thing to do. Better yet, his math seemed way off. The voices sounded close.

But maybe not. In the water, people could be over a mile away yet sound really close. So he resumed swimming. His chest felt like it was going to explode. His head stung and throbbed. He told himself: *Ignore the pain; dig deep; it's just water.*[38]

After a few minutes, something brushed against his calf. He didn't know what it was. *Probably just some debris from the plane, or seaweed.* It annoyed him more than anything. He reached down into the water intending to sweep it away, but then the back of his hand felt . . . *the raft's lanyard!* While Murray couldn't see the raft on account of an enveloping swell, he knew it was nearby the same way a sport fisherman can tell he's hooked a marlin.

As he grabbed the lifeline and prepared to winch himself in, he heard a voice behind him: "Help . . ."[39] It was Helga Groves, the German newlywed, still searching for her husband.[40]

The pilot turned around to look, saw her flailing, let go of the nylon rope and swam back for her. He hooked his right arm under her right shoulder, buddy-swam back to the lanyard, then began winching them toward the raft, hand over hand. They were the only two in the water.

Murray tried to reassure the distraught teenager: "You're going to be okay," he said.

> *I called for help from the raft to assist her in the boarding, and was suddenly shocked by a voice from the raft, "There are too many people on this raft already, go find your own raft."*
>
> *No doubt the raft was pretty crowded, but it didn't seem unreasonable to believe that I could get the two of us aboard without such objections from some who had got there first. While I felt completely confident that nothing or no one would prevent my getting us on board, it was a little irritating to find that there was someone who preferred we would stay in the water. I had no idea whether the objector contemplated physical force in keeping us off, but I certainly intended to find out.*[41]

Once Groves was close enough, Raúl Acevedo pulled her aboard. Her addition to the already badly overcrowded raft triggered a chain reaction that began with Fred Gazelle tumbling into and knocking over Sammy Vasquez, who in turn "fell and landed on top of Helga's legs, and she started crying: 'Please get off my legs!'" But "I couldn't get off of her legs because Little Animal was on top of me."[42]

Murray waited his turn, bobbing beside the raft. As the unwelcoming paratrooper glared down at him, George Brown pushed past his comrade and reached down for the pilot. Just as their hands clasped, a wave hit the raft and Murray fell back into the sea.

Alabaman Joe Hofer, who'd bravely positioned himself near the raft's edge to face the oncoming swells that'd been rolling in like liquid earthquakes ever since Michael Murray and Hard Luck Sam had clambered aboard 20 minutes earlier, drawled: "Get ready . . . here comes another one. Hold on!"[43]

But the 50 souls crammed into the upside-down raft designed for 20 had nothing to hold onto other than arms, ankles and clothes. As it shot up high, people shrieked, and Captain Murray was ejected further out to sea.

Yet he clung to the rope. Once the raft crashed back to the surface, the pilot winched himself back over to Brown. The soldier with the really bad head wound hoisted the civilian with the really bad head wound up and aboard. Murray collapsed on top of Fred Caruso.

(Top) The Swiss freighter *Celerina* rounds the Cape of Good Hope, undated. (Bottom) September 23, 1962: a still from an 8-mm film clip of waves washing its deck 35 feet above sea level, taken by 19-year-old deckhand Pierre-André Reymond just hours before receiving Tiger 923's Mayday. COURTESY REYMOND.

Chapter 6

All We Had Was Hope

Pierre-André Reymond was impressed but not surprised that his captain hadn't hesitated to respond, and had done so with great skill. Though the youngest member of the *Celerina* crew, the Lausanne native had the sea in his DNA, paternally and maternally, so he was well aware that his employer wasn't just Switzerland's oldest shipping company but one of the country's most respected firms that had rescued many people since its founding in the 1870s. While "the law of the sea" was supposed to govern the conduct of all mariners (basically drop everything to help anyone in need), few took it to heart like Suisse-Atlantique. Company president (and Pierre-André's uncle) Henri E. André often reaffirmed the corporate motto: "*Être et non paraître*" ("To be, not just appear").[1]

Yet the deckhand felt Captain Lugli's efforts were for naught. Reymond was no pessimist, just a realist. Not long before the Mayday, the amateur photographer shot some 8-mm film. "I wanted proof to show my family and friends, who otherwise wouldn't have believed me when I told them how terrible the conditions were."[2]

In the 63 minutes since the first Mayday, and the 30 since the ditching, conditions had grown worse. Given the fact that the heavy steel freighter seemed like it'd topple whenever its 6 million pounds of non-containerized wheat shifted in the hold, and assuming the plane's hitting the water hadn't killed everyone instantly or the aircraft hadn't sunk in seconds, taking the rafts with it, Reymond didn't see how all the small rubber rafts he suspected were the plane's equipment hadn't already capsized. What's more, if they had, he knew that righting them would be next to impossible in such violent water, and given how cold it was, and the wind chill, he doubted anyone could last out in the open for more than half an hour, let alone the five, six, or however many hours it would take to reach them.

Distress messages like Murray's occurred fairly often in the North Atlantic. Searches often lasted days. The typical result was a trace of oil clinging to the surface of the sea.[3]

On board Tiger 923's packed emergency raft: given the darkness and immobility, few knew the identities of the occupants or extent of their injuries. Had an inventory been taken, it would have revealed that about a third barely had a scratch to show for hitting the water at 120 mph (Fred Caruso's ankle bruise); a third had at least one significant injury (Captain Murray's head gash and possible concussion); and the remaining 16 or 17 were clearly in bad shape (Art Gilbreth's gouged-out calf, several broken vertebrae, extensive blood loss).

Everyone agreed that the water in the raft felt a lot colder than the ocean, despite the thermal body heat. "This was not just a raft out in the cold, though. It was a horror. We were so numb with shock and fear, with no idea how soon anybody would find us. Sometimes a trick swell would ride under us and it would seem like we were tipping over."[4]

The raft's being upside down made it highly unstable, especially given the fact that "the waves were gigantic."[5] Each time one hit, "the sea would sweep over the raft and completely drench everyone."[6] The inversion also exposed the coarse rubber flooring, siding, and nylon stitching, resulting in more cuts and abrasions.

Most felt the raft would capsize or come apart every few minutes. When the sea folded it, it would creak and seem about to snap like an old rubber band. Most suffered brutal cramps because their arms, legs, and necks were stuck at unnatural angles, and they couldn't move an inch.

While some found hope in the sound of plane engines droning in the sky above and sight of searchlights poking down through the clouds, most despaired. In the absence of running lights, flares, and flashlights, everyone knew the raft was essentially invisible.

The grit impressed Hard Luck Sam. "There wasn't any undue shouting or panic. For the most part, people just . . . took their medicine."[7]

Recalling from her Tiger training how important it was to maintain morale, and how her Sunday school songs had helped soothe the hurt inflicted by her dad when he'd skipped out on her and her mother, stewardess Carol Gould started singing: *"Oh, Jesus loves the little children of the world . . . All the children of the world . . . Red and yellow, black and white . . . They are precious in His sight."*[8] Others joined in. She also led renditions of "Battle Hymn of the Republic."

When Captain Murray said, "Any doctors aboard?" and the Air Force OB-GYN said, "Yes," Gould "turned toward Doctor Figueroa-Longo and did my best Bugs Bunny impression: 'What's up, Doc?' But not everyone appreciated my attempt at comedy."

Murray asked her if she remembered any of her first-aid training. "Some," she said. He asked her to help Figueroa-Longo. "I'll do my best."

Figueroa-Longo said he couldn't see much because he'd lost his eyeglasses. Gould said: "It's okay, I'll be your eyes."

> *I made my way over to George Brown, who pulled me aboard. Saved my life. His head was bleeding really bad. When I noticed Doctor Elander was nearby, I asked him how to stop it. He told me "Keep the head elevated and tilted back as much as possible, and maintain as much pressure as possible." Easier said than done—with the raft tossing and turning the way it was.*
>
> *Then I noticed the captain, who was near George. He was mumbling, incoherent. He'd nod off, then bolt upright and shout instructions: "Soldier! Remove your cap, and use it to bail!" He was drifting in and out, waking only when his head fell into the water in the raft. "Captain!," I yelled. "Your head! You're bleeding really bad!"*
>
> *I don't know what I used, maybe one of the soldiers' caps or something. All I remember is holding whatever it was against his head, then placing his hand over mine, then sliding mine out from under his, and saying, "Don't let go. You need to stop the bleeding!"*

He was so exhausted. His eyes kept closing, his hand falling to his side. The blood oozed out. It was dark, this I could tell even in the dark night.

"Sit still for a minute, will ya! You don't want this to get infected."

But Gould knew Murray couldn't possibly sit still. No one could, what with the raft gyrating and folding, rising and falling, and moving inexorably away from the last position reported by navigator Hard Luck Sam.

Art Gilbreth had nearly passed out several times owing to fatigue and the horrible pain of a grave calf wound and a broken back. He could sense his life force seeping out into all the other blood, tears, vomit, urine, and gasoline. His location in the center of the raft forced him to ingest the disgusting fluid often, which he regurgitated, adding more vomit. Advancing hypothermia was playing mental tricks, telling him to *Close your eyes and sleep . . . sleep.* The paratrooper was now much closer to expiring than he'd been on the plane or in the sea.

When a wave tossed another soldier onto his chest, he yelled: "Get off!"[9] But the guy just sat there, staring blankly. Gilbreth started punching him in the face as hard as he could in his weakened state. The guy didn't try to defend himself. He sat there taking punch after punch until Little Animal crabbed his way over and pushed the soldier off his buddy's chest. Gilbreth passed out before he could say thanks.

Fred Caruso was wedged in tight and tangled. "Murray's life vest was slimy with blood and gasoline, and it kept rubbing up against my face every time he moved. But no complaints from me! He'd saved us."[10]

The pilot's eyes were closed, his body slack. Some felt he was unconscious. Others felt sure he was dead.

Carol Gould's bartering woke him: "If you let me live, God, I'll become a nun, never do anything wrong, go to church every day. I'll even get married and stop having fun."[11]

Murray said: "We'll take you to China, and you can get everything you need for the wedding. You're getting married."

Thank God he's safe, thought Caruso.[12]

Murray's delirious thoughts drifted back to his own wedding day, then to each of his five children. He tried to wriggle his left arm free from between a pair of burly paratroopers, one of whom was "constantly praying in a low voice."[13]

But "nothing could distract the soldier." Not Gould's bartering with the Almighty, bad jokes, or passable singing; not the exclamations of relief when the sea grew calm or shrieks when a huge swell seemed certain to capsize the raft. The stoic African-American kept repeating over and over: "Oh, Lord, into Thy hands I commend my spirit."

"It was deeply humbling: this young man, not much older than my son." While John Patrick Murray was on his way to study at a first-rate university, his father wondered if he'd attain as much wisdom as (based on his Deep South dialect) "this soldier who'd probably only graduated high school. I was deeply appreciative of this young man's quiet leadership, and the comfort he was providing to all who could see him, and hear him."

Maybe five feet from the pilot, paratrooper Joe Hofer shouted: "Searchlights! A plane! Headed straight for us!"[14]

Murray looked up. He recognized the silhouette and lights: a C-118 Globemaster; likely with Air Force lieutenant Joe Lewis at the controls.

Most on the raft yelled and waved. Many burst into tears of joy. Some tried to stand up, but it was like they were on a waterbed: they'd stumble and fall over others who were trying to do the same thing. "Ouch!" "Hey!" "Watch it!" "Sorry."

A soldier landed on Murray, who snapped: "Sit down! It won't help to capsize!"[15]

But elation quickly gave way to despair as people remembered they were invisible. "They'll never see us from way up there! With the clouds and no lights!"

"I've got a flashlight," Murray mumbled.

"Hurry!" Hofer yelled.

Murray tried to dig into his pants pocket to retrieve the light . . . but he was too hemmed in. "I can't get at it. People need to move!"

However, it was unclear who should move and who should stay put given the fact that 51 people were completely interlocked. A paratrooper to Murray's right rose, wobbly legged, only to collide with another to the pilot's left, who'd done the same thing. They both fell back down, splashing.

"Hurry! The plane'll be here any second!"

"Got it!"

It was too late. The searchlight missed the raft. As the plane rumbled into the clouds, Raúl Acevedo spoke for many when he said, "I might as well jump overboard."[16]

But the articulation was often silent, like the young black soldier near Captain Murray who was "sitting bolt upright, his eyes wide open in a fixed stare that never wavered, his body immobile as though cast in bronze. His position never changed and his attitude never varied. He was evidently in a state of deep shock."[17] As wave after wave drenched everyone and the wind further chilled the already bitterly cold water before washing it back into the sea, more of the collective will to survive seemed to empty out too, in addition to the body heat necessary to prevent hypothermia. Thirty-four minutes after the plane's impact with the water at 120 mph, morale was at its lowest point.

Then things got worse. On top of all the cracked vertebrae, gashed heads, and profound trauma, a new ailment began to present and spread: chemical burns. Aviation fuel and oil and hydraulic fluids had seeped into the wounds, of all sizes, adding toxicity to the blood and other secretions. Rather than washing away the organic matter and cleansing the wounds, the saltwater made matters much worse, akin to drinking it when thirsty. And the rocking raft transformed the thick wool Army trousers into scouring brushes.

Acevedo was suffering the most. "All over, my skin first tingled, then itched, now it's like someone set a match to it. Blisters . . . burning, popping. The pain's so bad! It's getting worse, second by second. There's nothing I can do about it."[18]

But at least Captain Murray had finally gotten the flashlight out of his pocket and it worked. Out of position and essentially blind, he handed it to Joe Hofer then passed out.

Hofer said aloud: "What's the S-O-S?"[19]

Vasquez yelled: "Hof: three short, three long, and three short. I was in the Boy Scouts."

The Tiger 923 search-and-rescue operation involved 9 countries, 5 rescue centers, 12 air traffic control centers, and 61 military and civilian planes and ships, ranging from an Alitalia jet to a Turkish freighter; and more than 10,000 people, ranging from the Pentagon's telegram supervisor to the 1,200 sailors on-board *Bonaventure*, Canada's lone aircraft carrier. Three hours into it, the operation wasn't going well.

As for the maritime facet, U.S. Navy lieutenant commander Richard Knapton, who'd flown south from Keflavik, Iceland, reported that there were so many "ships in the area that they were having trouble getting out of each other's way. Things were quite confusing."[20]

As for the aviation side of things, Air Force lieutenant Bill Tripp said the sea was too "mean-looking" to discern much of anything.[21] Knapton added: "I have never seen so many aircraft all working in precision but unfortunately finding nothing."[22] Eleven planes were now orbiting the ditching site, including Knapton at 6,000 feet and Air Force lieutenant Joe Lewis at 1,300 feet.

With Lewis reporting "visibility extremely poor and gales whipping up big waves," an Air Force colleague in another plane dropped ten "one-million candlepower flares, two 20-man rafts and three survival kits."[23] Yet, according to an RAF spokesman, "it was like looking for a speck of grease in a foam bath."[24] Though three "amphibians had hoped to land alongside any rafts they spotted, the stormy seas made this impossible"; thus, despite having been scrambled in Cornwall at 8:35 p.m., they returned to base, their dejected crews feeling it was a lost cause.[25]

It wasn't just the darkness, weather, and incompatible radio frequencies that hampered the effort. According to *Stars and Stripes*, "there was a lot of competition for news . . . at the time: The Cuban Missile Crisis was coming to a head, [and] the East Germans with Soviet aid began reinforcing their 866 mile long death zone barrier along the eastern border."[26] Public relations was a critical theater in the Cold War and given how badly the U.S. had been embarrassed by the U2 shoot-down over Russia and the Bay of Pigs fiasco in Cuba, the brass desperately wanted to avoid the bad PR that would result should the North Atlantic Treaty Organization be unable to locate, let alone rescue, 76 men, women and children in the North Atlantic. Especially since so much of the communication was via HAM radio, Morse code, and other unsecured frequencies, the U.S. Army, Air Force, Coast Guard, and Civil Aeronautics Board officials seemed to spend almost as much time redacting information, tinkering with semantics, and composing carefully worded press releases as directing first responders.[27]

Washington wasn't just vexed by Moscow. London wasn't helping as much as it could, according to the U.S. Coast Guard, which felt the British Admiralty's "policy regarding no rendezvous procedures may be the reason no one tried to help the Flying Tiger pilot find a motor vessel."[28]

The turf wars weren't just military and international. Since Tiger 923 was a commercial flight, the U.S. Defense Department had to coordinate with the Commerce Department (via the Federal Aviation Agency, Civil Aviation Authority, and Civil Aeronautics Board) and Treasury (via the Coast Guard). As a consequence, transmissions were often relayed too late to be of any use or facts got garbled. For instance, though a U.S. Navy communications station in Ireland intercepted a Scottish air traffic controller's report that "all women and children are off the aircraft and 7 survivors picked up," no survivors had even been seen, let alone picked up.[29]

USAF 246 was still the closest plane. Joe Lewis was just 10 miles away from the raft and 51 survivors, though the first-time pilot didn't know. All he really knew was that the search grid encompassed more than 10,000 square miles, there were no maritime rescue planes in the vicinity, the Canadian aircraft carrier was 325 miles away, the Swiss cargo ship was 45 miles out, and he had four and a half hours of fuel remaining.

None of his 8 crew members or 19 soldier-passengers saw any blinking lights or yellow rubber, but it was hard to see anything in the darkness, cloud cover, and wild, misdirecting whitecaps.[30] According to official Air Force records, Lewis "had considerable difficulty in setting up an orbit pattern." Having circled above the presumed ditching site twice and concluding that either the Lockheed had sunk or the Tiger navigator's estimated coordinates had been off or got garbled, Lewis suggested they look elsewhere.[31]

Copilot Michael Burnett suggested Lewis orbit one more time. Seconds into it, Burnett discerned a sequence of pinprick flashes: *S . . . O . . . S.* He informed Lewis.

Moments later, Joe Lewis, the rookie pilot from Tuscaloosa, Alabama, connected his searchlight with the flashlight held by Joe Hofer, the rookie paratrooper from Tuscaloosa.

Carol Gould said:

> *When the spotlight hit us it was like daytime on the raft. It was good . . . but also it wasn't. I could see everyone around me and they were bloody. And the water in the raft was turning a sickening red.*
>
> *But it was the first good news for a long time. People I thought might be dead, 'cause they hadn't moved or said a word now opened their eyes and started to cry and yell, wave and whistle. Some tugged on my sleeve, some started to crawl over towards the edge of the raft.*
>
> *Most felt our nightmare was nearly over. I knew otherwise, but as my training taught me morale was really important, I wasn't about to start correcting people. We didn't have any food or water. All we had was hope.*[32]

Murray knew the nightmare wasn't over, not by a long shot. He knew the Air Force prop couldn't help much and there was no telling how long it might be before a seaplane, amphibian, or helicopter might arrive, and they were the only aircraft that offered any hope of rescuing the survivors from the air. As for the Swiss freighter, he had grave doubts it would arrive before the raft capsized. It was just too far away.

Bob Eldred clung to the hope that his wife had either made it onto another raft or was somewhere on his, too far to see and hear above all the noise, maybe beside one of the other spouses he couldn't see but could hear every now and again. Yet he "didn't dare to call out" Edna's name. "I was afraid she wouldn't answer."[33]

Dr. Elander could sense hypothermia gaining the upper hand. With the wind chill, he figured his core temperature was probably in the danger zone but he no longer felt cold. He took note of his sluggish heart rate, labored breaths, leaden eyelids, and numb toes.

While the Army major was struggling to keep his own head above water, he was far more concerned with his wife's safety. Though he could tell Lois was in pain, given her groans, the more pressing concern was that she was pinned beneath two big bodies at the very outer edge of Dick's reach, often beyond it; every time a wave crashed over the sides of the raft, she'd slip out of his grasp and fully submerge.

"You can do it, Lois! Keep holding your chin up, as high as you can."[34]

Raúl Acevedo was really relieved the raft had been found. "But I'd feel better if I could actually see the plane."[35] He was so crammed in he couldn't see the light, just hear the rumble overhead. "I wish it would hurry! My leg feels like it's on fire!"[36]

While the crowded sky above the raft was mostly a cacophony of prop planes (the Alitalia jet had left because there was little it could do), Murray discerned a different rumbling amidst the din. He hoped it might be a seaplane (designed only for water takeoffs and landings), an amphibian (that could operate on land and water), or one of the retrofitted anti-submarine bombers he'd see in Prestwick whenever he found himself at the U.S. Air Force's Military Air Transport Service base. But even if it were designed for water rescues, Murray knew it was likely outmatched. Not only was it really dark, and not only were the whipping winds gusting near hurricane strength (65 mph, versus Cat 1's 74 mph), but also the waves were averaging 15 to 20 feet, yet the operational feasibility of even these specialized aircraft was only 4 to 10 feet. The sea was simply too rough.

So his reaction was decidedly different when the orange spotting flares began streaking overhead. People shouted "Hallelujah!" and "We're saved!"[37] He knew otherwise.

The U.K. Royal Air Force bombardier was good at his job. But his job was to drop depth charges that blew big Soviet subs out of the water, which sonar had pinpointed, not drop wooden crates of food, potable water, and medical supplies onto a small raft no one could see, hoping they'd land not in the raft (as that could inflict more injury), but close enough to retrieve.

The now-moonless nighttime sky turned bright purple in spots as dozens of flare-affixed crates parachuted down. But every flare soon fizzled out and every crate missed its mark, most by a wide margin. Out of crates and low on fuel, the RAF plane returned to base.

Captain Murray wasn't surprised all the flares had died out, with no sign of any floating provisions. It was dark and cloudy, the winds were brutal, and by the sound of it the plane had been several hundred feet up, if not a thousand. Anything short of a bull's-eye and the water would instantly engulf anything that had been dropped and sweep it away.

But provisioning wasn't John Murray's main concern. Seaworthiness was. He was amazed the raft hadn't already sunk in the 50 minutes that had elapsed since Michael Murray was the first aboard.

Were the raft to capsize, righting and reboarding it would be difficult. The now-inverted sides were nearly three feet high and really slippery from fuel, oil, hydraulic fluid, and seawater. The pilot knew how tired, hungry, and thirsty everyone was, because he was. He knew that many were badly injured, because he was. And he knew it was getting harder and harder for everyone to hold their heads up high one moment and then, the next moment, when the waves swallowed the raft, hold their breath underwater, because he was experiencing the same difficulty.

And once in the open sea, people wouldn't last long. Hypothermia kicks in at 95 degrees F. The vests were flotation devices, not heating pads. It wouldn't take long for the 48-degree water to lower the body's core temperature 3.6 degrees.

Plus, the vests wouldn't last forever. They were only designed to get people from point A to point B: from plane to raft. A few cubic feet of CO_2 were no match for the relentless battering by such forceful waves.[38]

Despite the indication of life inherent in Murray's flashlight, a "feeling of helplessness crept over" the passengers and crew of USAF 246.[39] As Joe Lewis "stared at the lonely light and prayed that it would not go out, he found that he could not take his eyes from the light or he would lose sight of it. The strain of flying in this manner began to tell."

The 32-year-old had passed his initial line check with flying colors. He had responded in the nick of time, persevered until he intercepted Tiger 923, then never lost track of the flashlight, despite the darkness, clouds, and choppy gray waves that would swallow the raft for minutes at a time. Such a pilot's exam would have challenged the skills and nerves of the most seasoned of aviators. Now, prudence dictated a change: Major Guthrie relieved Lieutenant Lewis and Lieutenant Matthews relieved Lieutenant Burnett.

The frigid blasts that defied Walter Wunderlin's heavy slicker made it impossible for the ship's carpenter to do repair work on the motorized lifeboat or anything else above deck. The Swiss had planned to set off for Madras after unloading a cargo of Manitoba wheat in Antwerp but now, as the *Celerina*'s overtaxed engine belched smoke in a desperate diversion, Wunderlin didn't know what lay ahead. He passed the time by writing a letter to his parents. "Time goes by slowly. A violent storm sweeps across the sea. We know people are still waiting for rescue in the pitch-dark night. Everybody hopes for the rescue of the survivors, but nobody believes that the 72 [*sic*] shipwrecked people could be saved. It's a hard test of nerves for all of us."[40]

The *Celerina* had made great time since the Mayday call, averaging 15 mph. However, the weather had just taken another turn for the worse, which meant that once again Captain Lugli found himself battling "house-sized waves."[41] The thick chop cut the Swiss freighter's speed back down to 8 mph and added two more hours to her ETA, which now stood at 2:47 a.m.

The *Juliett* was much better equipped. However, the atrocious weather had delayed the floating British Navy weather station's ETA to 3:48 a.m.

Fortunately, the 20,000-ton *Bonaventure* didn't need to make it all the way to the raft, just to within range of the Royal Canadian Navy's planes and helicopters. Unfortunately, the ETA of the carrier's fastest aircraft was 8:00 a.m.

Captain Murray had never been so tired in his life. The cold, pain, thirst, and even fear took a back seat to his longing for sleep.

Knowing hypothermia wanted him to close his eyes, he'd pinch his thigh, wiggle his toes, and work his jaw. Anything to stay awake. Sometimes it worked, sometimes it didn't.

When awake, a sense of responsibility weighed on him. He wasn't sure how many others were on the raft with him but he knew there weren't 75. Where were the others?

On the other hand, a dawning realization was easing some of his burden. Perhaps it was because weight and balance were things pilots often thought about, or because ballast was vital in sailing, or because he was a trained engineer. Whatever the prompt, he wondered: *Instead of a curse, might this terrible overcrowding actually be a blessing?*[42]

Thus far, hundreds of swells had hit the raft since Murray had pulled up beside it.[43] Like everyone else, as he watched them thunder in and felt so utterly at the mercy of their terrifying, humbling power, he believed it was only a matter of time before the upside-down raft capsized. Though it would seem to contort well beyond its breaking point, it always managed to snap back into place. Although the specs said the raft should be right-side up and hold 20, Murray began to wonder if true optimality just so happened to be upside down and precisely however many souls had made it aboard.[44]

But while Murray felt the uncomfortable crowd of survivors was an asset in the form of ballast, he also knew the lack of flashlights was a very serious liability. While Betty Sims had said she'd gathered lots, just one made it aboard: his own. He figured the *Celerina* was by now sweeping the sea with its projector beam, hoping to spot USAF 246's searchlight (basically, a lighthouse in the sky), yet the efficacy of Lewis' light depended entirely on Murray's flashlight holding out. The Tiger pilot worried the batteries might not last.[45]

He passed the word that it was more important to look out across the sea as opposed to up into the sky, to try and locate one of the four wing-stowed rafts. If any were still upright, their running lights would be visible to the rescue ships and planes. The other rafts were also stocked with flashlights, flares, medical supplies, food, and water. If one were close enough, it might even make sense for someone to swim over to it, connected to a human chain in life vests and knotted clothes, lest the swimmer be swept out to sea by the current.

Seven feet from the Tiger pilot, Dick Elander was praying for the health and safety of his friends John and Naomi Devlin. The ophthalmologist-major hadn't seen the psychologist-major or his psychologist-wife since exchanging quick, fraught glances with them a few moments before the plane slammed into the sea.

Major Elander was also worried about his own health and safety. He could feel his skin burning. He knew that, if not treated in time, he could lose a leg, or worse.

But Lois remained his top priority. Most of her small body was trapped under two feet of water; often her mouth, for extended periods. She hardly made a sound.

Especially when Lois was beyond reach of Dick's outstretched hand, which was most of the time, he tried to stay upbeat and exhort her not to lose heart. "You can do it! Hang on!"[46]

By late September 1962, the world was wondering not so much if but when the Cold War would get hot. In recent years, the USSR had exploded history's most powerful hydrogen bomb, crushed the Hungarian Uprising, downed the supposedly unseeable Lockheed U2 spy plane and paraded its pilot on the world's stage as the poster child of American inferiority, helped install Fidel Castro and easily repulse the CIA-led Bay of Pigs invasion, and caught the CIA napping by erecting the infamous Berlin Wall almost overnight, resulting in Fred Caruso, Art Gilbreth, and 28 other paratroopers boarding Tiger 923 at McGuire AFB earlier in the day. This was why the Pentagon didn't want the Kremlin to know the whereabouts of its elite paratroopers, Canada didn't want the Soviet Baltic Fleet to know the location of its lone aircraft carrier, and Britain didn't want the Russians to know the location of their sub-tracking aircraft.[47]

It's also why Moscow was monitoring the Tiger 923 search-and-rescue operation via its Northern Fleet subs, surface ships, aircraft, and air traffic control centers, and the last thing it wanted was a success. Khrushchev would have loved nothing better than to embarrass Kennedy again, and humiliate NATO. The way things were going, *Pravda* wouldn't even need to create and propagate fake news. The Soviet media could simply state the truth: "North Atlantic Treaty Organization unable to save soldiers, women, and children in North Atlantic."

Monday, September 24, 1962
1:00 a.m.

The 51 survivors had been in the water for almost three hours, most of the time aboard an upside-down, un-provisioned rubber raft built to hold 20; all the time soaking and shivering in the 48-degree water, 55-degree outside air temperature, and winds gusting to 65 mph. While a few people saw some searchlights poking through the clouds every now and again, and heard some engines rumbling, no one ever saw USAF 246 or any of the other planes that arrived and orbited above the ditching site. No one saw any of the dozens of bright purple parachute flares or any of the wooden crates of provisions to which they were attached.

The survivors had contended with swells rolling in every nine seconds on average. Some were gentle, barely rippling against the rubber sides. But others were powerful surges that lifted the raft up 20 feet or more before the sea would suddenly disappear beneath the raft and everyone would crash back to the concrete-like surface. Most felt sure that capsizing wasn't a question of if, just when. No one had ever experienced anything remotely as terrifying, including decorated, battle-scarred veterans of the Normandy invasion and the Korean War.

Fingers were numb and lips were blue. Most were suffering bad cramps. Many wanted it all to end. Most expected it would, soon. Some managed to doze off, despite the sea's relentless pounding. The raft grew quiet as more and more yielded to exhaustion . . . and fate.

Stewardess Carol Gould tried staying awake by leading another round of hymns. Once the song was over, she said to the soldier with the bad head wound who'd saved her life, whom she'd thanked several times, "Hey, I never got your name."[48]

"George Brown, from Oshkosh."

"Never been. Maybe you'll show me 'round some time?"

"Maybe."

The Italian captain of the Swiss freighter had expected a relaxing trip from Port Churchill to Antwerp. That's why Domenico Lugli had brought his wife and teenage daughter along. He figured his girls would enjoy the fresh sea air, followed by shopping in the diamond district; then the three of them could take in some of the city's many fine restaurants, which would be a welcome change from herring, soup, and bread. But the relaxation had stopped soon after leaving Hudson Bay, and it showed no signs of abating.

When the *Celerina* was 30 miles from Murray and the 50 other survivors, a cry rang out on the bridge: a sailor said he saw a light, suggesting a raft. Captain Lugli raised his binoculars, fingered the dials to get the best resolution, and studied the sea. After a minute, he lowered the device and shook his head. "Just a light buoy, dropped from one of the rescue planes."[49]

While a rescue center report said a raft had been spotted, with lights emanating, the news was stale. Lugli wasn't sure how close the raft might be to the ditching site or if anyone was still on board and alive. Given the wind and waves, not only could the raft have capsized but also the buoys could have missed by a wide margin. Given the fact that it had been three hours since the ditching and the current was 4 mph, that added 12 more miles to any initial errancy.

To make matters worse, the first mate informed Lugli that rescue planes had dropped not too few parachute flares but too many. Rather than help guide the Swiss, the fizzling flares had mixed with the moist air to create a purple fog that the brisk westerly wind was blowing right at the freighter, further obscuring visibility.[50]

Radar could often compensate by picking up a distinctive mass, but the heavy sea spray had rendered it inoperable. So the Swiss had to rely on their lone searchlight to hunt and peck for survivors. That meant it couldn't be used to search for other rescue ships or aircraft or spot and avoid the upper Atlantic ice shelves that at this time of year had the nasty habit of calving, floating about in the dark, and crippling the propellor, if not sinking the ship altogether, as one had the *Titanic* about 200 miles from the *Celerina*'s current location.

Incompatible communications made things worse. Since the *Celerina* lacked the equipment to patch into NATO's frequency, over which most of the search-and-rescue updates traveled, the radioman had to try to stay abreast and keep others informed via the antiquated and very slow Morse code, hoping his tap-tapping would be picked up by a nearby ship that had access to the longer-range frequency and could act as a go-between.

In addition, the chief engineer informed Lugli they were headed straight for even stronger winds and heavier seas. So their ETA would be further delayed. Finally, even if the motorman and carpenter managed to repair the motorized lifeboat, it couldn't be lowered. The conditions were too treacherous.

and there you are, your flower scented
fragrance makes me hold
my breath, for fear you will be gone
before the story's told

Only extant sonnet and pen-and-ink drawing of the sort Bob Eldred regularly sent Edna while away on business (here in Fayetteville, NC), with hauntingly prescient concluding stanzas: "and there you are, your flower scented fragrance makes me hold / my breath, for fear you will be gone before the story's told." COURTESY KAREN ELDRED-STEPHAN.

Chapter 7
Speechless

Four hours after the ditching, the search-and-rescue operation had little to show. The U.S. Coast Guard and British Admiralty struggled to keep up with the blizzard of sitreps from their many assets in the sea and sky. Some were timely and accurate; many were not. One summary making the rounds was:

1. The main search area was three times the size of Manhattan;
2. Including the two rafts dropped by a U.S. Air Force plane, there were now at least seven in the sea, and maybe eight;
3. There were no *confirmed* reports of survivors aboard *any* raft, only of some lights;
4. The specialized rescue seaplanes en route from Scotland and Cornwall had begun turning back because they weren't capable of operating in such rough water;
5. A Swiss merchant vessel was 9 miles away from the ditching site but given the 4 mph current and the freighter's slow speed it was probably at least two hours away from the faintly lit raft; and
6. A Canadian aircraft carrier's helicopters wouldn't be within range until seven hours after that, at the earliest.[1]

The mood aboard the emergency raft lifted as 12 more planes rumbled overhead behind the clouds and began dropping flares and provisions.

"It's lit up like a big city at night," said Carol Gould.[2] Her stomach grumbled at the thought of a Hershey bar, while others licked their lips at the prospect of potable water, or stronger beverages. Other hopes centered on the arrival of pain medication.

But the mood sank again when the new arrivals fared no better. The cloud cover was too thick, the winds too strong and gusty, the raft but a speck in a dark night and unruly sea. The few times a crate splashed nearby, the sea would swallow it or the wind and current would carry it beyond reach. Lest they run out of fuel so far from land, one by one the reinforcing aircraft departed the area. No one knew how long it might take the nearest rescue ship to reach the raft, but as the flares fizzled out and the sound of engines receded, Major Elander summed things up: "We're living, really, from one wave to the next."[3]

"At first we'd be lifted with amazing speed to the dizzy heights of a swell," was how Captain Murray described it.[4]

> *Then across the top as the raft bent and buckled, rubbing our already sore limbs against each other to the accompaniment of moans and cries. Next the crazy drop of the spinning raft down the endless sheer steepness of our watery mountain, culminating in the even more painful reshaping of our rubbery vessel at the bottom. Here, we were thrown about in every which way, continually slapped in the face by the icy hands of the inundating white caps as we waited our ride up the next swell.*
>
> *Although the raft remained upright, I dreaded the approach of each new crest. Surely, anything larger than what we had experienced would flip the raft.*
>
> *And then it came . . .*

A semi-delirious Murray stared in horror as "the largest wave of them all started out with a deceptively slowly rising force, and then its steepness and its size accelerated until near the top it seemed as though we were poised at the rim of a bottomless chasm. The waves are toying with us. Surely the raft could not survive this monster."

The paratrooper beside Murray, who'd been calmly praying all along, "continued to intone in an even voice: 'Oh, Lord, into Thy hands I commend my spirit.'"[5]

Hofer cried out: "Get ready! Hold on!"

People shrieked as the raft rose three stories high and a breaking wave engulfed it. The terror intensified as the quickly receding sea sent the raft crashing down to the surface, to fold like a taco shell.

It immediately snapped back into shape, and the sea filled the raft above Lois Elander's and Elizabeth Dent's mouths. Murray yelled: "Bail! We've gotta clear this water out!"[6]

Gould thought but didn't say: *With all the water pooled in the middle and no one able to move, bail how? And with what?*[7] But as she looked around, she saw people using their hands, hats, wallets, and empty cigarette packs.

Dr. Elander's "entire activity was using his arms, keeping people away from pushing Lois under. The water was up to her chin the whole time." The major "kept calling for her . . . but he couldn't see her . . . just feel her. Every so often she'd go 'I can't breathe!,' and he'd give her a little jerk, and she'd go 'Oh.'"[8]

At least the risk of hypothermia seemed to have abated somewhat as the combined body heat of exertion mitigated the frigid conditions. However, the endless flexing of the raft against the woolen uniforms had further scoured the skin. More toxic chemicals and organic matter had leached into and infected wounds, from Gould's minor thumb abrasion to Gilbreth's mauled calf. Drs. Figueroa-Longo and Elander suspected that many of the wounds were dangerously close to becoming gangrenous.

Having orbited for five hours, USAF 246 was low on fuel. It didn't have nearly enough to make it to Harmon AFB in Newfoundland, where it had intended to refuel before completing its journey to McGuire AFB. It would have to return to Scotland.

Before doing so, however, Major Guthrie and his crew helped several other aircraft locate the Tiger 923 emergency raft by use of flares, and helped guide the *Celerina*. But USAF 246 left the area knowing "nothing of the fate of those on the sea below."[9]

Aboard the raft at 3:30 a.m., a voice rang out: "I see a light! It's a ship!"[10]

Fred Caruso found the repeated false sightings "really annoying."[11] Every one had been USAF 246's searchlight, a flare dropped by some other aircraft, the unveiled moon, or floating phosphorescent plankton, leavened by wishful thinking. "We get excited, crane our necks to look, and it turns out to be nothing."

Hard Luck Sam didn't think it was nothing, but he didn't let on for fear of getting people's hopes up. He'd been tracking a light beneath a reference point on the Big Dipper's lower lip, and once he felt sure it was a ship, he informed Captain Murray.

Murray didn't doubt his navigator. Besides, given his bloodied eye and lost eyeglasses, he had little choice but to trust Sam. What he doubted was whether his flashlight would last. The ship's searchlight was a long way off. Plus, based on the information relayed prior to the ditching, he felt it was probably the Swiss freighter, which he reckoned wasn't the fastest of vessels.

While PFC Joe Hofer had done a great job "babying the flashlight," it wouldn't hold out forever, which is why Hofer was turning it on less and less, and keeping it on for shorter periods of time.[12] If the Swiss couldn't see the flashlight, they'd never find the raft.

The mood aboard the *Celerina* was somber, especially on the bridge, where Captain Lugli felt that given how the violent sea was tossing his big freighter around, the small rubber raft someone reported as having seen hours ago had likely capsized; any survivors had almost certainly drowned. Yet he scanned the horizon, peering through his binoculars, before stopping abruptly.

He touched his first mate's elbow, pointed southeast, and handed him the binoculars. The two men saw the same thing. "At last! Between the floating flares . . . the feeble light of the raft was at times emerging on top of the big waves."[13]

The good news yielded to practical considerations. First, it'd still take the *Celerina* an hour or so to reach the raft. Second, the motorized lifeboat was out of order.

Thirty minutes later, and much closer, Lugli realized his pitching 12,000 tons might flip the raft or his giant propellor might chew up the survivors. Knowing he needed to position his ship so as to shield the raft, he yelled: "Full stop! Reverse engines!"[14]

Bob Eldred noted how "a searchlight began to play, went past us, came back, back and forth. Then, just like in a movie about a prison break, it hit us full, went by, and then swung back and held us. We knew we were seen. Then the searchlight went out."[15]

Given the distance and darkness, no one on the raft could make out the Swiss flag, so a soldier inferred a Cold War explanation: "It's a Russian ship! It's seen we're American, and it's leaving us here to die!"[16]

Fifteen minutes later, at 4:31 a.m., a ship's green running lights and 30-foot-high prow emerged from the dark swells and spray, 50 yards from the raft. No Russian ship, it was the *Celerina*. As its searchlight lit up the shiny yellow raft, the survivors waved and shielded their tearful eyes from the powerful beam.

Captain Murray spread the word that everyone needed to stay put, lest their excitement or desperation lead them to rush over (as best they could) to the side that faced the ship. "The last thing we want to do now is capsize."[17]

Captain Lugli said that off-loading the crowded jumble would be "almost impossible and very dangerous on account of the strong sea and wind."[18] He struggled to maneuver in the 40-mph wind gusts and 25-foot waves. The crew on deck lost sight of the survivors as the raft kept disappearing in the troughs.

As Lugli inched closer, Reymond was "able to distinguish their faces looking up, blinded by the search beam and trying to see us in the night." The 19-year-old watched as soldiers his age, and men and women twice his age, fought to hold on. "Such a scary sight," added carpenter Walter Wunderlin. "So many people crammed together in that life-raft, all desperate."[19]

From the bridge Lugli issued orders to his first mate, chief engineer, and others. "Rudder starboard! Engines half forward! Make ready the Jacob's ladder!"[20] Sailors crowded along the railing, holding heaving lines and rope ladders.

But the *Celerina* couldn't get close enough to commence an off-loading operation. It would sidle two or three feet toward the raft, only to be pushed away six or ten feet by a swell. "Wait!" several survivors screamed. "Don't go!"[21]

Lugli tried again. The engine growled and smoked. As an auspicious swell pushed the ship closer, two sailors heaved the thick rope-cable used for docking, but the wind was too strong; the heavy cables bullwhipped back, nearly knocking out some teeth.

But "our second attempt was the good one," said Reymond.[22] When a swell lifted the raft high into the air, just as a contiguous ebb dipped the ship, two sailors heaved a rope and a soldier caught it. Other survivors fastened onto Joe Hofer's legs or the heaving line.

After a rope ladder was unfurled, some on the raft started to make their way over to the lowest rung, but almost seven hours of an emotionally draining ordeal in harsh conditions without food or water had left everyone depleted. Meanwhile, the wind whipped and twisted the rope ladder as waves elevated and then dropped the raft the equivalent of three stories. Climbers struggled just to hold on to the coarse ropes and keep their feet on the slick rungs, let alone ascend. Even the fittest paratroopers couldn't make any headway. Some barely managed to stay on the raft.

Above them, the Swiss hurriedly formed a human chain that stretched from railing to raft. Depending on the up-and-down movement of the sea, the closest sailor was between 5 and 35 feet from the nearest survivor.

During a lull in the waves, two paratroopers rushed the ladder, bumped into each other, then began elbowing each other as they ascended in close formation. The first officer shouted down from the railing: "One person after the other!"[23] But no one on the raft could understand him because the wind and waves were too loud.

Before the lead paratrooper had stepped off the highest rung, Carol Gould had stepped onto the lowest. She paused midway up the ladder to catch her breath. Seconds later, another explosive swell lifted the raft nearly up flush with the deck. Wunderlin reached over and clasped on to her forearm. When the swell receded and the ladder fell away, Gould was left hanging midair with nothing but the carpenter's grip preventing her from plunging 25 feet into the sea.

After the wind blew the rope ladder back to her, Gould grabbed ahold, inched her way up, and, with Wunderlin's assistance, clutched the cold wet iron with her right hand. He helped her over the railing. She collapsed in his arms and laid her head against his chest. "Thank you!"[24]

Six hours and 40 minutes after Tiger 923 had slammed into the ocean, more than 10,000 first responders on 61 ships and planes had rescued 3 people. The upside-down raft still held 48, sunrise was more than an hour away, and the weather had grown worse.

At 4:53 a.m., aware of the danger and the fact that the human chain wasn't sufficient, chief steward Jean Unghy coiled a thick rope around his forearm, lifted his legs over the railing one at a time, stepped onto the ladder's highest rung, then paused for a moment staring down, wondering whether it was insane for him even to think about jumping into the bucking raft. Reymond and Wunderlin watched. *If he jumps,* thought the carpenter, *that would probably be the end.*[25] He'd likely miss the raft entirely or bounce off a side into the sea, then get sucked under and ground to bits by the propellor. "Don't do it!" yelled Reymond. "It'd be suicide!"[26] Unghy balked, then retreated back over the railing.

It took the Swiss human chain five minutes to get six more survivors up and aboard. But the winds now gusted to 50 mph, the waves topped 35 feet, and the current now exerted its own 6-mph pull. The Jacob's ladder whipped about violently as the raft rose and fell erratically. As the removal of nine people left it lighter and less stable, it seemed closer than ever to capsizing.

Dick Elander said, "The rescue from the raft was a series of disconnected snapshots. Bright lights shining down from the ship—ropes and a Jacob's ladder dangling, I can't possibly climb those—the water in the raft, vile with blood and vomit—a dead man laying across Lois."[27]

As Wunderlin helped the tenth survivor over the railing, it dawned on him why things were proceeding so slowly: the life vest straps were tangled, the effect being that rather than hoisting one person, it was as if he was trying to hoist thousands of pounds. He turned to Unghy and said: "I cannot watch this any longer!"[28] He asked permission to jump down into the raft. Before Unghy could reluctantly nod his assent and tell Wunderlin to hitch himself to the heaving line with a carabiner to avoid getting knocked into the sea, the carpenter had stuck a jackknife between his teeth and begun racing down the rope ladder toward the raft. When a gust whipped a wooden rung into the knife, knocking out two front teeth and sending him splashing down to land inches from Fred Caruso, the paratrooper said to himself: *He looks like a madman!*[29]

Trying to prioritize by women and apparent injuries, Wunderlin made his way over to Lois Elander. As he prepared to cut her tangled life vest straps, the sea boiled over again, hurling him across the raft and flat on his face. He was back up on his feet fast, but rather than continue to assist Elander, he started assisting survivors in the order in which he came across them. He worried that if triaged he'd not get many off before the raft overturned, which seemed imminent.

Seaman A.B. Spampinato crabbed his way down the ladder and stood on the lowest rung. He and Wunderlin tried to work fast but carefully, cutting the knotted vests without puncturing the bladders. The process was still going too slowly for Wunderlin, so although he'd jumped down to separate the knotted survivors, he now reversed course. He and Spampinato started bundling people together in twos by their straps, then shoving the couples up the ladder, to be grabbed by an outstretched arm.

Ten minutes later, there were still 8 survivors on the raft. The human chain had shrunk: there was just Unghy at the railing, Spampinato on the bottom rung of the rope ladder, and Wunderlin in the raft. The other 30 crew members were on the bridge, in the engine room, or had peeled away to help the 43 already off-loaded find warm clothes and get something hot to eat and drink.

Caruso watched as Wunderlin escorted Captain Murray over to the ladder. The pilot "could barely keep his eyes open let alone haul himself up into the wind on the thrashing rope-ladder. His right hand would inch up and fasten on, his left hand would follow, then, just as slowly, his right foot would step up, then his left. All the while the wild waves kept battering him, rocking the ship and raft, and shaking the ladder."[30]

On the penultimate rung, when he was just beyond reach of Unghy's outstretched arm, as Murray paused to catch his breath, a volcanic wave swept him off the ladder, down into the sea. He disappeared, resurfaced, bobbed, then floundered in the churn, equally terrified of being swept out to sea or under the ship's hull, toward the huge propellor's spinning blades.

Fortunately, he'd splashed within reach of Caruso. With an assist from the carpenter, the paratrooper lifted the pilot up and into the raft, escorted him over to the ladder, and handed him off to Spampinato.

Murray inched his way back up. He made it all the way this time, over the railing and on board. The hard metal deck beneath his water-logged socks felt wonderful. He wanted a cigarette, he wanted out of his wet and reeking clothes, he wanted to sleep for a week, and he choked up at the realization that, despite what he'd believed seven hours earlier, he'd not seen the last of his wife and five children.

Wunderlin carried Lois Elander over to Spampinato, who escorted her up the ladder, handed her off to Unghy, then descended back down into the raft for her husband, who was by now delirious. "Every time I tried to reach for the rope, it seemed like people on the ship were trying to keep it away from me. That every time I reached for it, it'd get out of my reach."[31] But Dr. Elander made it up and aboard, too.

Bob Eldred was next. After limping his way up and easing his shattered knee over the railing, he looked down despairingly into the nearly empty raft. He'd hoped his wife would show up during the off-loading, the way Carmen Figueroa-Longo had surprised her husband: neither had known the other was aboard the same raft. But there was no sign of Edna.

Though darkness and immobility had made it impossible for George Dent to see his wife at all during the 21-mile raft journey, the ship's bright projector beam lit her up, and sank his heart. Her eyes were shut, her body limp. "Elizabeth, darling. Stay with me!"[32]

George tilted Elizabeth's head back and tried mouth-to-mouth, but he knew it was too late. Wunderlin tenderly separated the couple, handed her to Spampinato, helped the Air Force officer start his ascent, then returned for the final five survivors.

Art Gilbreth looked dead too. His eyes were shut. His lifeless body moved with the sea. An hour earlier, he'd "huddled down in the water to get warm but because of the loss of blood I was passing out a lot."[33] His eyes opened when "a huge guy with the longest beard I'd ever seen [Spampinato] rushed down the ladder, swung from the bottom rung and started yelling at me in a thick accent: 'Grab the ropes!'"[34]

But the paratrooper from Big Bear Lake, California, couldn't grab anything on account of his broken back, mangled leg, and exhaustion. He passed out again.

When jostled by Wunderlin, Gilbreth felt "a bright light on my face and saw what looked like snakes, but they were ladders, and I grabbed hold of one, and I was going up and down with the swells, and I'd see shadows climbing up, and it was people, and the raft dropped out from under me. But I finally reached over and grabbed the rungs of the ladder. I don't know how I got up that rope."[35] He passed out within seconds of boarding the ship.

Caruso was the only survivor still on the raft. He made it up the Jacob's ladder and on board without complication. He was greeted by tears, hoots, and handshakes. "There were my buddies, Stewart and MacDonald. God they looked beautiful. I wanted to hug them and hold them just to see if they were real. We did. They were real. Thank God! The Lord truly is with me. Miracles do happen."[36]

Someone handed him a hot drink. "I shook so hard, I couldn't hold the coffee cup. I heard of the stove upstairs. I went with a guy who was the navigator. We were naked but for shorts. The stove was so beautiful. So beautiful . . . He swore to me that he would never fly again. It was too much. He was getting too old . . . Never again."

Two sailors escorted the dazed Tiger pilot to a small room with a bunk and a medicine chest but left as soon as Pierre-André Reymond arrived because he spoke much better English. The youngest member of the crew was struck by three things. First, "Captain Murray had a deep cut on his head" that looked infected.[37] Second, he was in shock: his bloodied blue eyes were dilated and darting, he paced restlessly, and he resisted any attempt to treat his gash. Third, Murray "insistently asked me to meet our captain."[38]

Reymond wasn't sure why Murray was so insistent. He wondered whether he had some critical information to share, such as the location of another raft. As radio operator George Stöckli had told Reymond the rescue planes overhead had spotted five rafts but the *Celerina* had only found the one, perhaps Murray had some information as to their whereabouts.[39]

The 19-year-old was sure of a few things, however. The 44-year-old needed medical care, Lugli was really busy, and if the deckhand were to escort the airline captain up one floor to the bridge, Reymond had better have a really good reason for disturbing his commanding officer.

Reymond proposed a deal: he'd take Captain Murray to see the ship's captain if the pilot allowed the teen to attend to his head wound first.

"Fine," Murray said.

"So I gave him some rudimentary care. I cleaned the wound, applied some ointment, and wrapped it."[40]

Ten minutes later, Reymond felt like a nuisance on the bustling bridge, where his captain was focused on trying to locate more rafts and more survivors. Captain Lugli barked orders in his native Italian as the crew mumbled about the dubious prospects in French, German, and Dutch. The brisk sea air whipping through the open portholes didn't fully dissipate the strong aroma of the favored Turkish cigarettes. Lugli was unaware of the presence of Murray and Reymond but when he caught sight of them as they approached, he looked perplexed, not piqued.

"Please excuse me, Meister," said Reymond in Italian.[41]

Murray was self-conscious about his appearance and odor. The water trail wrung out by his socks and clothes pooled against Lugli's shoe. The pilot somehow still reeked of gasoline despite the North Atlantic's incessant washing. As he approached, his trousers sounded like sheets of wet sandpaper rubbing together.

But Murray was mostly self-conscious about his existential insignificance and continued good fortune. "I felt the joy of being alive; the overwhelming incredible feat of mere (how could it ever be called mere?) existence."[42] For some reason, he knew Providence had spared him yet again by putting Lugli exactly where he needed to be with the precise skills and crew needed to effect the rescue.

The American stepped forward and extended his hand. The Italian smiled and shook it. Neither spoke.

"No words were needed," according to Reymond. "The handshake between the two captains was an emotional moment that revealed a lot about the thoughts of both men."[43]

Wunderlin was the last off the raft, at 5:50 a.m. "I have helped over 35 people . . . get pulled up. Finally I tied myself to the heaving line and had me pulled up. I was exhausted, on my own I could not have climbed up the ladder any more."[44] Once aboard the freighter, he glanced back down into the "water red from blood and about two feet high."

Art Gilbreth accounted for much of the blood. The carpenter said the paratrooper looked to be in "terrible" shape, and indeed he was, with a back broken in several places, most of one calf gone, his leg badly infected, and much of his body chemically scalded. As Gilbreth slipped in and out of consciousness, two sailors carried him to the galley, laid him on a stainless-steel table, and held a mug of rum to his lips. Though in his shivering delirium far more liquor was spilled than swallowed, the sweet burning potency of what went down his throat felt and tasted wonderful, as he passed out . . .

He woke to the tugging sensation of someone cutting off his wet Army pants with a pair of shears. The guy smiled and said in accented English: "Hello, Baby."[45]

Bob Eldred was fretful that he'd not seen Edna or heard her voice, but as dozens of people had gotten off before him and the raft had been so dark and jam-packed, he still nursed hope. *Had she gotten off before me?*

Shortly after he'd boarded the freighter and the crew "got me peeled down" and dressed in a sailor's long john underwear, "which became my bandages until I got to a hospital," Eldred received some wonderful news: "A sailor came along and told me, in very bad English, that my wife had sent me a message that she was all right."[46]

A few minutes later, however, when inquiring as to his wife's precise whereabouts, he learned the sailor had mistaken Lois Elander for his wife. "That was the worst time of all. I can't describe how the discovery that he did not mean me, and that Edna was not aboard, hit me."

But Elander hadn't seen his wife, either. "I blacked out. The next thing I knew, I was in this room, people were around me, and I was extremely thirsty. The ship was pitching. I didn't know where I was. No one spoke English. It was very dream-like. I drank some Coke, and slept."[47]

When the ophthalmologist awoke later Monday morning, since he was one of the last off the raft, the wardrobe pickings were slim: all his hosts could scrounge up was underwear and a blanket. Still, he happily removed his wet, torn clothes, stepped into the Swiss skivvies, wrapped himself in the blanket, and "hopped upstairs, three levels." He arrived as the list of survivors was being compiled.

"Name?" a sailor asked, his mien and tone compassionate.[48]

"Dick Elander."

The sailor put a check beside his name.

"My wife, Lois, got on-board too."

"You sure?"

"I'm sure."

"I'm glad." The sailor checked her name.

Dick asked: "May I see the list?"

The sailor nodded.

Major Elander saw no marks of any sort beside John or Naomi Devlin. He closed his eyes and said a quick, silent prayer, asking that God look over them and their family. Then, though "badly injured himself, he dragged himself from cabin to cabin aboard the ship to give expert help where he could."[49]

Fred Caruso wanted to help too, starting when he nearly stepped on a paratrooper who was flat on his back on the steel floor. "He just laid there with a glassy stare."[50] Caruso bent down and began performing mouth-to-mouth, "swapping spit with a dead man. Let him live God! We lived. Please let him live."[51]

Sammy Vasquez approached and said: "This guy's dead." He could tell because the lifeless soldier "was all grey and had foam coming out of his mouth."[52]

But Caruso kept at it. "I was so amped up. I was bouncing off the walls."[53]

Dr. Figueroa-Longo approached, knelt down, felt for a pulse, and pronounced death.

Caruso sobbed. "He's dead. I could be him."[54]

Wunderlin escorted Caruso to his cabin and "gave me his bed. He shut the door so I could cry in peace."

Because the *Celerina* was near the end of a planned three-week journey and had only been provisioned for 35, the 83 hungry people fed mostly on bread. Fortunately, at least in the opinion of Pierre-André Reymond, it was "the tastiest, crunchiest bread ever."[55] The ship had its own baker. Just the aroma of the baking bread was analgesic. The famished survivors devoured it, along with all the remaining cheese, bacon, eggs, potatoes, and fried cod sticks.

The crew, plus Captain Lugli's wife and daughter, did what they could. They wrapped the survivors in blankets and showed them where they could curl up in the boiler room; relinquished their beds; shared their clothes, chewing gum, and toothpaste; and served hot soup, strong rum, milk, Coca-Cola, and Orangebom, a Dutch beer. The few bars of Swiss chocolate were rounded up and distributed to Helga Groves, Lois Elander, Carmen-Figueroa-Longo, and Carol Gould.

Though all of the survivors were exhausted, few could sleep because most of the bunks were shared by two survivors and the rough sea kept tossing them into one another, aggravating their fractures, sprains, and lacerations. The crew improvised: "I slept in a broom closet," said Wunderlin.[56] Insomniacs roamed the ship, many limping around on crutches made of broom handles or moccasins made of hemp thongs, their arms in slings made from strips of denim.

While most of the 48 survivors were suffering to some extent from chemical burns, Raúl Acevedo had it the worst. His torn wool trousers had been especially receptive to the foul fluids and abrasive scouring. "The pain was unbearable."[57] Dr. Figueroa-Longo gave him morphine from the ship's medicine chest, but it didn't help much.

Helga Groves' pain was of a different sort. "That gal'd lost her husband and was pretty hysterical," said Dr. Elander compassionately.[58] Walter Wunderlin added: "The poor lady is close to madness. She keeps going to all the cabins asking whether her husband is there. We keep her under permanent observation."[59] Carol Gould tried to comfort the distraught teenager and keep her from jumping overboard, "which she kept saying she wanted to do, to join sergeant Groves."[60]

It was clear to Captain Lugli that dozens of survivors were in need of urgent medical care. He'd arrived beside a raft with 51 survivors but within minutes 3 had died. Yet the nearest ER doctor was 9 hours away via Royal Canadian Navy helicopter, and the nearest hospital at least 36 hours away in Cork, Ireland.

Huge waves continued to breach the ship's railings and drench anyone unlucky enough to have to be on deck as the fierce winds converted the cold sea spray into an icicle shower. Poor visibility increased the threat of running into the sort of lethal icebergs that had sunk the *Titanic* after its visit to Cork.

Lugli ordered the flag be flown at half-mast, then set sail for Cork. Survivors began trickling back on deck, peering over the railing, "looking very anxious into the water."[61]

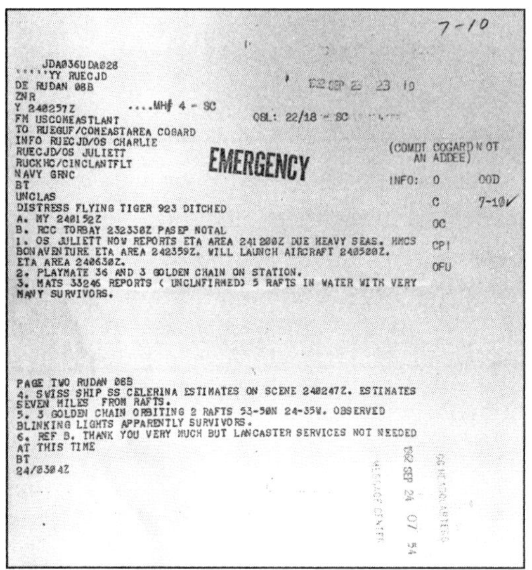

7-10

JDA036UDA028
'''''YY RUECJD
DE RUDAN 08B
ZNR
Y 240257Z ....MH# 4 - SC
FM USCOMEASTLANT
TO RUEGUF/COMEASTAREA COGARD
INFO RUECJD/OS CHARLIE
RUECJD/OS JULIETT
RUCKHC/CINCLANTFLT
NAVY GRNC
BT
UNCLAS
DISTRESS FLYING TIGER 923 DITCHED
A. MY 240152Z
B. RCC TORBAY 232330Z PASEP NOTAL
1. OS JULIETT NOW REPORTS ETA AREA 241200Z DUE HEAVY SEAS. HMCS BONAVENTURE ETA AREA 242359Z. WILL LAUNCH AIRCRAFT 240520Z. ETA AREA 240630Z.
2. PLAYMATE 36 AND 3 GOLDEN CHAIN ON STATION.
3. MATS 33246 REPORTS (UNCLNFIRMED) 5 RAFTS IN WATER WITH VERY MANY SURVIVORS.

QSL: 22/18 - SC

EMERGENCY

(COMDT COGARD NOT AN ADDEE)

INFO: O OOD
C 7-10
OC
CPI
OFU

PAGE TWO RUDAN 08B
4. SWISS SHIP SS CELERINA ESTIMATES ON SCENE 240247Z. ESTIMATES SEVEN MILES FROM RAFTS.
5. 3 GOLDEN CHAIN ORBITING 2 RAFTS 53-50N 24-35W. OBSERVED BLINKING LIGHTS APPARENTLY SURVIVORS.
6. REF B. THANK YOU VERY MUCH BUT LANCASTER SERVICES NOT NEEDED AT THIS TIME
BT
24/0304Z

1962 SEP 24 07 54

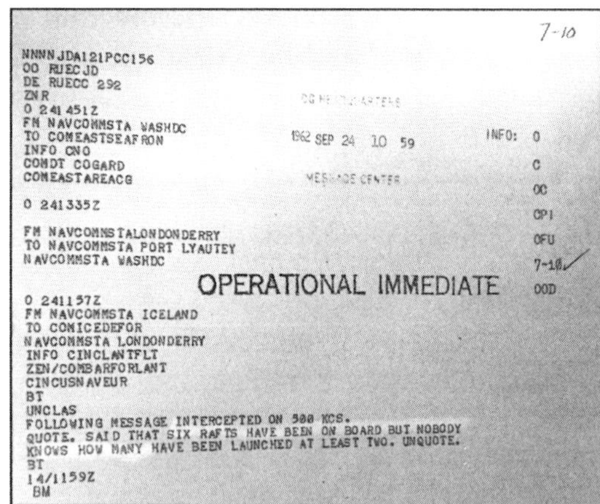

7-10

NNNNJDA121PCC156
OO RUECJD
DE RUECC 292
ZNR
O 241451Z
FM NAVCOMMSTA WASHDC
TO COMEASTSEAFRON
INFO CNO
COMDT COGARD
COMEASTAREACG

1962 SEP 24 10 59

INFO: O
C
OC
CPI
OFU
7-10
OOD

O 241335Z

FM NAVCOMMSTALONDONDERRY
TO NAVCOMMSTA PORT LYAUTEY
NAVCOMMSTA WASHDC

OPERATIONAL IMMEDIATE

O 241157Z
FM NAVCOMMSTA ICELAND
TO COMICEDEFOR
NAVCOMMSTA LONDONDERRY
INFO CINCLANTFLT
ZEN/COMBARFORLANT
CINCUSNAVEUR
BT
UNCLAS
FOLLOWING MESSAGE INTERCEPTED ON 500 KCS.
QUOTE. SAID THAT SIX RAFTS HAVE BEEN ON BOARD BUT NOBODY KNOWS HOW MANY HAVE BEEN LAUNCHED AT LEAST TWO. UNQUOTE.
BT
14/1159Z
BM

Two of the 41 telegrams contained in a March 1963 U.S. Treasury Department (Coast Guard) study. The "Emergency" telegram's ETAs would prove erroneous. The "Operational Immediate" telegram says Tiger 923 had six rafts on board, not the five stipulated in the U.S. Commerce Department (Civil Aeronautics Board) report. COURTESY U.S. DEPARTMENT OF HOMELAND SECURITY.

PART III

MISSING PERSONS

An excellent regulation in itself, innocent of the infinite variables, cannot be accepted with complacency by a conscientious pilot.

—Capt. John Murray[1]

Chapter 8

I Don't Know What We'll Do Without Her

The 1962 press corps did a commendable job getting the facts straight and out, especially given the military's propensity for need-to-know dissemination.[1] Within hours of the crash hundreds of millions around the world were following the saga, including President Kennedy.[2] Sometime late Sunday evening, after Ed Sullivan had signed off for the night and at least the younger three Murray children (7-year-old Steven, 3-year-old Ellen, and 14-month-old Barbara) were in bed (15-year-old Kathleen and 14-year-old John might have been doing homework or studying for a test), Dorothy was probably reading in the upstairs living room, but the family can only recall two things. First, she switched on the TV (no one's sure which station, for though she preferred ABC news, it was late and the kids could have had it on NBC because *Walt Disney's Wonderful World of Color* moved there in 1961). Second, the news "bulletin" was very brief; not just because the initial reports were spotty but because American news was still dominated by print journalism. (Most large cities had morning and afternoon editions. CBS was the first of the three major networks to expand its nightly news from 15 to 30 minutes, in September 1963.)

There were no pictures, just a few words from some up-and-coming anchorman:

- A Flying Tiger charter taking American GIs and dependents to Germany made a "forced landing at sea" more than 500 miles from land;
- The Pentagon wants to inform the next of kin before releasing the names listed on the flight manifest;
- There are unconfirmed reports of at least a few survivors but none has as yet been identified or picked up; and
- A Swiss freighter and Canadian aircraft carrier are among the many ships converging on the ditching site.[3]

Dorothy called Carey Bowles, Flying Tiger Line's chief pilot in Newark, just before he was about to call her. While he couldn't tell her more than what the Pentagon had told the networks, he confirmed that her husband had been piloting the plane that crashed.

Dorothy didn't want to tell her children until she knew whether their father was alive. She'd been nervous before but "I knew it when I married him, and I accepted it a long time ago."[4] Now terrified, she called a close friend in her hometown of Detroit. "We were up all night. We were so worried we couldn't sleep."[5]

Early Monday morning, she told her two eldest. They should know, she reasoned, and she couldn't bear it alone any more. "Mom did her best to stay positive," John Patrick recalls, "and I remember thinking to myself: *Of course Dad would have done an excellent job—he's my father.* "I'm not worried in the least," he told his mother and sister.[6]

While no one can recollect exactly how Dorothy kept the news from Steven, Ellen, and Barbara, she did. It's unlikely she sent Steven off to school, lest he find out there. Perhaps a friend came by and picked them up to get them away from the media. "Either the NY Daily News or NY Post (possibly both) reporters staked out our house, hanging around looking for a story. Mom kept them at bay. These guys were old school reporters in rumpled suits. We took the phone off the hook and wrapped it in a pillow to block the annoying beep, beep sound that an off-hook phone makes."

Later that morning, it was likely a *Long Island Press* reporter who broke the good news to Dorothy.[7] "It's wonderful, wonderful," she said, adding, "He's flown so many miles, that after a while they stop counting. I'm so thankful he's alive."

The children were as relieved and thrilled as their mother that their father had survived. Though John Patrick was every bit as joyful as his mother and four siblings, "I had no doubt," he recalls. "I had seen Dad handle the crises that can hit any family and was confident in his ability."[8]

Tiger 923 was the world's top news story. The massive *New York Daily News* headline read "GI PLANE DITCHES AT SEA WITH 78[sic]." The *Philadelphia Inquirer* banner led with "one of the most stirring rescues in history." The *Detroit News* devoted nearly all of its first two pages to the ditching and search for survivors. The broadcast and international media coverage were just as extensive.

The telephone switchboard at McGuire Air Force Base was overwhelmed by an "endless stream" of calls from family members and other loved ones.[9] Operators were told to do their best to allay concerns, buy time, and keep the media at bay until the Pentagon's lawyers could confer with its public affairs people, issue press releases, and inform the next of kin.[10]

The Army did a commendable job contacting family members. While it sometimes took hours to track down the designated contact, the first telegram went out 84 minutes after the last of the 48 survivors was on board the Swiss freighter. While it took five hours longer to reach Maj. Dick Elander's father in Seattle (his mother was in West Point, watching Dick and Lois' three young children) as it did to reach Pvt. Gordon

Thornsberry's father in rural Arkansas, the missives all said the same thing:[11]

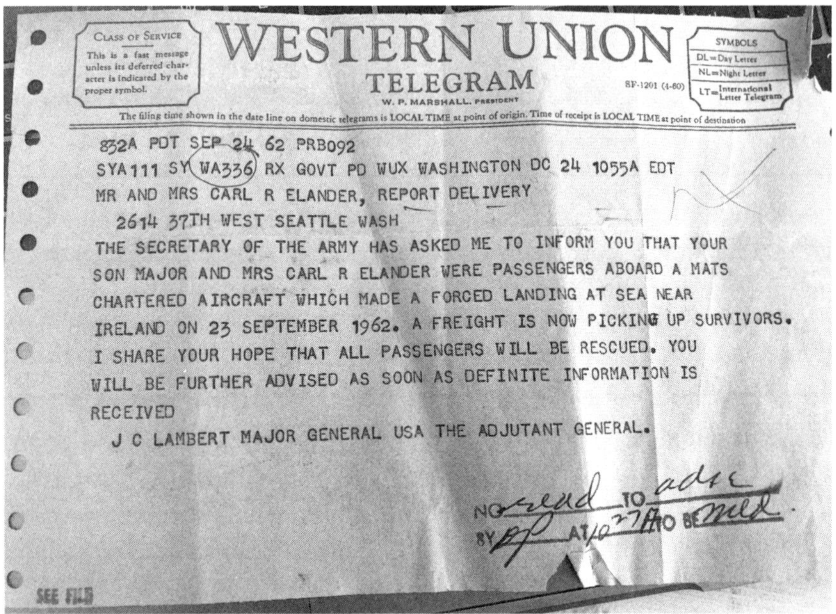

CLASS OF SERVICE
This is a fast message unless its deferred character is indicated by the proper symbol.

WESTERN UNION
TELEGRAM
W. P. MARSHALL, PRESIDENT

SF-1201 (4-60)

SYMBOLS
DL=Day Letter
NL=Night Letter
LT=International Letter Telegram

The filing time shown in the date line on domestic telegrams is LOCAL TIME at point of origin. Time of receipt is LOCAL TIME at point of destination

832A PDT SEP 24 62 PRB092
SYA111 SY WA336 RX GOVT PD WUX WASHINGTON DC 24 1055A EDT
MR AND MRS CARL R ELANDER, REPORT DELIVERY
2614 37TH WEST SEATTLE WASH
THE SECRETARY OF THE ARMY HAS ASKED ME TO INFORM YOU THAT YOUR SON MAJOR AND MRS CARL R ELANDER WERE PASSENGERS ABOARD A MATS CHARTERED AIRCRAFT WHICH MADE A FORCED LANDING AT SEA NEAR IRELAND ON 23 SEPTEMBER 1962. A FREIGHT IS NOW PICKING UP SURVIVORS. I SHARE YOUR HOPE THAT ALL PASSENGERS WILL BE RESCUED. YOU WILL BE FURTHER ADVISED AS SOON AS DEFINITE INFORMATION IS RECEIVED
J C LAMBERT MAJOR GENERAL USA THE ADJUTANT GENERAL.

SEE FILE

Though the telegram worried Thornsberry's father, Elmo, he was philosophical but also practical. While he said, "My wife and I believe something greater than human beings took part in this," the carpenter wondered what "now picking up" meant.[12] Did it mean a freighter was in the process of pulling people out of the water or just en route to the ditching site? Even after a second telegram arrived, saying his son had survived, Elmo still fretted. "I'd give anything to know how Gordon's doing. If he's injured."

As Raúl Acevedo had listed his brother as the contact person, Refugio was the first to receive word that his younger brother might be dead. It seemed surreal. Raúl's postcard of the Empire State Building had just arrived. He'd jotted: "Refugio, Greetings from the pueblito of New York. I will write more as soon as I get to Germany."[13]

"If only we had told our parents the truth," said Refugio. He now regretted having surreptitiously helped his brother remain in the U.S.

rather than return to Zacatecas, as his parents expected; yet he again decided to withhold the truth, hoping and praying that the Army would soon be the bearer of better news.

After six gut-wrenching hours, a second telegram arrived at Refugio's home in San Pedro, California. Refugio was terrified to open it but seconds after he did he started to cry and pump his fist in the air. "What does it matter now? He's alive! That's the important thing. Thank God I don't have to tell our parents that Raúl is dead."

The news traveled more slowly to Mexico. The following day, Raúl's father, Roque, was opening up his general store when from behind the familiar voice of an attorney friend startled him: "Have you seen this?"[14]

The mayor of Zacatecas didn't like being startled. He had a heart condition. His doctor had told him he had to avoid all stress. Roque turned around. "Seen what?"

The attorney held up the latest edition of the *Los Angeles Herald-Examiner.* Beside a photo of Raúl in a soldier's uniform, it read: "Missing at Sea."

The mayor's first reaction: *This is some sort of a crazy mistake. Raúl's in Monterrey, in a basketball tournament.* But then the father began processing the news. *Oh my God! That sounds just like Raúl!* His second-youngest son had snuck across the border once before and was always in the thick of some adventure. *I've got to get home and tell his mother before a reporter gets to her!*[15] But the mayor collapsed on the sidewalk before he could take another step.

Though some of the relatives were "too grief-stricken to talk to reporters," Carol Gould's mother did, albeit with mixed emotions.[16] After having been informed that her only daughter might be one of the people some ship was now picking up, Paula Ziegler wanted clarity yet feared it. She'd not been so worried since fleeing Syria in 1921, nor so disconsolate since her first husband and Gould's father skipped out on them, wreaking havoc. Ziegler's angst gave way to sobbing, dark imaginings, and referring to Gould in the past tense. "I just don't know what we'll do without her. She was so cheerful and she brought such brightness and light into the house."[17]

Guilt exacerbated the dread. Ziegler now rued not having tried much harder to dissuade Gould from flying for a living. She now knew she'd made a grievous error in telling Tiger personnel where they could find Carol when they'd called at 4:30 a.m., hoping she'd fill in for a sick colleague. The mother felt complicit in the nightmare. She wondered how she'd be able to live with herself.

But Ziegler's angst abated significantly when she received word that Gould was one of the 48 survivors. Now the question was: *How badly hurt is she?*

In Massachusetts, on Monday morning, before Dorothy Murray had received word her husband had survived, 17-year-old Karen Eldred "was given a message that I should go to the headmaster's office, which of course immediately made me think I had done something wrong. With a bit of interior panic," she can still recall vividly, 57 years later,

> *I made my way there. I was met by Northfield School Headmaster and the President of the Schools. They broke the news that both my parents were in a crash and that no one as yet had been found. They brought me to the infirmary, where I stayed for the next few hours, then contacted Middlebury College in Vermont where my brother Bob was and they told me that he was being brought to Northfield by a sort of police cruiser Pony-Express (blue lights and all).*
>
> *They were getting information funneled to us by my uncle Jim (mother's brother) who was a Navy Commander. Somewhere I got the news that my father had been found but they gave no info on his condition or whereabouts. My mother was still missing, but the search was still ongoing. By this time my brother had arrived.*
>
> *It had been arranged that the dean of students would drive us down to Cape Cod. I can still remember, her car was a VW Karmann Ghia. My brother, nineteen, was in the passenger seat and I got to ride all bunched up in the luggage area where in other autos there would be a back seat. I didn't mind though, I was actually in shock. We were brought to the house of some family friends who lived down the street from us.*

On Tuesday, Uncle Jim called, apologized for not being there in person, and broke the news: his sister and Karen's mother was presumed dead;

though technically, Edna was one of the seven still missing at sea. "I don't remember how many days it was till we had enough info to schedule an overseas call to England. At that time it was the only possibility to call abroad. I think we reserved three or four days ahead actually. A few days later, I spoke to my father, but neither of us could say much."[18]

The prior afternoon, about 2,800 miles northeast, Captain Lugli had been adjusting his binoculars while looking out over the horizon: he spied a helicopter heading straight for the freighter. He told the first mate to sound the horn.

The news traveled fast. People flocked to the railings. More survivors rolled out of bed and ventured on deck. Murray, Gould, and Nicholson joined them.

A minute later the chopper was 50 feet off the bow, 100 feet above, fighting gusty winds. With its bulbous fuselage and yellow striping, it resembled a bumblebee trying to force its way through a gale. It'd move a little forward, shoot sideways, bob up and down.

Murray and Nicholson eyed each other knowingly, aware that they were witnessing an act of uncommon bravery and consummate skill. The pilot would not have been ordered to fly in such conditions. He'd have volunteered. The Tigers prayed for his safety.

Murray also flew helicopters but never in such dangerous weather. He imagined how the Navy pilot must have been struggling to orchestrate the cyclic and collective in such forbidding conditions. He wished he were up there beside the Canadian to lend a hand, or at least try to. It would've been less stressful.

Pedro (stenciled on the fuselage) hovered erratically. The freighter's deck was too small and obstructed for a landing. The pilot was trying to maneuver close enough but not so close that he'd clip a mast or rigging with one of his rotor blades, crash, and add to the casualties.

A hatch opened, a rope unspooled, and Dr. Jamie Ferguson half rappelled and half rode a litter basket. The wind toyed with the principal medical officer. He swung back and forth more than he descended.

Along the railing, 60 riveted survivors and crew members cheered, held their breath, and clutched each other's arms. When the end of the rope dangled within reach, a sailor grabbed it. Others followed suit, adding ballast.

The doctor's foot touched the deck at 3:15 p.m. A medical attendant followed shortly thereafter, carrying more first-aid supplies.

A second helicopter arrived and began hovering. *Fallen Angel* lowered crates of medical supplies, blankets, food, water, cigarettes, and toiletries.

Pedro's pilot told Captain Lugli he didn't think he could hover much longer. He urged the captain to coordinate with Dr. Ferguson, select those most in need of medical attention, and get ready to place them in the baskets they'd soon lower.

Lois Elander was tapped to go first. She was borne "on a stretcher, strapped into a horse collar, hooked to a hoist in two spots, and lifted high in the air."[19]

The wild wind whipped her about. From 50 feet below her husband watched his wife's injured back and dislocated shoulder bump up against *Pedro*'s door frame, again and again. "It caused me a great deal of anxiety, but eventually they got her in."

Dr. Elander was next. He winced as he limped barefoot toward the hoisting spot. His leg burns weren't excruciating but the pain was getting worse and the lesions were spreading. At least one of the crew had found him a pair of dungarees, though they were 48 inches at the waist, to his trim 32. He tried not to trip over the billowing jeans. He was quickly strapped in, and as he was pulled up into the whipped-up air: "I kept my legs together to keep my pants from falling down." He made it aboard, and *Pedro* banked out to sea and returned to the carrier.

Pedro returned for Art Gilbreth. As his minimally effective painkillers had worn off by the time two crew members escorted him to the hoisting point, every step exacerbated the nightmarish pain of his broken back and gouged-out calf. "For the first time I could really see the high seas. It looked like something out of the movies. Everyone was wearing foul weather gear . . . bent over me, talking in a language I couldn't understand."[20]

The sailors eased Gilbreth into the litter basket, covered him with another blanket, and strapped him in. The whorl of rotor blades disheveled his hair. The warm sun felt good against his face.

> *A crew member said: "Good bye, Baby." And then I shot up into the air.*
>
> *But I kept banging against the bottom of the helicopter landing bars. I was swinging over the ocean from what looked like a hundred foot of rope under a helicopter. And I could see the whitecaps, below. I kept slipping out of the stretcher.*
>
> *I finally wiggled my fingers through the blankets and hooked them onto the lip of the helicopter.*

Dr. Ferguson grabbed ahold of Gilbreth's hand as the medical attendant grabbed the stretcher. They pulled him in. As he turned to thank the pilot, he was struck dumb: the wind had blown open a tartan kilt, exposing considerably more than Gilbreth cared to see. The Scottish-Canadian aviator smiled and said: "Aye, that was a sticky wicket."[21]

It took 81 minutes to get just four survivors onto the carrier: Major and Mrs. Elander, PFC Art Gilbreth, and PFC George Brown. They were joined by the remains of Elizabeth Dent and two others (yet to be identified). Return trips brought more provisions, while two more carrier-based helicopters and a plane searched the area for other survivors.

While there are no extant records of why just four people were flown to the aircraft carrier, it was likely a combination of the belief that most if not all of the other survivors were in good enough condition to make it to Cork, or even Antwerp, coupled with the treacherous weather. In any event, the *Bonaventure*'s commander felt compelled to ground the airlift operation at 4:36 p.m., after which Captain Lugli headed for Cork with the remaining 44 survivors.

Tuesday, September 25, 1962

By 5:50 a.m., a full day after the Swiss had rescued 48 people, the prospects of finding any other survivors seemed dim. None of the U.S.,

Canadian, British, Italian, German, Dutch, or Turkish ships involved in the search found anyone else alive.[22]

Nineteen more bodies were retrieved: those of stewardess Jackie Brotman, copilot Bob Parker, flight engineer Jim Garrett, paratrooper Hal Lesane, and 15 yet to be identified. While some "showed evidence of mechanical trauma" along the lines of "contusions, abrasions and lacerations of the face and extremities, all of these injuries were considered minor."[23] Drowning was the official cause of death for all 19.

Three more rafts were recovered. Two had been occupied, one by Brotman. A third was found empty apart from "bloody clothing and bloody water sloshing around."[24]

The death of Brotman was especially poignant. Like Betty Sims, Carol Gould, and Ruth Mudd, all the 24-year-old Chicagoan ever wanted to be was a stewardess, according to her father.[25] Brotman had been tragically prescient when she told Carol in the Gander terminal that she had a bad feeling about the flight.

That left just 6 of the 76 on the flight manifest unaccounted for: Rachel, Uilani, and Luana Hoopi; chief stewardess Betty Sims; stewardess Ruth Mudd; and Army specialist John Groves. The British Air Ministry, which by agreement had been leading the operation, began to consider calling off the search.

Though London knew it was possible more survivors "could still be drifting helplessly," as Brotman had for some time, that didn't mean it was likely.[26] Cooler heads needed to weigh the risks against the rewards. It wasn't just a matter of wasting fuel: the improbable search was also keeping soldiers, sailors, and aviators from their posts and their loved ones, like USAF 246 copilot Michael Burnett's Brazilian newlywed, who'd anxiously waited for hours in New Jersey before being told of her husband's role in the rescue operation. Also, it was peak season for maritime Maydays, Plymouth was the U.K.'s most active rescue center, and resources were stretched thin. Plus, since all the rafts appeared to have been retrieved, the search would now almost certainly net at best one or two more drowning victims.

So, at 4:50 p.m., just shy of 43 hours after Tiger 923 hit the water, the search was called off. After first noting that the RAF had logged 170 air-hours, the U.S. Air Force had logged 166, and the Royal Canadian Navy had logged 89, an Air Ministry official said: "We decided most reluctantly that there is no further hope."[27]

The survival of the 48 who had been rescued was not a foregone conclusion. This was as true for Dick and Lois Elander, Art Gilbreth, and George Brown, who were receiving first-rate treatment on the *Bonaventure*, as it was for the 44 on the *Celerina*, whose care was rudimentary. Almost everyone had been chemically burned to some extent; every case had worsened. Some had burns on 20 percent of their bodies. Sammy Vasquez saw "blisters hanging down, like two inches long."[28] The agony caused by the insidious, spreading lesions occasioned more moaning and crying than at any time since Tiger 923 left Gander.[29] There were also severe lacerations, broken bones, and rampant seasickness, owing to a violent sea and the ravenous survivors overindulging on beer, canned meat, chocolate, and cheap cigars.

After conferring with the only medical doctor still aboard the *Celerina*, Captain Figueroa-Longo, and Captain Murray, Captain Lugli issued a new Mayday, informing the rescue control center in Plymouth that at least a dozen were in need of urgent medical treatment, and some of the cases might be life-or-death. Lugli also said that those able to make it all the way to Antwerp could use considerably more ointment, gauze, and painkillers.

The control center's RAF commander replied that, unfortunately, there were no feasible aircraft in the vicinity. However, once the *Celerina* drew closer to Ireland, he'd scramble some British and Irish helicopters.

Though the four survivors who'd been choppered to the *Bonaventure* had received far better care, they also needed to be transferred to a hospital, partly because the six-ship Canadian Navy battle group had to rejoin a NATO exercise. However, the Canadians told the RAF that the RCN helicopters would get their guests to Cork via *Fallen Angel* and *Pedro*.

Given the condition of his burned legs, Dick Elander should have been flown straight to the U.S. Army's Berdrup Park Hospital in Swindon, 55 miles west of London. But in light of the rumors floating around about shoddy life vests and missing life rafts, apparently someone in the

Pentagon's public affairs office felt a detour was warranted. The U.S. military wanted a credible advocate and spokesman, and the 31-year-old major seemed straight out of central casting. He was a highly respected medical expert, a loyal Army officer, and deeply grateful to NATO allies Canada and the U.K. He was affable, handsome, and folksy. His 32-year-old wife, Lois, was a perfect leading lady: smart, accomplished, and delightful. The brass knew them, liked them, and trusted them. Who better to speak as the military's official eyewitness than the United States Military Academy's chief of ophthalmology?

However, as the Canadian naval officers and American Army couple had become fast friends, the aircraft carrier's commander wasn't about to release his guests of honor without a proper send-off. That Lois felt she didn't have anything to wear wasn't a problem either: the commodore of the Eastern Canadian Fleet ordered curtains in the State Room cut down and repurposed as a dress. Though at first embarrassed at the thought of wearing a curtain, stylish Lois approved of the ingenious couture. Then, when she said in passing that she didn't suppose a ship with no women aboard had any lipstick lying around, the commodore made a PA announcement and 23 tubes appeared.

Major Elander called the send-off a "marvelous, delightful" affair.[30] To commemorate their visit, the commodore gave them each a *Bonaventure* shirt, beret, and watch.

Later that same night, the commodore and the ship's chaplain visited the couple in their room for a nightcap: Dick had brandy, Lois, an old-fashioned, in bed. They all stayed up until 2 a.m., talking and laughing. Relaxed by pain meds and alcohol, Dick and Lois ruminated and waxed about how the ordeal seemed like it'd been in some novel, not a real-life nightmare.

The next morning, the Elanders were up at 6 a.m. and on deck by 7:30 in their official *Bonaventure* attire, feeling the effects of too little sleep and too much alcohol. With *Pedro*'s whirling blades mussing Lois' hair (she tried to hold it in place; Dick's beret corralled his), they looked up and around to see 1,200 sailors standing at attention, saluting. "It was very moving and impressive."[31]

The commodore hugged Lois, shook Dick's hand, then said that by unanimous consent they'd been inducted into "the Ship's Company," meaning they were welcome on any Royal Canadian Navy ship and in any officer's mess. The American Army major understood it to be a "tremendous honor."

The chopper departed at 8:15 a.m. The flight to Shannon Airport took 45 minutes. "It was an Emerald Isle to be sure, of neatly stacked haystacks and evenly partitioned farms."

When they arrived, "We were invaded." Several U.S. Air Force colonels greeted them and placed Lois in an ambulance and Dick in a limousine "amidst the flashing of flashbulbs and all sorts of activity." He sat in the back seat "waving to photographers, repressing the impulse to flash the V for victory sign."

When they arrived at the airport, though Dick was in considerable pain, he tried not to show it, saying he didn't need a wheelchair. He walked slowly into a makeshift briefing room, the dimensions of which he likened to an "Olympic sized swimming pool." It was "jammed with people and spotlights, perhaps eighty reporters and photographers, each with pencils and pads, from all over, many tape recorders and microphones being shoved in my face."

He opened with prepared remarks, an Air Force colonel invited questions, and a reporter asked what had gone through the major's mind after the second engine died. "Captain Murray said there was no need for alarm, that the plane was well able to fly on two engines, which was very true. Major Devlin and I discussed this. The fact that the pilot was still climbing after this second engine went out . . . was evidence to us that the plane still had plenty of zip to it." Elander said it was only as a precaution that people were told to review "the ditching manual in front of us, and try the life vest on again."

There were more questions and answers, a tea break, then more Q&A. After 80 minutes, Lois was carried in "on a litter. She was the big point of interest for lots of TV programs, movie newsreels, and an ABC interview."

After the last reporter was gone and the last photo was snapped, Dick limped his way to a waiting C-47, alongside Lois, whom two Army medics carried on the litter. About 90 minutes later, as they neared the coast of Scotland, Dr. Jamie Ferguson, who'd hitched a ride, said, "I can taste the whisky and hear the pipes playing."[32]

When they arrived at the sprawling Air Force hospital in Swindon, Lois was put to bed in Ward 41, while Dick, though assigned to Ward 14, was rushed to radiology for X-rays. When he got out and learned Lois was the equivalent of six city blocks away, he asked to be relocated to a bed beside her, saying that, as a doctor, he could be of assistance in monitoring her recovery. But an "unpleasant" American nurse responded: "Yes, but it's against the rules."[33]

Dick appealed to a fellow M.D., who said: "Well, in that case, we'll just have to change the rules, then." Dick was relocated to the women's recovery ward in the bed next to Lois.

The surgeon on call wanted to operate right away on Elander yet couldn't because the major needed general anesthesia but it couldn't be administered because he'd just eaten. For some reason, the next available surgical slot wasn't until Sunday, September 30.

Meanwhile, Elander could tell his body was failing, not responding to the penicillin. He began to worry terribly about what the future might hold for his wife and three children, absent a father. But as he didn't want to worry Lois, he did his best to suppress the urge to wince as he limped around on crutches with a big smile on his face, saying things like "I'm feeling better, really."[34]

He at least took comfort in the fact that Lois' prognosis was for a full recovery. Though she was confined to bed, her shoulder dislocation had been reset and X-rays had revealed that her back pain was the result of a bad sprain and minor stress fracture, not a clean break.

Art Gilbreth was barely airborne before the doctor on the RAF chopper realized Ireland's newest hospital was overmatched. The soldier's back was broken in several places, his calf was a pre-gangrenous mess, he had second-degree burns, and he was running a temperature of 104 degrees F. After the pilot confirmed he had enough fuel to reroute to the U.S. Air Force hospital in Swindon, he brought his chopper around and sped toward England.

The first thing that happened when Gilbreth arrived was he was handed two documents and told he'd have to sign both before he could be admitted. One was a standard release form, absolving the doctors and Air Force of liability if something went wrong, they had to amputate his leg, or he died on the operating table. The second was an Army gag order preventing him from talking to anyone about Tiger 923 unless authorized by his superiors. Woozy on morphine, he scribbled his name, then passed out.

Wednesday, September 26, 1962

Cobh, adjacent to Cork city, has played an outsized role in history and tragedy. Two and a half of the six million Irish who emigrated to America between 1848 and 1950 set sail from County Cork's principal harbor. In 1912, it was the *Titanic*'s last port of call. Three years later, after a German U-boat sank the *Lusitania,* locals cared for 761 survivors. Now residents awakened to another spectacle: a big warship just off shore, flying a Canadian flag; and, closer in, one half its size, flying a Swiss flag at half-mast.

The skies were alive with helicopters hovering and planes orbiting. The plan was for the *Bonaventure* to offload its four Tiger 923 survivors and the 15 sets of remains, then resume its NATO mission, and for the *Celerina* to offload whoever else needed hospitalization, then resume its mission of delivering wheat to Belgium.

Numerous skiffs, rowboats, and fishing trawlers wanted to lend a helping hand. Some of the more enterprising journalists chartered other vessels in order to get in close for some photos and human interest quotes. Given the fact that the *Bonaventure* was a warship and further out, the press converged on the freighter.

Captain Lugli knew reporters had a job to do, but so did he and the media were impeding his. His communications officer pleaded over the ship's radio while the crew yelled and waved from the railings, indicating that now was not the time for press interviews but the time to get the injured and traumatized survivors to hospital.

The media flotilla continued to advance until hit by the *Celerina*'s water cannon. As the journalists retreated, several British and Irish military helicopters began airlifting 17 survivors to two hospitals in Cork and one in Shannon, while others lowered onto the freighter more than a ton of meat, rice, chocolate, beer, whisky, soft drinks, milk, and potable water.

Raúl Acevedo was the first survivor flown from the *Celerina* to Cork, which lay about a mile northwest of the freighter. Unfortunately, the city's new Mercy Hospital couldn't help him. Swaths of skin from his ankle to his groin had been burned off. The copious morphine barely dented the excruciating pain. Sleep was impossible.

All the caregivers could do was try ever so gingerly to unwrap his fused bandages, daub the pus from the exposed flesh, reapply ointment and gauze, and pray. They knew the 22-year-old GI needed to get to a hospital that was better equipped, staffed, and experienced, so the plan was to fly him to the U.S. Air Force hospital in Swindon ASAP.

The next morning, as Acevedo was being loaded via stretcher onto an ambulance, it felt like someone had doused his legs with Sterno and set them alight.[35] He didn't see how he could endure the pain another second.

The drive to Cork Airport was short, bumpy, and painful. Then, as Acevedo was being helped off, when he saw the tiny prop plane he'd be flying sitting on the tarmac, staying in the ambulance struck him as preferable. Another awful night in Mercy Hospital suddenly didn't seem such a bad idea, compared to a three-hour flight in a plane not much bigger than a hearse, in foul weather. In 12 hours, Ireland had regressed from green and sunny to gray and dreary.

The flight was delayed when several high-ranking U.S. Army officers called ahead to say they wanted to hitch a ride to England but were held up. By the time the brass arrived, so had impenetrable fog and lashing rain.

The plane sat on the runway for three hours. Acevedo's marginally effective morphine wore off in two. He was in agony.

When the PA system crackled with the announcement that his plane was about to depart, Acevedo couldn't understand why, for the weather hadn't cleared up. "My private parts were in my neck from fear."[36]

The puny plane commenced rattling down the small airport's short strip. "It was terrible. Everybody thought we were running out of runway space for takeoff."

The nose lifted—but then the pilot aborted, leveled off, and descended. The front wheel pounded the tarmac, screeched, and inflicted more pain. "It was such a nightmare."

The pilot tried again. But he had to abort again and return to the tarmac.

He tried a third time, also without success.

His fourth attempt was successful.

Sort of.

The plane ran into heavy turbulence immediately, and Acevedo experienced a new horror: watching the red emergency beacon right outside his window swirl "every time we ran into an air pocket. It was such a small plane . . . in such horrid weather. My thoughts were, 'I'm not going to make it a second time.' I was sweating blood and hung on to a Rosary that one of the nuns gave me in Cork's hospital. The nurse on the plane had to administer some shots to one of the Brass . . . to relax him."

But Acevedo made it to England, where "they were waiting for us with fire engines, ambulances and lots of people. They had received a 'Mayday' and thought that we were not going to make it. All of us in the plane didn't think we were going to make it, either."

Fred Caruso was the 17th and final survivor flown via helicopter to Cork. He didn't know why he wasn't heading to Antwerp along with the 27 others, but he didn't object. He might have, however, had he known what lay in store: five weeks of mysterious nighttime trips to hospitals in Ireland, England, and Germany, accompanied by needles, nurses, and ax-murderers.

At least things began on a high note, on

a day like no other I have ever seen. The countryside was a magnificent and majestic green. The Royal Air Force rescue helicopter flew at just a hundred feet, and, like all military choppers, it had a noisy way of

> *announcing its approach. It is an awesome, deep and throaty "whoop, whoop, whoop" of the propellor blades . . .*
>
> *An Irish farm woman stepped out of a tiny cottage to see the source of all the noise. She held a broom in her right hand and cupped her left hand over her eyes. I could see her so clearly I can remember the color of her dress. I am certain she had red hair.*
>
> *A small flock of sheep in the field behind the cottage, hidden from view, began to panic and race to safety, moving at a frantic pace, first running one way and then the next. What a hoot! What a glorious view! What a show! My heart was racing wildly.*[37]

The chopper landed. Caruso climbed into an ambulance and headed for Mercy Hospital. As he didn't appear injured, the paramedics asked him if he wanted a tour, "as if they might have been working for the local visitor's bureau. Of course I wanted to see all I could, so the driver took the long route to the hospital. We passed a beautiful lake with giant white swans. It was Lough Cork."

As Caruso was stepping out of the ambulance, a reporter for the British *Daily Mail* asked for an interview. The paratrooper replied, "I told all about it in this letter to my folks. I'll give it to you if you promise to get it to them."[38] A deal was struck: the reporter jotted down Caruso's home phone number in Nanuet, New York, snapped his photo on the hospital steps, and left.

It soon became clear that he couldn't remain in Ireland, though he wished he could, as he was smitten with the Irish nurses, all of whom were nuns. But the Sisters of Mercy couldn't catch Caruso. He'd race from room to room, hiding under gurneys and tables, in closets and bathrooms. "I could hardly stop laughing. I was wild." The nurses tried to sedate him, "clutching oversized needles. I gave them a good run, but I didn't mind getting caught. It was just a little poke in the butt."[39]

In "The Epidemiology of Post-Traumatic Stress Disorder after Disasters," Sandro Galea, Arijit Nandi, and David Vlahov suggest the origin of Caruso's mania. Though Tiger 923 isn't cited in the 2005 study, the aquatic focus is remarkably germane: "being blocked while trying to escape flood waters and having prolonged exposure to flood waters were important correlates of PTSD."[40] Though Caruso was the first one off the plane, he was one of the last to break free from the sinking plane's suction, as 20-foot waves battered him for 10 minutes.

Then came the grueling swim to the raft and the fight to the death with the soldier who'd latched onto him and dragged him under.

Then, when he arrived beside the packed raft, he was told there was no room for him.

Then came six hours of terror on the raft.

Then, just after boarding the freighter, a buddy of his was pronounced dead while Caruso was performing mouth-to-mouth.

It didn't help that Caruso had been traumatized before, at an early age. The same study says that repeat victims almost always suffer more than first-timers. He'd been severely affected by a fire that engulfed a next-door neighbor's house, nearly killing a family of seven. Two of his friends wore ski masks to school to hide their charred disfigurement. Then a gruesome car crash nearly killed Caruso and another friend. These prior, vivid traumas, welded onto his psyche, set the soldier up for a hyperreaction to the Tiger 923 ordeal.

So it was no surprise that Ireland's newest hospital wasn't equipped to care for Caruso, either. Sometime during the night, the staff managed to sedate him and put him aboard a fight to Swindon.

He remained in England about two weeks, along with Art Gilbreth, Raúl Acevedo, Bob Eldred, Lois and Dick Elander, and several other survivors. But Caruso's mania worsened. One day he'd be cracking jokes and "racing wheelchairs along the vacant ramps and deserted hospital wings," the next he'd be "in my hospital bed all day, with the drapes pulled around me. I got up only once to use the toilet when I knew no one was around to do me any harm. The rest of the time I used a bedpan. Nurses brought meals to me."[41]

When it became obvious the U.S. nurses were having no more luck than the Irish nuns, the Air Force decided to send Caruso to a "*special* hospital in Frankfurt . . .where I didn't want to be. Whatever it took—tranquilizers, restraints, a stretcher, walking, I just don't know—" they got him there. "I didn't remember the trip. I didn't care. It seemed to be all one big blur."[42] All he knew was the new nurses didn't speak any English and he was surrounded by people who all "had some kind of bizarre story . . ." or had committed a "shocking . . . crime, mostly murder," including someone beside him who'd "killed someone with an ax."[43]

It was rough at first. "I was slipping." He slept 24 hours straight, then not a wink over the next 24 on account of "vivid flashbacks" and delusions. "In the middle of the night, freezing water would lap up on the sides of my hospital bed. I was all right as long as I stayed in the middle of the bed, but if I fell out, the waves would get me. Icy fingers would claw at me, trying to drag me under . . . the waves. I couldn't breathe. I couldn't keep my head out of the water."[44]

However, by the end of the first week, and to their credit, the doctors and nurses realized Caruso wasn't deluded. The psychological response to what he'd endured was a sign of spiritual toughness and grit, not infirmity.

> *The Army said I was okay for duty. My vacation was over. The staff at the hospital gave me the necessary paperwork, and I was free to go. No one even showed me the way out. "Just follow the signs to the hospital exit."*
>
> *I was met on the street by a smartly dressed paratrooper driving an open Army jeep. We drove some 35 miles toward Mainz-Gonsenheim and the base known as Lee Barracks, home of the majority of airborne troopers in Europe. That must have been a well-kept secret. I had never heard of Lee Barracks.*

Caruso arrived at a compound that was home to two battle groups, but as they were on maneuvers for 30 days, south of Munich, it was deserted. "The buildings, made of concrete and generally unpainted, all looked very cold, institutional and hardly welcoming." He received his first official posting: to C Company, of the 505th Infantry Division.

He acclimated fast and maneuvered his way into a job as a typing clerk at the base reenlistment office. He started seeing a therapist and the base chaplain, who was also Airborne. The two Catholic paratroopers got on well. The support system helped Caruso land a promotion to the Public Information Office, where he was deemed mentally sound enough to receive secret clearance and write for the 8th Infantry's newsletter, the *Arrow*.

★ ★ ★ LATE

DAILY NEWS

5¢

NEW YORK'S PICTURE NEWSPAPER®

Vol. 44. No. 78 — New York 17, N.Y., Monday, September 24, 1962★ — WEATHER: Fair, seasonable temperatures.

GI PLANE DOWN AT SEA WITH 78

2 Life Rafts Sighted in Storm

(Top) Tiger 923 dominated the news for days. COURTESY NEW YORK DAILY NEWS. (Bottom) As a bomber pilot in WWII, Richard "Wit" Witkin was awarded the Distinguished Flying Cross and the Air Medal with five oak-leaf clusters. In 1962, his superb investigative reporting for *The New York Times* pertaining to Tiger 923 was a harbinger of the Pulitzer Prize–winning work he'd do pertaining to the NASA *Challenger* space shuttle disaster 25 years later. COURTESY GORDON WITKIN.

Chapter 9

Praise Galore

The *Celerina* made good time as it steamed past Cornwall on Wednesday night, favorable seas helping it sustain 18 knots. At this rate it would be in Antwerp by Thursday night, four days after the ditching.

Having been generously replenished on the outskirts of Cork, few of the 27 survivors still aboard had ever seen such a spread, let alone one they didn't have to pay a nickel for. They took full advantage, gorging themselves and smoking.

Captain Murray missed his Pall Malls but the airlifted Marlboros did in a pinch. He ate mostly soup and bread. Though he was really exhausted, the still-crowded ship wasn't conducive to sleep, nor was his throbbing head, though it looked a lot worse than it felt on account of it not having been sutured.

But it was the stuff inside his head that was most inhibiting sleep. While profoundly grateful to be alive and harboring no doubts as to his conduct, he was deeply saddened by the fact that not everyone had survived. As he strolled the deck, gazing up into the sky and out across the sea, whenever something occurred that he didn't want to forget during the debriefing he knew awaited him in Antwerp, he scribbled it in the small notebook Pierre-André Reymond had given him. The two kept bumping into each other. They talked about their shared passion for sailing and what it was like growing up near lakes (Lake Michigan and Lake Lausanne).

The 44-year-old veteran pilot again thanked the 19-year-old rookie deckhand for helping to rescue him, for treating his wound, and for brokering a meeting with the ship's captain. "My pleasure and honor," said Reymond, while rebandaging Murray's wound and extolling his "extraordinary feat, especially given such rough weather."[1]

The pilot said, "Thank you for saying that but if I had to do it over I might've tried to lay her down closer to a ship, if it had been feasible."[2]

Reymond stopped wrapping the bandage and shook his head. "No! You're not being fair to yourself, captain. Second guesswork is the easy work. The sea could have been worse at that spot or moment. Some other ship could have capsized the raft."

"Maybe you're right," said Murray. "We'll never know, will we?"

Dick and Lois Elander appeared on TV Wednesday night throughout Ireland, the U.K., Germany, Switzerland, Belgium, and most importantly the United States. The couple came across as credible, delightful, and brimming with moxie. Their Shannon press conference rebutted any innuendo that a callous military had used substandard equipment. Why would the Army fly such wonderful and highly valued people on a faulty plane?

Thursday, September 27, 1962

Millions of Britons awoke to see Fred Caruso's face staring back at them from the cover of the *Daily Mail*, the U.K.'s most widely read newspaper, beside the headline "Oh, Thank God!" and excerpts from the letter he'd written to his parents.[3] (Mailed by the reporter Caruso had met on the steps of Cork's Mercy Hospital, it was read by Britons before his parents.) Rather than the Army major's account of the engines having run fine until the flight engineer's mistake, the Army private, who'd been sitting closer to the engines and had a better view (window, as opposed to aisle), wrote of having heard "tremendous strain on the motors" well before then, starting not long after departing from New Jersey.[4] His account riveted Britain.

A few hours later, *The New York Times* added more intrigue. In response to his questions as to why the life vests didn't have lights, and didn't their absence contribute to the death of 28 people who'd evacuated, investigative reporter Richard Witkin elicited the following comment from a Federal Aviation Agency official: "There was no light available that met what were considered minimum requirements."[5] When Witkin dug deeper, he discovered that the U.S. was the only one of 98 International Commercial Aviation Organization member countries that permitted unlit vests on overwater flights; many U.S. carriers did equip overwater flights with lighted vests; the two largest, TWA and Pan Am, did not; Air France, British carriers, and scores of other airlines did; so did every U.S. Air Force–piloted Lockheed Super Constellation.

Witkin's background yielded the insight.[6] His 33 combat missions as a B-24 bomber pilot during WWII had not only earned him the prestigious Air Medal and Distinguished Flying Cross but also taught him the importance of lighting. Because most of his sorties had been at night and most of Germany was blacked out, he recalled how even a few candles in a church window stood out, even from a few thousand feet up. That's how he discerned why 61 planes and ships had such trouble finding 51 survivors: in discord with industry best practices, a United Nations aviation treaty, and common sense, Tiger 923's life vests didn't have "a means of electric illumination."[7]

Another voice chimed in: that of the Air Line Pilots Association, the world's leading aeronautical guild. While the ditching occurred too late for inclusion in the October edition of *The Airline Pilot*, the 14,500-member union issued a press release in which president and Capt. Charles Ruby wrote how Captain Murray had exercised "exceptional judgment," and his "feat of bringing his crippled aircraft down in the storm-tossed 15-foot waves with three engines not running was an extraordinary display of airmanship."[8] Ruby added how the Tiger pilot had "set the huge aircraft on the water with such skill and precision that it remained afloat long enough for the complete evacuation of all of its passengers. Captain Murray's airmanship was the only thing which prevented the accident from becoming a complete tragedy. Forty-eight passengers and crew survived the ordeal." Ruby added that Tiger 923 was the first successful ditching since U.S. carriers began flying the Atlantic.[9] *The Philadelphia Inquirer* likewise hailed "the first successful 'controlled' water landing" since 1946.[10]

There was immediate governmental pushback against the Caruso-Witkin-Ruby narrative. When a Civil Aeronautics Board (CAB) investigator was asked what had caused the ditching and deaths, he said that since a "triple-engine malfunction is so rare as to be almost unbelievable," the "first speculation" was fuel contamination, which led to a somewhat xenophobic investigation of the British-Dutch firm Shell, Canadian service personnel, and "the six aircraft which had drawn fuel from the same pit" as Tiger 923.[11] He added that since "the failure of three [engines] reported by the Flying Tiger Line crew was considered a 1-in-10-million chance . . . the fuel system" was another likely culprit.[12] When the Bureau of Standards found no evidence to support the CAB's fuel-related theories, Rep. Jack Brooks (D-TX), chairman of the cognizant House Governmental Oversight Subcommittee, said he intended to look into the matter. But nothing came of his investigation either.[13]

On the outskirts of Antwerp, at 9:15 p.m., as Captain Lugli neared the perimeter locks and saw the city's twinkling lights, he should have been smiling because he should have been only 90 minutes from a hot bath, followed by a hot meal, a good bottle of wine, and a good night's sleep, given the fact that he, his wife and daughter had relinquished their quarters to Carol Gould and Helga Groves and bunked in the mess with most of the crew. But Lugli was frowning because the locks had shut at 9 p.m., so he dropped anchor.

Friday, September 28, 1962

At 8:30 a.m., the first mate informed Lugli that the harbormaster still wouldn't allow the *Celerina* to enter the port. No explanation was given.

Meanwhile, the less-injured began to relax somewhat, even enjoy themselves. Soldiers toasted their rescuers, teased each other, and revised history, insisting they'd never actually been afraid. They draped the poorly designed life vests around their necks like garlands of honor and scribbled on each other's arm and leg bandages. Pierre-André Reymond went around taking photos.

Captain Murray and Hard Luck Sam were in no mood to celebrate. They huddled away from the crowds, their thoughts centered on the 28 lives lost (as they'd been informed), which included, in addition to 23 passengers, copilot Bob Parker, flight engineer Jim Garrett, and stewardesses Betty Sims, Ruth Mudd, and Jackie Brotman.

After the clock on the bridge chimed three times, Lugli began to wonder if Antwerp's harbormaster had forgotten about him. However, at 3:30 p.m., the Swiss got the green light to pass through the city's two outer locks and enter the restricted Customs Zone.

Once the *Celerina* was about 150 yards from its assigned berth, no. 123, Lugli was struck by how static everything seemed. There were lots of ships of all types and nationalities, yet they were inert.

At 100 yards, Lugli could see that most of the vessels were decked out in their finest riggings, brass gleaming in the afternoon sun. He saw his peers, captains from all over the world, standing at attention; their crews strung out along the railings, clustered on bridges, or perched in crow's nests.

The cameras started flashing at 50 yards. The blast of a ship's horn triggered a raucous cacophony of protracted honks and exultant bell-ringing. Some people waved Swiss flags as others shot off flares that whooshed and danced and painted the spires of the old city.

Lugli tried not to cry in response to the encomium. His wife bit her lip as she clenched her husband's arm, as his daughter kissed him on the cheek, and whispered into his ear.

Walter Wunderlin told his parents how "all of Belgium and reporters from all over the world and a delegation of paratroopers gave us a stormy reception."[14]

Stormy, yes, but also circumscribed, as two parked Army buses stood between the pier and the 300-plus that had gathered quayside. While most of the crowd was kept behind the buses and a cordon of military police, a few reporters broke through, asking if anyone onboard spoke French. Pierre-André Reymond waved. "The radio, television and newspaper journalists fire questions at me. But they are disappointed, for we had been asked by the U.S. Army not to speak until later and the officer in charge frowns at me gently to remind me of the orders."[15]

As she disembarked, "Helga Groves covered her face with her hands. But Paul Stewart waved cheerfully to reporters as he was carried to the ambulance."[16] When a journalist saw how young Stewart and several of the other paratroopers looked and in fact were, he exclaimed, "Oh my God, you're just a boy!" but a different journalist said, "No, he's man. They're all men. There're no boys here."[17]

Lode Craeybeckx was the longest-serving mayor in Antwerp history (1947–1976) not just because he could smell an opportunity but also because he could seize upon it with celerity and panache. He knew the world's eyes would be upon his fair city, and he wanted people to know it had more to offer than diamonds and chocolate. As soon as he'd confirmed the *Celerina*'s likely arrival day and time, he'd ordered his staff to get to work.

The Dock Hotel would host the gala. It wasn't the Ritz but it was nice and very close. While the guests of honor would be the 27 survivors who'd arrived on the *Celerina*, the 33-man crew, and Lugli's wife and daughter, other VIPs would include NATO representatives from its Brussels headquarters, U.S. military and diplomatic officials, and plenty of media.

Wunderlin described the opening cocktail reception: "The thanking and shaking hands seems to have no end. A high American general thanked me personally . . . doused with plenty of whisky. In the midst of all the happiness, the survivors and the rescuers, each praying to God in their own language, held each other by the hand. A unique and unforgettable moment."[18]

A grateful paratrooper pinned his Army Airborne wings on Captain Lugli's lapel. Another pinned his on Lugli's wife's lapel. A third pinned his daughter.

Carol Gould had already given her stewardess uniform to Lugli's daughter to thank the family for their remarkable hospitality, including letting Gould use the well-appointed captain's quarters. However, because most of her time on the ship had been spent not sleeping but trying to keep the inconsolable German widow, Helga Groves, from jumping overboard, Gould wasn't in the ballroom but in her hotel room, fast asleep.

A rap on the door woke her. It was Captain Murray telling her the mayor wanted her to sit beside him during dinner. "Okay," she said, "I'll be down in a sec."[19]

Gould sat between Murray and the mayor. The rest of the head table included Captain and Mrs. Lugli, their daughter, Hard Luck Sam, a Belgian official, and U.S. Army officers. Reymond recalled how "sailors and soldiers mixed and ate and drank together till exhaustion. We laughed, we sang, we exchanged addresses and caps and swore that we would meet again and would never forget one another."[20]

In the U.S., prompted by *The New York Times* exposé, more journalists began to switch from regurgitating the Pentagon's press releases to searching for the truth. More troubling facts began to emerge. Wasn't this the third Tiger–Army–Air Force plane to crash in just six months? Weren't they all Lockheed Super Constellations? How on earth had the FAA just certified Flying Tiger Line, Inc. as a "carrier capable of continuous safe operation"?[21] Why was the military still contracting with the airline to transport soldiers and civilians, period, let alone on such seemingly dangerous equipment? Hadn't several new Boeing 707 jets been sitting empty on the tarmac at McGuire AFB? Why hadn't those been used? And what about the stories of missing life rafts, unlit life vests, failing engines and "secret military cargo"?[22]

Saturday, September 29, 1962

Antwerp: The survivors slept late in the hotel, the Swiss crew late in their bunks. Most of the rest of the day was spent swearing out affidavits to CAB officials.

When not being debriefed, the U.S. soldiers were confined to their rooms, which didn't seem right to PFC Gordon Thornsberry, "especially on account of they'd given us all a hundred dollars. We couldn't much use it in our room, so though a lieutenant colonel was assigned to watch over us I managed to give him the slip, find a liquor store, invest my hundred, sneak back into the hotel, and triple my money in two hours."[23]

Mayor Craeybeckx treated Gould, Murray, and Nicholson to lunch at a fancy restaurant. Just the four of them. When the preordered first course arrived, Gould made a face, turned to the pilot, and whispered, "What's that?"

"Escargot," Murray replied.

"What's that?"

"Snails."

"Snails! I don't know if I can handle snails!"

"Given what you've been through, I think you can manage a few snails."[24]

On September 30, the fancy food with the funny names resumed on the Sabena flight back to the States. Gould loved the first-class treatment. She said, "Why, don't mind if I do!" whenever a stewardess offered to top up her glass of champagne. She'd never been tipsy seven miles up. "But it's something I could get used to."[25]

Neither she, Nicholson, nor Murray had any qualms about flying so soon after the tragedy. "Stepping on a plane so soon after the ditching didn't faze us. Then again the champagne may have helped."

Because Gould sensed from her seat across the aisle in first class that the Tiger pilot and navigator were preoccupied, she wanted to lift their spirits. "I'm having a heckuva time deciding which of the two of you were braver." Murray and Hard Luck Sam would either ignore her, or curl back their thumb at the other guy, or point at her.

The two men stared out the window a lot, slept little, and argued as to whether Indian or Harley-Davidson made a better motorcycle. Occasionally they discussed the incident or jotted down some notes while things were still relatively fresh in their minds, knowing they'd be held to account at a public hearing once home.

They also discussed the irony of their situation and how they were convenient PR props. Sabena Airline was still reeling from a famous crash of its own that occurred on February 15, 1961. All 72 aboard died, including all 18 members of the U.S. Figure Skating Team who were en route to Prague for a competition. It was the first crash of Boeing's 707-320 jet in three years of operation. The cause was still a mystery. The same make and model plane was now flying Gould, Nicholson, and Murray. This flight could help redeem the Boeing and Sabena brands. Belgian officials realized the world's eyes were on the drama that had wound down in Antwerp, three of the main players were headed back to New York, and Sabena was the Belgian state airline. It would have been most ungracious not to fly the Americans home, gratis, given the U.S. role in NATO and how vital the Alliance was to Belgium's economy and security.

But the plush seats, fancy victuals and luxe service couldn't exorcise Murray's demons. Confined with his thoughts for eight hours, on a plane no less, he couldn't stop turning things over in his head: obsessing about what he'd done and not done, what he should have or might have done differently.

At 2:20 p.m., the scene at Idlewild Airport (JFK since 1963) reprised Cork and Antwerp with all the reporters and bystanders milling about, only this crowd was bigger, yet also more intimate, with many friends and family in the mix. These were local heroes (New York, New Jersey and Pennsylvania), not foreigners, and Idlewild was typically packed with travelers, unlike Cork's tiny airport or Antwerp's quay.

Tiger 923's introverted navigator didn't want to be the first to face the throng but as Carol Gould was swapping phone numbers with the Belgian stewardesses, who promised her a really good time wherever else their paths might cross, Hard Luck Sam was again out of luck, for Murray lagged behind, possibly flashing a wry smile, as if to suggest: captain's prerogative. But it was Sam's prerogative not to have to answer any of the questions being fired at him, so he smiled shyly as he brushed past the media and disappeared into the crowd.

Gould stepped off the jetway feeling bloated. "I'd gained ten pounds in five days on the ship to Antwerp, and that was before the shindig at the hotel, the lunch with the mayor, the to-die-for waffles and chocolate, and the flight home, where I ate and drank like a queen."[26]

She scanned the crowd, then choked up as her mother ran toward her, arms spread wide, mascara streaky. "We hugged each other really tight and cried a lot of happy tears but didn't say much, apart from my mom saying 'I was so worried!,' and me saying 'Me, too!'"[27]

As Gould's uncle and surrogate father kissed the top of her head, she saw Eddie Hansen, one of her two main boyfriends. He was holding a bouquet of roses. "He was so handsome! He looked just like a Viking god!" She ran to him.[28]

While hugging Eddie, she caught sight of Tommy Kopalak, whom she'd also been dating. He had a bouquet too. "Tommy was a really sweet guy but I'd decided to marry Eddie. I'd just not told Tommy yet, or Eddie for that matter."

John Murray clomped down the ramp shortly after Gould, a cigarette dangling from his lip. He was nattily dressed because some of his Tiger colleagues in Belgium had sprung for a new outfit, including fancy shoes. "They sort of teased him," said Gould, "'cause, you know, he wasn't exactly a clothes-horse."[29]

His left cheek was still black and blue. His forehead gash was still dark red and raw-looking, though a week had passed since his head had slammed into the plane's glare shield.

His family rushed forward. He hugged and then kissed his wife, Dorothy, embraced his 15-year-old daughter, Kathleen, then shook hands with his sons, Steven (7) and John Patrick (14). When 3-year-old Ellen sprang into her daddy's arms, he cradled her and kissed the top of her head as 14-month old Barbara protectively tugged his trouser leg. The gutsy man who seemed never to choke in a crisis choked now.

He struggled to speak. While recollections are hazy, John Patrick recalls his father saying something along the lines of: "I . . . can't tell you how great it is to see you. Every one of you. I can't wait to get home. But . . . maybe your mother could drive?"[30]

That same night, though most of the 40 million Americans who'd tuned in to *The Ed Sullivan Show* (the country's number-one-rated program) probably did so to see the New York Yankees' Mickey Mantle just before he suited up to play Willie Mays and the San Francisco Giants in the upcoming World Series, the host threw a curveball, kicking things off by asking a special guest—a hero pilot—to stand and be recognized. U.S. Air Force lieutenant Joe Lewis stood, followed by his wife, his crew, and their wives. Mantle joined the live audience in giving a big round of applause to the flight crew that had so skillfully intercepted Tiger 923, then orbited the area to direct the search-and-rescue effort, almost running out of fuel in the process.

No one in the Murray household saw the *Show*. No one recalls if Captain Murray had been invited. But a few recollections are clear.

First, the Tiger pilot had no desire to be in the spotlight in New York, any more than he had in Antwerp when U.S. Army officials and the Swiss deckhand were running around snapping photos. Second, Murray was glad Lewis was getting the recognition he deserved: he'd told all who'd listen that the Air Force pilot had saved his life and the lives of 47 others; it was a mutual admiration society, with Lewis having told reporters: "The passengers rescued owe their lives to Captain Murray."[31] Third, Murray never regarded himself as a hero: he "dismissed his own competence," saying "God's hands were in control of the plane."[32]

Maybe Sullivan hadn't invited him because the Air Force, Army, and CAB hadn't wanted Murray on TV, for various reasons. Or maybe someone had called to invite him but the phone had been taken off the hook. Or maybe he'd answered but politely declined, preferring to spend his time hearing all about his children's new school years and new friends, and to give his wife a breather so she could get out of the house, play tennis or bridge with her friends, or paint.

Murray's friends and neighbors couldn't understand why he hadn't appeared on the *Show*. He was, they insisted, cut from the same cloth as former Oyster Bay resident Teddy Roosevelt. The town's boosters pointed out how the Miracle Pilot's home on Seawanhaka Place sat directly across the Bay from the Rough Rider's on Sagamore Hill.

The locals clamored for a parade. And, as the holidays were just around the corner, why not also remind the New York–New Jersey catchment of the town's many great places to dine, shop for that special Christmas present, or buy that car they'd had their eyes on, at end-of-year-prices way lower than all those high-rent dealerships?

Murray demurred. He worried that a parade might be construed as unseemly, disrespectful, given the fact that 28 people had died on his watch. Dorothy told him he was being foolish, too hard on himself.

Carol Gould reveled in the attention, from all the WELCOME HOME, CAROL! signs that awaited her when she turned onto Chase Street in Lyndhurst, to all the kids and their parents with Kodaks who wanted their picture taken with the heroine, waving newspapers, holding up pens. She laughed and complied. "I signed more autographs than I can remember."[33]

On October 4, the Murray family rode in a Chevy convertible lent by the local dealer, bedecked in roses donated by the local florist, beneath the OUR HERO! banner that stretched across Main Street.[34] The procession wound its way to Oyster Bay High School, where a packed gymnasium saw Ethel Roosevelt present her neighbor, whom she was meeting for the first time, with a scroll. Teddy Roosevelt's youngest daughter said she knew that had her father been alive he would have loved to have been the one accorded the honor of praising a fellow "arena" combatant. Murray was visibly humbled. He didn't say much other than "Thank you . . . but I'm not a courageous man."[35]

He spent the next week or so trying to answer the nonstop questions posed by his inquisitive children in a way that lessened anxiety about what he did for a living, and would continue to do, and was life-affirming. He went sailing with Barbara, clamming with Ellen, rowing with Steven and John; talked politics with his canniest and eldest, Kathleen; and let Dorothy get out of the house to decompress, but also took her out to dinner, so they could discuss: What now?

But there was one question 14-year-old John Patrick didn't ask.

> *One of Dad's Tiger friends in Belgium had bought him some shoes that were extremely pointed in the toes. Well, don't you know, that was the absolute height of fashion in high school, and, without asking, I often "borrowed" his ultra-pointed shoes. He NEVER would have bought them himself! But, for me, they were in the stratosphere of style: the most pointed toes anyone had ever seen. I felt soooo cool wearing them to high school. When the cool kids start asking you where you got your shoes, you know you're on to something!*[36]

As for how the pilot and his family were affected emotionally, "Dad was a good father but not one to share emotions with his kids. While the loss of life troubled him and he probably ran the images of the event through his mind repeatedly, recalling details, questioning the actions he and others took that night, he wasn't moody or detached, and life was more or less normal. We were all very proud of him and the attention he was getting."[37]

The phone rang off the hook. Reporters continued staking out the house, showing up unannounced, ringing the doorbell, asking for an exclusive or at least a quote. Murray always politely declined, saying he had been asked to hold off on making any comments until the CAB Board of Inquiry hearing that, he just heard, would convene on November 14, 1962, at Idlewild Airport.

On October 14, at an altitude of 72,000 feet, a Lockheed plane snapped the first photos of what up until then had only been a suspected Soviet nuclear missile base on Cuba. But now the evidence was rock-solid.

Not that the public knew about it. Very few did, apart from President Kennedy, the NSA, CIA, Joint Chiefs of Staff, and Lockheed Aircraft Corporation.

It's unknown if the photos had any bearing on the Tiger 923 investigation. But this much is known: a Lockheed plane was playing a key role in the brewing, terrifying Crisis; Lockheed's top-secret "Skunk Works" were located just up the road from its headquarters in Burbank; Flying Tiger Line's headquarters were in the Lockheed Air Terminal; and with Washington and Moscow on the brink of nuclear war, the Lockheed planes flying above Cuba were a lot more important than the wreckage of one at the bottom of the Atlantic.

How The Miracle Pilot Saved 48 From Ocean

Plane Put Down Skillfully in Atlantic

Tears of Joy, Tears of Sorrow Over Crash

49 Safe After Plane Carrying GIs, Families Ditches at Sea

House OKs President's Call-Up Bill

WASHINGTON (UPI) —

EUROPEAN EDITION

THE STARS AND STRIPES

ARMY NAVY AIR FORCE

Unofficial publication of the U.S. Armed Forces in Europe, North Africa and the Middle East

Volume 21, Number 160 D 5 cents daily, 10 cents Sunday Tuesday, September 25, 1962

14 Missing, 11 Bodies Recovered

From Press Dispatches

LONDON—A little Swiss

Courtesy *Indianapolis Times*; the U.S. Air Force's *MATS Flyer* ("Good Show"); *Stars and Stripes.*

Antwerp, September 28, 1962. (Top) Captain Murray aboard *Celerina* beside two appreciative U.S. Army officers. (Bottom) Captain Lugli, flanked by his wife and daughter, wearing U.S. Army Airborne jump badges. COURTESY PIERRE-ANDRÉ REYMOND.

Antwerp, September 28, 1962. (Top) Three hours before they were fêted by the mayor of Antwerp at the nearby Dock Hotel, surviving paratroopers look out over the railing they'd climbed over four days earlier at the crowd of generals, military police, media, and bystanders (bottom). Names courtesy Pierre-André Reymond, Fred Caruso, and Gordon Thornsberry. PHOTOS COURTESY REYMOND.

Antwerp, September 28, 1962. Top and Bottom photos taken aboard *Celerina* (wth Pierre-André Reymond's camera). Names courtesy Reymond, Fred Caruso, and Gordon Thornsberry. COURTESY REYMOND.

Antwerp, September 28. (Top) Surviving crew members John Murray, Carol Gould, and Sam Nicholson observe the gathering at quayside. (Bottom) U.S. Army buses and military police block the media from getting near the survivors. COURTESY PIERRE-ANDRÉ REYMOND.

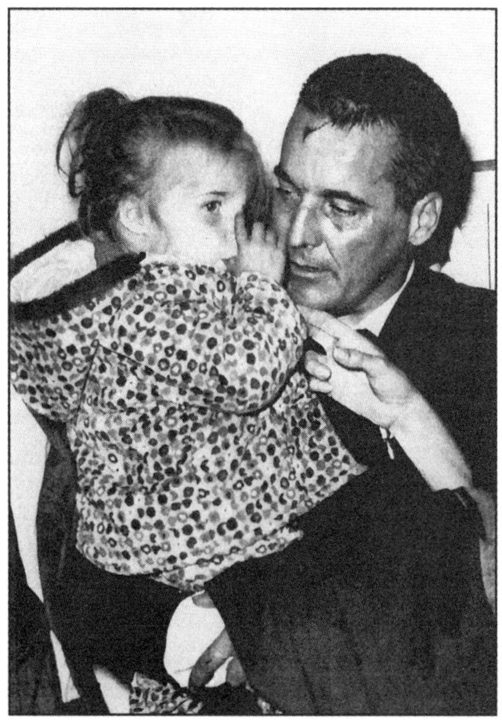

(Top) Idlewild Airport (now JFK), September 30, 1962: John Desmond Murray, 44; Dorothy, 42; Kathleen, 15; John Patrick, 14; Steven, 7; Ellen, 3; and Barbara, 14 months. (Bottom) Ellen in the captain's arms. COURTESY JOHN P. MURRAY.

Chapter 10

Having Second Thoughts

Idlewild Airport International Hotel
Jamaica, Long Island, New York
November 14, 1962
9:30 a.m.

The ballroom was packed, the stakes were high, and the 20-year-old from Russellville, Arkansas (population 8,979), was nervous. "It was intimidating," said Gordon Thornsberry. "Here I was just a private in the Army, surrounded by generals, TV cameras, and reporters from all over the world."[1] The occasion was the Civil Aeronautics Board (CAB) hearing into Tiger 923, and joining Thornsberry, the brass, and the media were another 14 survivors scheduled to testify, family and friends of the 48 who survived and the 28 who died, lots of pilots and other members of the aviation community, congressional staffers, and New Yorkers who'd been following the dramatic tale and had time on their hands now that their Bronx Bombers had won another World Series.

Thornsberry wasn't alone in his anxiety. Captain Murray's livelihood and reputation were on the line: the CAB could insist that the Federal Aviation Agency revoke his airman certificate, airline transport pilot rating, and/or commercial pilot privileges. It could also ground Flying Tiger Line, putting 2,500 people out of work and disrupting the travel plans of thousands more. Lockheed's stake was the billions of dollars it got to maintain hundreds of military Constellations strung out in the sky to defend against an incoming Soviet nuclear attack; for scores of its U2 spy planes; and to fund the top-secret SR-71 "Blackbird" spy plane the aerospace firm was hoping to persuade lawmakers to greenlight, at a price 35 times that of the U2. Others on edge included officials of the companies that made Tiger 923's problematic engines; of those that serviced, maintained, and fueled the plane; the Coast Guard; and NATO.

Formed in 1938 as a unit of the Department of Commerce, the CAB was in the business of promoting and defending the U.S. airline industry, primarily by regulating air fares and routes. (It would be gutted in 1967 when the Department of Transportation was created, and fully abolished in 1985.) While it also investigated accidents (until the National Transportation Safety Board took this over in 1967), according to former Marine aviator and Connie pilot Dick Rodriguez, who was hired by the CAB's Bureau of Safety as a hearing and reports officer in August 1962, the presidential appointees weren't as interested in reviewing crash data as they were in getting "schmoozed by mayors, city councils, legislators, et cetera as to whether Northwest should fly to Helena, Montana. That's the kind of thing the five Board members did."[2]

One thing most members did not do was overly concern themselves with trying to build safer aircraft. While not as blatantly callous as the aerospace executive who said "The more they crack 'em up, the more planes I build," the CAB tended to agree with the aerospace engineer who said his planes were already "*oversafetied*," despite a string of crashes.[3]

The result was safety personnel who were overworked, underpaid and underappreciated. "Each report writer was carrying a load of five to seven accidents, simultaneously," according to Rodriguez. "We were like the red-haired step-child kept hidden in the basement."[4]

The CAB first learned of the Tiger 923 ditching via its LA field office 67 minutes after impact.[5] The Bureau formed three investigative groups: operations, human factors and records review.[6] Six investigators fanned out to New York, London, Antwerp, Gander and Cork.

As chairman of the "Board of Inquiry," CAB member G. Joseph Minetti sat up front on a dais, flanked by 17 other men and 35 exhibits. The 53-year-old attorney from Brooklyn was clever: he had served in Army intelligence during World War II. He was tough: as a prosecutor, he'd successfully taken on the mob, crooked lawyers and war profiteers. And he was bipartisan: appointed or reappointed by two Republican presidents and three Democrats.

Chairman Minetti introduced the other three members of the Board of Inquiry sitting beside him at the main table: the CAB's safety bureau director, its deputy general counsel, and the acting chief of hearing and reports. Then Minetti introduced the three air safety investigators who'd be doing most of the questioning, noting that, collectively, they'd logged 15,000 hours as pilots in command. Then he introduced the inquiry's four advisors: the safety bureau's supervisor of investigations, chief aeronautics engineer, chief meteorologist, and public information officer. Minetti's final introductions were the seven men he'd invited as official guests, who represented the U.S. Air Force; the FAA; Flying Tiger Line, Inc.; the Air Line Pilots Association, on behalf of John Murray; the Flight Engineers International Association, on behalf of Jim Garrett; the Transport Workers Union, on behalf of Sam Nicholson; and Lockheed Aircraft Corporation.

Minetti explained the hearing procedures, starting with: because it had been convened "solely for the purpose of developing facts," as opposed to finding fault, participants were "not permitted to express any opinions."[7] Nor would he permit questions he deemed immaterial or redundant, "tolerate" cross-examination, or allow the media to disrupt the proceedings. After saying that "no objections to my decisions will be permitted," Minetti asked one of the three CAB investigators to kick things off.

The investigator described how, three hours after the ditching, he'd rushed to Flying Tiger headquarters in Burbank, housed in the Lockheed Air Terminal, to secure all relevant records and hold preliminary meetings with Tiger, FAA and Lockheed personnel. He said that right off the bat he'd uncovered numerous "deviations" from "required" protocol by the Tiger 923 crew and others, which he hoped the inquiry would clear up.

When Chairman Minetti called Murray as the first witness and he rose from his chair and kissed his wife, Dorothy, heads turned, fingers pointed and flashbulbs popped. He had decided to wear his funeral suit rather than his Sears knockoff uniform, and to refrain from smoking, at least until recesses. As he'd lost 15 pounds in the seven weeks since the ditching, he was near his college football–playing weight. His hair was short. The crimson scar above his left eye was faintly visible. He looked like a Marine brigadier general who'd seen a lot of action. The tidy stack of papers before him suggested he was girded for battle.

The leadoff investigator asked the pilot to summarize his background and credentials, the flight and accident, and help everyone understand the deviations to which he'd just referred. Murray said he would try.

He didn't get very far before Chairman Minetti interrupted: "You sound like you have a cold this morning. Do you?"

"Yes," said Murray.

The CAB investigator resumed: "Captain Murray, on November 14 last, were you captain of N6923C when it was ditched in the Atlantic Ocean?"

A: That's September 23, sir.

Q: September 23, sir. I am sorry.

Q: Prior to departure from McGuire . . .

A: I didn't leave McGuire. I got on the airplane at Gander.

Q: Were you not on this plane that went from McGuire to Gander?

A: No, I wasn't.

The exchange sparked some muttering and muted guffawing, but the room fell silent when the chairman rapped his gavel, as it hadn't been 30 minutes since he'd warned those in attendance that he'd not tolerate any disruptions.

The opening exchange was indicative of the CAB's "trial strategy." Investigators first sought to gauge Murray's basic cognitive functioning in the present. Could he cite chapter and verse of all four parts of the federal laws that governed his profession? Explain the difference between FAA form 666 and CAB hearing exhibits 2-Q, 2-R, 2-S, 2-U and 2-V?

Summarize the Lockheed L-1049H's fire warning and suppression procedures? The ditching procedures? He could and he did.

Investigators then turned to Murray's judgment at the time: at Gander Airport, in the air, and after impact. Was taking off with an unsealed main cabin door wise? How thoroughly did he inspect the plane? Why did he delegate so much authority to his crew? After impact, could he really have conducted a thorough search for any and all injured survivors? Wasn't it too dark? How, exactly, had he helped Helga Groves get over to and aboard the raft? Was he the de facto captain of the raft, or unconscious most of the time? He explained himself as best he could.

While most hearings spent a lot of time on weather and equipment, Tiger 923's focused overwhelmingly on the pilot.[8] This came as no surprise to Murray given the fact that the CAB told the *Los Angeles Times* and *New York Times* that "a triple engine malfunction is so rare as to be almost unbelievable;" and "for three to fail was a chance in ten million."[9]

Still, as compared with other CAB hearings, the focus on the Tiger 923 crew, and Murray in particular, was striking. Though the pilot was just 1 of the 24 witnesses, questions put to him or pertaining to him accounted for about 90 percent of the forensic inquiry over the course of three days and 31 hours of testimony.[10] When not asking the pilot to explain his actions, the hearing's 18 members, investigators, advisors, and guests were asking the other 14 survivors and 9 expert witnesses to weigh in on what Captain Murray did and didn't do, and how it bore on the outcome. The remaining forensics pertained to how well the airline had serviced and maintained the plane, engines, life vests, and life rafts; how well it had trained the Tiger 923 flight crew; and how its overall safety record compared to that of the industry at large.

The hearing ran so much longer than expected that it had to be relocated to a different venue to make way for another booking.[11] The transcript runs 959 pages.

The investigator continued questioning Murray: "You came up with a total gross take-off weight of 134,394 pounds?"

Murray corrected him again: "Three hundred *seventy*-four."

Q: Did you have any flares aboard this aircraft?

A: No.

Q: Would flares aboard the aircraft have been of any help to you in the ditching?

A: Not in this case.

Q: Why?

A: I didn't have time.

Q: Have you ever refused to take an aircraft because of a maintenance difficulty or because it did not have the required equipment aboard?

A: Yes.

Q: More than once?

A: Yes.

An investigator asked Frank Sargent, the Flying Tiger Line mechanic on duty at Gander Airport when Tiger 923 arrived, if the pilot who'd flown up from New Jersey had commented as to the condition of the plane or the nature of the flight. Sargent said that "Captain Luccio . . . remarked when they came in that the aircraft was in really fine shape. There was no report of any difficulties."[12]

The investigator asked if it was Murray's or Garrett's duty to confirm that the plane was "airworthy" via a physical "walk-around check." Sargent said, "This is completed by the flight engineer wholly," that the pilot only gets involved if something seems amiss and is brought to his attention. He added that he saw Garrett climbing on the wings, "sticking the fuel tanks," etc.

An investigator asked Murray: "Now regarding the weather, it was noted that you picked up the forecasts and studied them. It was also noted that you did not go to the weather office. Do you make it a practice to visit the weather office?"

A: Only . . . if problems are indicated en route.

Q: Were you satisfied that this was not the case in your analysis of the weather folder in this case?

A: Yes.

Edward Bechtold's official role was to represent the Air Line Pilots Association and its 14,500-plus dues-paying pilots. Unofficially, he was most interested in representing one pilot in particular: his friend John Murray. The 43-year-old Eastern Airlines pilot was a good friend to have. He'd flown nearly 16,000 hours as pilot in command (more than the three investigators combined), he'd received the Army Air Medal in WWII for meritorious achievement, his fellow pilots had awarded him the prestigious Safety Award in 1962, and the Port Authority of New York and New Jersey had appointed him to head its Air Safety Committee.

After noting that the record reflected that the misaligned main cabin door was clearly not a major issue or otherwise germane to the ditching, Bechtold asked: "Captain Murray, was there any, any malfunction indicated prior to takeoff in the aircraft, the engines, or anything else?"

Murray replied: "None."

After a break, an investigator delved into how well Murray had supervised Jim Garrett, whom Flying Tiger Line had hired shortly after Eastern had let him go. "Do you know what the flight engineer does?"

"Yes," Murray responded.

Q: Did you talk to the incoming engineer?

A: No.

Q: Can you briefly give us what the emergency procedure would be for an engine failure or fire in flight?

A: I—

Q: Physically what do you do?

A: I would be flying the airplane. I would take it off the autopilot.

Q: All the controls other than the flight controls then are handled by the engineer, is that correct?

A: Yes. Would you like me to read my statement?

Q: No. Do you have any mixture controls at the pilot's station in the FT 1049H?

A: No.

Q: Where are they located?

A: Flight engineer's station.

Q: Are they visible to you?

A: Yes.

Q: Yes?

A: Yes, turn around and look at them.

Q: Would it not seem reasonable to do a visual inspection of the engine?

A: It would be helpful.

Q: Might it not have helped to go over things with the flight engineer.

A: If the flight engineer hadn't been absent from the flight deck.

When the investigator asked if Murray felt Garrett knew what he was doing, the pilot replied: "He appeared to be one of the most competent engineers I have flown with."

Q: Was he a tall man or a short man or medium height?

A: He was a tall man.

The investigator pivoted to the supervision of Hard Luck Sam: "At any time when positions were being sent and so on, did you have time to leave your station and oversee the navigator's work?"

A: No, I certainly did not.

Q: Would you care to state whether you made any effort to see whether his positions on the interceptions and the ditching and the headings to Keflavik and all that sort of thing were correct?

A: This wasn't necessary. I was convinced that they were correct.

Q: Captain, how were you convinced that they were correct?

A: I'm glad you asked this. My job in flying an airplane consists principally of evaluating the performance of others and I can't tell you how I do it except through experience.

Q: Had you ever flown with Mr. Nicholson before?

A: No, I have not.

Nearly four hours were devoted to the ditching, with an investigator beginning: "Are you in any disagreement with any of the procedures that are outlined in the Flying Tiger manual?"

A: Yes.

Q: Would you say which procedures you are in disagreement with?

A: Ditching procedure.

Q: Could you see the waves and swells?

A: Yes, very clearly.

Q: Could you tell the direction of the swells?

A: Yes.

Q: Was there more than one system of swells?

A: I couldn't determine this. The sea was covered with whitecaps.

Q: Now in your manual . . . Does it give you procedures or information concerning an undesirable type of approach, or a type of direction you would not land under except in the most grim circumstances?

A: Yes.

Q: What is that?

A: Exactly the way I did it.

Q: Had you run the ditching checklist?

A: No, we had no opportunity to run the check list.

Q: Captain, you said that the exits were not removed prior to this ditching?

A: Yes.

The investigator waved the Tiger manual. "Now these are the pre-ditching instructions. Do you agree with these instructions that these exits be removed prior to the ditching?"

Murray: Yes, if you know you are going to ditch, I think they should be open.

Q: Could you give us any reason why they were not removed?

A: Yes. We didn't have time.

Q: Could the first officer have given these instructions or did he have time?

A: I beg your pardon? Could he have what?

Q: Or did he have time, the first officer, to give these instructions?

A: No, no one had time to leave the cockpit from the time the number two engine quit.

While reading from another piece of paper, the investigator asked the pilot: "There was no command given to the passengers to, and I quote now, 'Brace'? This term was not used?"

"No," said Murray. "Can I go into this a little bit?"

Q: I would like for you to, yes.

Captain Bechtold raised his hand and said: "Mr. Minetti, is this an exhibit?"

The investigator answered instead. "This is not an exhibit."

Bechtold: Could you tell us what it refers to, please?

Minetti: Mr. Bechtold, I understand that this is available for inspection if you care to inspect it.

Bechtold: Well, all right, sir. I'd like to know what they're talking about. We don't have it, sir.

Once handed a copy of the non-exhibit, the Eastern pilot, New York safety specialist, and Air Line Pilots Association spokesman said: "I do not see any requirement or any provision for the captain or other crewman announcing the ditching."

Murray explained his rationale for not saying "Brace!" over the PA system. First, he'd instructed the stewardesses to conduct three full sets of ditching drills, and they'd stressed the importance of bracing once it was clear the plane was near impact. Second, it was very clear they were near impact: the moon having recently emerged to light up the surface of the sea. Also, he'd devised a supplemental way of alerting the passengers to the imminent impact: as witness Edward Apanel confirmed, even way up front, he could hear Hard Luck Sam counting down at the very back of the plane; even over the landing bells, that provided further notice of proximity to touch-down. Most important, the pilot stated that had he used the PA it would have had the opposite effect of the investigator's implicit supposition: it would have endangered lives. Doing so "would have been impossible. I couldn't possibly have reached over and picked up the microphone, let go of the controls. I needed one hand free to chop number four. There was no way this could have been done."

The investigator said: "Could the first officer have made this announcement for you?"

A: No.

Q: Why not?

A: The microphone was over on the left side. He would have to turn around to pull the microphone and cord across to him. I probably could reach it, but the first officer was quite busy at this time looking for the sea. I was on instruments. I don't believe it could have been done by either one of us.

Q: How long after number two engine was lost before you ditched?

A: Two or three minutes.

When Air Force lieutenant colonel George Dent was asked how much time elapsed between the no. 2 engine dying and the plane hitting the water—Murray's intercom announcement that they were in fact ditching separating the events—the Air Force officer responded crisply: "Two minutes."

> The investigator said: "Are you fairly certain?"
>
> Dent replied: "I am positive."

The next line of inquiry focused on how well Tiger 923 had kept the rescue control center informed of the unfolding emergency. An investigator asked Murray: "Is there any method by which you can communicate with any of the surface vessels in your area from the aircraft?"

> A: Yes, you can bring up the Gibson girl, contact them on five hundred kilocycles.
>
> Q: What procedure would you go through using the Gibson girls to use the five hundred kc?
>
> A: I don't think you're being very practical. You have to bring it up and attach the antenna but you would have a choice then of S.O.S. or CW. There is no voice there.
>
> Q: But it would have been possible to get locations of ships or this message passed back to you in case you did have to ditch, would it not?
>
> A: I wouldn't want to rely on my ability to read Morse code at a high rate of speed.

Possibly diverting or dumping fuel came up in the context of an investigator suggesting how, had Murray done either, it may have reduced engine strain enough to avoid a ditching. The pilot was asked: "From what points were Iceland's sea conditions reported? Can you recall?"

> Murray: I didn't pay much attention to anything once I got the sixty-five-knot wind.
>
> Q: Do you recall what the wind conditions were on the surface at the ditching site?
>
> A: A good thirty knots.
>
> Q: Can you tell us why you did not dump fuel?
>
> A: Yes, because I intended to reach Shannon.

Q: At any time during the descending did you make a decision to dump fuel?

A: No.

Q: Did you ever consider how much fuel you can dump and still make Shannon?

A: We would not have had any reserve fuel if we had dumped it.

Q: But at any rate this was never considered?

A: Yes, it was considered. I had the dry tank time . . . which changed at every power setting . . . in advance of our ETA. . . . It wasn't a safe operation to dump.

About two hours were spent trying to make sense out of the hash of accounts regarding what it felt like to hit the water, and the immediate aftermath. Knowing that dozens had sworn out affidavits or testified that the crash was violent, saying they'd been hurled forward and/or knocked unconscious, the investigator asked Murray. "Was the impact severe?"

"No," said the pilot.

Q: Was it more or less severe than you anticipated?

A: Quite a bit less severe.

Q: Did you pad the glare shield?

A: Pad what?

Q: Pad the glare shield with pillows or blankets in front of your face, the glare shield, before you ditched.

A: No.

Q: Did you consider doing this?

A: No.

Q: Are there any instructions in your manual for doing this?

A: You would have to let go of the wheel then, take one hand off the wheel.

Q: Were you wearing glasses at the time of this ditching?

A: Yes.

Q: Did the glasses stay on or did you lose them or did they break, or do you know?

A: No, they flew off.

Though he'd been seated at the other end of the plane, Hard Luck Sam concurred with the pilot. "It was not as severe as I expected at all. I received no injuries as a result of it. I did not feel like it was a severe stop at all. I mean, certainly a heavy one, but not as severe as it could have been."

Q: Did you utilize any protective devices to protect you from impact?

A: No, sir.

Q: No pillows or blankets, or anything?

A: No, sir, I didn't.

As there were conflicting accounts as to who boarded the raft, how, and when, Bechtold asked Murray: "Did anyone else get in the life raft after you did?"

A: No.[13]

The question irked the chairman:

Minetti: Mr. Bechtold, I must warn you we have gone over this area before. You are repetitious now.

Bechtold: Mr. Minetti, I would like the record to show that yesterday's examiners were not referring to a true transcript of what the flight actually recorded.

Minetti: Do you have any proof to support that? If you have, why, introduce it.

Bechtold: I think we just heard it. And we have Captain Murray's statement.

Minetti (to the investigator): Is this a true transcript, or a summary?

CAB Staffer: It is not verbatim in the words of Captain Murray.

Minetti: It is not verbatim?

Investigator: It is not.

Though the chairman did not look pleased, he let the investigator resume questioning the pilot. "Captain, based on your testimony, is it correct that you did not follow procedure?"

A: No, and I believe I had good reason not to.

Q: So would you care to state for the record your reasons?

A: Because of the critical situation I was in.

Q: Do you feel that the expenditure of a few seconds would not be worth the effort?

A: It is not the expenditure of a few seconds but what could happen to that runaway prop if it continued to increase its rpm in those few seconds.

Wendell Danielson was the last guest invited to ask Murray a question, but the president of the Transport Workers Union didn't have anything he wanted to ask. Yet he did want to say something, even though he knew it was in violation of the chairman's explicit ban on expressing opinions. "Captain Murray, I will ditch with you any time, but I don't want to."

"Thank you," said Murray.

After the FAA's John Frederic said he spent 100 percent of his time on the "inspection and surveillance" of Flying Tiger Line, and that he knew Murray well, an investigator asked him how he'd rate the Tiger 923 pilot's proficiency. Frederic said, "Standout."

Investigator: Why?

A: Because of Captain Murray's performance as a pilot.

After Murray's last trip to the witness table and a final set of questions, the chairman excused the pilot, but he wasn't ready to leave. "Mr. Minetti, could I say something?"

Q: What is it that you want to say, Captain?

A: I have to say it to tell you what it is.

Laughter broke out. Minetti rapped his gavel, pointed it toward the pilot, and nodded.

"Well," Murray began, "I would like to say that . . . I was putting too heavy a workload on the rest of the crew. I knew it was heavy at the time, and, looking back at the activities of the copilot . . . of the flight engineer . . . Mr. Nicholson . . . Miss Sims . . . the other stewardesses, I am not an articulate man, but I would like to get across that all the people did far more than I think they could reasonably be expected to, that I could not possibly have managed to ditch this airplane without the assistance of these people."

Minetti: Thank you.

Two hours were spent on how well the crew had been trained, especially in a ditching scenario. Stewardess Carol Gould said the training had been good but she'd made mistakes, including: though "required to carry a flashlight, two batteries, one knife and, I believe, in the time of my training, the instructress said to have two safety pins, so as to secure the knife to you, and/or your flashlight," she'd lent her flashlight to a friend. She also admitted to problems with the D-ring: "We did have a little difficulty. . . . Ruth and I were nervous."

Hard Luck Sam also said the training was good but he'd made mistakes too, including not making sure the emergency raft was anchored to the floor before throwing it out into the sea. When an investigator asked: "Did you physically observe the knot that was tied to the airplane, or was this underneath the raft?" the navigator replied: "No, sir, I did not observe the knot." After having given the lanyard "a tug," he thought it was secure, but it wasn't.

Q: At any later time did you ask Miss Sims, or any other person, to tie it?

A: No, sir, I did not. I thought I had adequately checked it myself.

Picking up on Gould's comment about how she was nervous, the investigator asked the navigator: "How did chief stewardess Sims appear to you? What was her mental condition? Was she nervous?"

A: Fine.

Q: Was she nervous at all?

A: I think I was more nervous than she was.

Q: Pardon me?

A: I think I was more nervous than she was. She was very cool and collected.

A different investigator asked head Tiger stewardess Violet Kushner if she could explain why rookie stewardess Jackie Brotman had not received her mandatory wet ditching drill. Her answer: the Coast Guard refused. It "insists that we have ten or more girls." Kushner added that Brotman was scheduled to be trained as soon as she returned stateside.

By 7:30 p.m. on Friday, day 3, Minetti had yet to call four witnesses. Next up was the airline's director of flight operations, whom an investigator asked: "How long have you known Captain John Murray?"

A: Since 1950, within a week after he came to work.

Q: What is your and therefore, the company's evaluation of Captain John Murray?

A: We feel, number one, that Captain Murray is a very competent captain. He is above average in all respects, and as an employee his record has been excellent with the company.

The hearing devoted just 17 minutes (1 percent) on the specifications, design, repair, service, and maintenance of Tiger 923's engines and life-saving equipment. Yet there were so many germane issues. For instance, an eight-page stretch of the transcripts details "a number of recurring write-ups" on engine no. 1 (which Jim Garrett mistakenly disabled, which catalyzed the crisis); how "the most numerous recurrent writeup involved the outward door"; problems with "the stowage and condition of sufficient life vests"; and other "non-routine discrepancies."[14] Despite the front-page story in *The New York Times* on September 27 that focused on the lack of lit life vests, the issue isn't mentioned once in the 959-page transcript.

John Dewey, the airline's superintendent of quality control, did spend a few minutes discussing the no. 1 engine's history of overheating, starting with cowl flap problems during a Chicago flight in July 1962. Then, on September 10, also on a flight to Frankfurt (from Madrid), just 13 days before Tiger 923 left Gander, the no. 1 got so hot during takeoff, and because it couldn't be corrected during climb-out, it had to be feathered. In Germany, maintenance technicians "replaced both spark plugs, leader and coils and injection nozzle on Number Eighteen cylinder unfeathered and ran." The log entry read: "Engine OK."

But it wasn't OK. On the same day, September 10, while flying from Frankfurt to Gander, the no. 1 engine ran "fifteen to twenty degrees hotter than other engines at all powers." Service wasn't performed until four flights later, in Newark. Both distributors were "re-timed."

Dewey then discussed how one of the rafts was removed on September 9 for repair, and how every life vest was inspected at each "turnaround operation." He concluded by saying that, despite many reports to the contrary, the vests weren't an inferior civilian knockoff. "The AD-Four is made to a military specification."

Chairman Minetti called the CAB's top meteorologist. The scientist began by describing his extensive background, including nine years with the United States Weather Bureau and several other jobs as a professional forecaster. Then he went into great detail about the many reports and charts Captain Murray had had at his disposal.

Once he was through discussing 500 and 700 millibars, 12-hour versus 24-hour forecasts, and the implications of "bases of cumulus, stratocumulus and scattered cirrus," Captain Bechtold pointed out that while the metrics sounded precise and thorough, the fact of the matter was: ice wasn't in the forecast; Murray intuited the possibility, based on his experience; hence, though the current witness and CAB investigators seemed to be implying Murray had been derelict by not going to the weather office, first, doing so was not standard operating procedure, and, second, had he, he would have been given additional *faulty* data and forecasts. Bechtold concluded by saying that had Murray made his decisions based solely on "the official forecast," 76 people may well have died instead of 28.

The head of the transport workers union asked the meteorologist: "Sir, would you care to express any opinion in your analysis of this weather why this flight encountered icy conditions and so on, which were not generally expected?"

Minetti objected: "Are you asking a question now, or making a statement?"

> A: Sir, I would like for this meteorologist to tell us why in his opinion—
>
> Minetti: He cannot give you an opinion.
>
> A: Very well, sir. That is all.

Minetti excused the meteorologist. He was the final CAB witness.

George Rounds was the last witness. At 9:30 p.m., the FAA maintenance inspector said it was he who'd certified that all Flying Tiger Line aircraft were "airworthy," including the Super Constellation Murray had flown.

A CAB investigator asked: "Was it common for a Tiger flight to have engine trouble?"

"No," said the FAA inspector.

But what about all the crashes and engine problems in 1962?

The inspector explained how 1962 was an aberration. The company prided itself on its safety. It was a core part of its mission. It had received awards from the U.S. government and its peers. The Guam crash in March 1962 resulted in the airline's first passenger fatality—ever—since its founding in 1948. In 1961, the airline logged 898,710 miles without a single mishap.

Though Tiger 923 spiked the airline's "engine failure rate" for the month of September 1962 to 0.342 "per thousand engine hours," for the two preceding quarters, while the industry's failure rate was 0.132, the Tiger rate was just 0.053. In other words, on average, an Eastern Airlines flight was more than twice as likely to experience an engine problem.

Minetti rapped his gavel at 10:13 p.m. and said: "Gentlemen, since there are no other witnesses to testify at this time, this part of our investigation is at an end."

He added that he'd "reopen this hearing" in the event "new and pertinent information" came to light. "In due course a report will be issued in which the Board's determination of the probable cause will be stated." The proceedings officially concluded at 10:15 p.m.

November 14, 1962: John Murray testifying at the CAB Board of Inquiry hearing in New York. COURTESY U.S. DEPARTMENT OF TRANSPORTATION.

PART IV

MISSING FILES

There are no more cowboys in airline transport any more. They have all either been killed or fired.

—*Capt. John Murray*[1]

Chapter 11

Final Verdicts

In the early '60s there were about 3 million commercial air trips each month in the U.S., and it wasn't unusual for there to be one or two crashes each month, and hundreds of fatalities. Sixty years later, pre-COVID, this figure had risen to about 85 million, yet it wasn't unusual for a year or two to go by without a single fatality.[1] Since the highly publicized Tiger 923 touched upon many safety shortcomings, it's reasonable to assume it spurred many improvements.

The sharp mid-'60s move away from piston engines to jet engines was almost certainly hastened by Tiger 923. That it was one of five Connie crashes over the course of just 14 months was part of it. That three of its four engines failed was a bigger part. Jet engines were far more fuel-efficient; they got travelers to their destinations much faster; and now, apparently, they were much safer. However, only three safety changes can be directly tied to Murray's ditching and its aftermath.

The first came weeks before the CAB hearing: the FAA suddenly reversed course and required every U.S. airline to retrain any crew member the airline hadn't itself trained.[2] While Eastern Airlines trained Jim Garrett in *its* engine shutdown procedure, when Eastern laid him off and Flying Tiger Line hired him, he was never taught the slightly different Tiger procedure.

Second, Richard Witkin reported that as a "direct outgrowth" of Captain Murray's hearing testimony, the CAB urged the FAA to make illuminated vests mandatory.[3] Witkin doesn't get into how he established causation, perhaps because the vest regulation reversal seems more an outgrowth of his own efforts, given the fact that the CAB hearing never touched on the issue.

The third safety innovation was also spurred more by an external investigator as opposed to the CAB. While the U.S. Coast Guard didn't cite its motives, its missive directing much closer inspecting of civilian airliner lifesaving equipment and procedures (rafts, vests, lighting, and egress) seems to rely more on Bob Eldred's November 1 newspaper interview than anything covered during the hearing.[4]

Two other exogenous factors bore on the Tiger 923 investigation. One involved another Tiger flight; the other, a key hearing participant. Both added to the Bureau of Safety's already crushing workload.

On November 30, just two weeks after adjourning from the Idlewild hearing, Capt. Edward Bechtold was en route to an Idlewild airport runway. While he and his good friend Capt. John Murray would have to wait for the official "Aircraft Accident Report" before they could fully relax, both men were hopeful. It seemed like they'd gotten through the CAB hearing intact, and the worst was over.

What the Eastern Airlines pilot was now trying to get through was thick fog. But he'd cut through such muck on countless occasions since the early 1940s, much of it before the advent of avionics and navigational aids. This navigating he understood. Barometry was infinitely more straightforward than bureaucracy.

Like Tiger 923, Eastern 512 wasn't supposed to encounter any bad weather but it did. While most of the short trip from Charlotte was uneventful, visibility deteriorated fast not long after Bechtold entered New York air space. At 9:45 p.m. he lowered his landing gear and descended to about 250 feet, trying to slip under the warm air, but it seemed rooted to the earth's molten core. His landing lights were impotent. Two months earlier, Captain Murray's left wing clipped the North Atlantic Ocean. Now Captain Bechtold's left wing clipped a mound of earth just off the New York runway. The big DC-7 broke into three pieces and exploded in flames. Passengers were ejected out into the night, still strapped in their seats. The darkness, dense fog, and muddy terrain delayed first responders. Bechtold and 3 fellow crew members died, along with 21 of 45 passengers.

Murray had hardly had a chance to mourn the loss of his good friend and fierce ally when, just two weeks later, on December 14, at 10:12 p.m., the same exact time he'd crashed at sea, a colleague en route to Burbank Airport from Chicago crashed his cargo plane in North Hollywood.[5] As the Lockheed plummeted, its fuel tanks sheared off and exploded and its propellors tore semicircular slices through two big billboards on either side of Interstate 5. The loud boom and bright blaze shook roofs, lit up the sky, and led many to believe the Russians had attacked, as JFK had been warning they might. Witnesses said it sounded like an atom bomb.[6] Deadly shrapnel whistled in the dark for miles, killing all five crew members and three bystanders on the ground, and injuring many others, some seriously. The nightly news showed images of screaming people fleeing burning homes, cars and factories.

Murray grieved for his friends, colleagues, and their families. He also wondered what effect the two disasters might have on his "Aircraft Accident Report."[7] Waiting just a month had been very hard for him and his wife. Would he now have to wait longer?

Yes, according to the CAB's Dick Rodriguez. Given the grisly images, Walter Cronkite commentary, and political pressure from the powerful California caucus, Tiger 923 was bumped back in the investigatory queue.[8] Though the North Hollywood accident, Tiger 913, occurred nearly eight weeks later, its report was issued seven months sooner.

What's more, February's Tiger 913 report faulted the flight crew and Tiger training, which was a focal point of the Tiger 923 hearing. When the Tiger 913 pilot had a heart attack, the copilot wasn't ready to take the helm. Worse, someone at the airline had falsified records to suggest he'd received sufficient training. Murray didn't see how Tiger 913's report could bode well for his.

Some good news arrived in March 1963, in the form of a Coast Guard study of Tiger 923. While the Commerce Department via the CAB was charged with determining the official cause, the Treasury Department via the Coast Guard had enormous credibility, for two reasons. First, a cutter wasn't just active in the search and rescue, it had been communicating with Murray hours before the ditching. Second, as it was not in dispute that all 76 aboard had evacuated but 28 died in the water, the systemic infirmities were mostly maritime in nature, not aviation; the rafts and ditching drills were under the aegis of the U.S. Coast Guard, not the FAA or CAB.

Treasury's investigation was far more comprehensive and opinionated. While CAB hearing chairman Minetti had said he'd disallow opinions (but allowed them, selectively), the commandant who'd commissioned the Coast Guard study solicited opinions. While Minetti didn't call upon any non-Americans, the commandant welcomed their input. While the Coast Guard also had difficulty sorting through the facts (given no black box, contradictory testimony, etc.), its 279-page study yielded one conclusion, and one illuminating piece of information.

Its conclusion: Murray's "ditching *into* the 30 knot wind and *into* the major swell system attests to the correctness of his decision."[9] The "hindsight" criticism was wrong, insisted the Coast Guard's Eastern area commander, noting that Murray didn't just ditch the best way but the only way, as "frozen controls" prevented any other approach.[10] Britain's RAF coastal commander concurred, saying the manual's instructions were "dangerously inaccurate."[11]

The study also noted how "various" (unnamed) parties were worried about "suits for damages."[12] (The legal aspects are discussed below.) The Coast Guard opined that the legal jeopardy might taint the CAB's objectivity.

The airline weathered 1962, a Chinese Year of the Tiger, and the worst in the history of an outfit born of the volunteer Air Corps that'd helped China repulse Japan. The FAA didn't rescind its 1961 finding that Flying Tiger Line was "capable of continuous safe operation," even though Tiger 913 was its fourth crash in nine months. What's more, Murray's employer didn't just retain its position as the number-one Pentagon contractor, it flew far more flights in the mid- and late 1960s than in the early '60s. (FedEx bought the airline in 1989.)

The airplane manufacturer didn't suffer any adverse repercussions either, even though Tiger 913 was the fifth Constellation crash in 14 months. Lockheed's commercial trajectory has been remarkable. Though unable to compete with Boeing's commercial jets, the company now doing business as Lockheed-Martin has earned hundreds of billions selling fighter jets to the Pentagon and foreign powers and managing red-light cameras for American municipalities.

But there was one corporate casualty: Curtiss-Wright. While the company still builds small engines, when Lockheed ceased production of the Connie, a huge chunk of Wright's prop-piston revenues dried up. Jet engines seemed safer. They decreased total travel time by as much as 75 percent. And as turbines were a lot lighter, they burned less fuel. Boeing now ruled the commercial aviation market, and it had no more need for Curtiss-Wright's piston-engines than Henry Ford's Model T had had for buggy whips.

As for the human casualties, did Tiger 923's survivors, their loved ones, and the loved ones of those who didn't survive share in the undiminished—even improved—financial success of Flying Tiger Line and Lockheed? How were they recompensed for such extensive pain and suffering?

Though missing records and decayed memories make it impossible to speak conclusively, four things are clear. First, some survivors received no cash. Second, some accepted an offered amount. Third, others filed suit. Fourth, most received in-kind benefits. Each group will be discussed briefly.

According to Carol Hansen: "Flying Tiger Line stopped paying me the instant I hit the water."[13] There is likewise no record of John Murray, Sam Nicholson, Bob Parker, Jim Garrett, Betty Sims, Ruth Mudd, Jackie Brotman, or their families receiving any compensation.

The Army went one step further: it docked the pay of one of the deceased. On October 2, 1962, eight days after informing mother-of-five (from newborn to age 7) Marjorie Baney that her husband had died, the following was added to Staff Sgt. Melvin H. Baney's personnel file: "The individual named in this report is held by the Department of the Army to have been absent in a pay status pursuant to the provisions of Section 2, PL 490, 77th Congress, as amended, from the date of death 24 September 1962 to 26 September 1962, date of receipt of evidence in the Department of the Army as stated in this report."[14]

"I think I got a thousand dollars [$7,500 in 2020]," says Gordon Thornsberry, who was an Army private at the time.[15] Then-retired Army captain and Bronze Star hero of Normandy Bob Eldred got $2,000 for his wife's pain, suffering, and death; his pain and suffering; and his family's trauma. "I was *shocked* by the low amount," said Karen Eldred-Stephan, Edna and Bob's only daughter, 58 years after the incident, which occurred when she was 17. "I was angry about that for a long time."[16]

In March 1963, an insurance adjuster representing Flying Tiger Line also offered Army PFC John Toole $2,000, though he wasn't nearly as injured as Eldred and didn't lose a spouse. Fred Caruso says the money was a "Godsend" because Toole had wanted to bring his wife over from Montgomery, Alabama, but he hardly had a penny to his name (his $90/month wage didn't go very far) and the Army had a rule about bringing spouses to Germany: before Toole could fly his over (often on a Tiger flight, like Rachel Hoopi), he had to prove he had $500 in the bank in case the Army brass wanted to ship his wife back home for whatever reason, or no reason.[17] While he entertained the thought of holding out for more money, an Army adjutant advised Toole to "take the money and run."[18]

Art Gilbreth didn't have an adjutant advising him. Fortunately.

Around the same time the adjuster in Germany was offering the comparatively uninjured Toole $2,000, another adjuster in North Carolina was about to offer some cash to Gilbreth. The U.S. adjuster said he wanted to compensate the Army private for having nearly died on several occasions; having nearly lost a leg after mauling it on a tailfin hinge underwater; having broken several vertebrae; having endured months of surgeries, traction, and rehab in English, California, and North Carolina hospitals; having to give up his dream of joining the Green Berets; his shell shock; and all his family's trauma.

The ex-paratrooper recounted:

> *We met in Fayetteville. Maybe at a diner. I can't remember. What I can remember is he asked me what I'd lost on account of the ditching. He told me to put a number on it. But how do you put a price tag on what I went through? So I exaggerated a bit, adding stuff I didn't own, like a camera. Then I padded it all. I said it added up to five hundred dollars. He made a face like I was nuts. Acted like I'd asked for the moon.*
>
> *"Five hundred dollars!" he says. "There's no way we can pay that much!"*
>
> *Well, that kinda pissed me off. Then he offered me two hundred. I said, "I need to think about it. I'll get back to you."*[19]

Instead of returning to base, Gilbreth lit a cigarette and loitered outside the diner on the sidewalk, wondering what his next step should be. When he took a drag and tilted his head to exhale, he noticed a sign above him: ATTORNEY AT LAW.

> *So I go upstairs, knock on the door that was ajar, push it open a bit, and it was like I'd stepped onto a movie set. Casablanca or something. There's this big guy behind a desk wearing a straw hat and seersucker suit, looking like Sydney Greenstreet. He doesn't even look up at me at first. Above him, a ceiling fan's hardly moving. The room's thick with smoke.*
>
> *I clear my throat. He looks up, finally. I say, "Do you have a minute? Can I ask your opinion about something?"*
>
> *He picks up his cigar, takes a puff, lays it down, then nods. "Sure, soldier. Have a seat."*
>
> *So I sit, and begin at the beginning. I can tell he's not really paying attention—until he hears that I was on Flight 923. It was front-page news in the North Carolina papers, too, 'cause the paratroopers belonged to the 82nd, stationed at nearby Fort Bragg.*

He starts asking questions. He got more interested with each answer and he got really interested when he learned that I didn't know where I was going, other than somewhere in Germany. I told him I didn't know where I was going because our sergeant wasn't on the flight with us, and he had my orders. In fact, I wasn't even given a ticket. None of us guys were.

He told me he'd look into it. Then maybe two weeks later he called me, and we met again. He told me he'd consulted with the leading aeronautical lawyer in New York, and that guy had invited me for a meeting. The North Carolina lawyer said if we went forward he'd give two-thirds of his one-third fee to the New York lawyer, because he figured having that guy on the case was key.

So I hitchhiked to New York, got dropped off at Grand Central Station, walked over, and asked a cab driver if he could take me to such-and-such address. He nodded, I hopped in, and he drove me around the block to the other side of the station, let me out, and told me how much I owed him.

"You mean," I asked during a phone interview in 2020, "that instead of saying 'Thank you for your service' and telling you that you could just walk straight through the Station and get to where you were going twice as fast without eating up a day's Army wages, he drove you around in bumper-to-bumper traffic?"

Exactly.

The New York lawyer said he thought I had a case. He said most countries followed something called the Warsaw Convention, that limited monetary damages for death and injury and pain and suffering, but as the Convention was, I was told, a contract, certain terms had to be met, including that each passenger had to have his own ticket, because it implied I'd accepted the damage limitation on the back. Because I didn't have a ticket, the lawyer said he could argue the cap on damages went out the window.

But he also said, "You should know that the airline and maybe the airplane maker and the government will fight us tooth and nail. It may take a long time, and we may not win."

I said: "Let's give it a shot." So he took my deposition.

Three years after rejecting $200, Gilbreth got a lot more. While he can't recall the exact figure, "and I'd rather not guess, I received enough to buy a car and put a down payment on a home."[20]

Over time, more details bubbled to the surface of his memory. "The first thing I did was go out and buy me a brand-new Corvette. First year of the 427 engine. Paid fifty-two hundred, cash."[21]

"And the color?" I asked in 2018, over coffee in Sunriver, Oregon.

"Sea-foam green."[22]

Tiger 923 generated a lot of media attention, from cosmopolitan Antwerp to rural Arkansas. However, fame was monetized differently in 1962. Carol Gould got free perms for a month. All Tiger 923 military survivors received free medical care from the Army, Air Force, or Veterans Administration. Much of the care has been excellent and compassionate. "They've treated me real good," said Thornsberry, when asked if there was anyone special he'd like to thank for how his life turned out.[23] Likewise, Caruso will forever remain grateful to the paratrooper priest in Germany who told him not long after the ditching: "Being bitter won't make you better."[24]

Carol has never seemed bitter. Despite having been hailed by the media as a "genuine heroine" for having led so many to safety in such forbidding conditions, having been such a good nurse and morale-booster on the raft, and having prevented the distraught teenager Helga Groves from leaping overboard, she never received a dime from her employer, the Army, or the Air Force.[25] When asked about the apparent injustice, she says "What of it? I'm alive. The Lord's been good to me."[26]

But Carol has never suggested she's a saint. She admits to enjoying with no pangs of Catholic guilt the free first-class tickets courtesy of Sabena; free first-class round-trip airfare to London, ritzy hotel accommodations and chauffeured limo, all courtesy of Thames TV, when they invited her to appear in a 1979 *This Is Your Life* episode to celebrate one of the RAF helicopter pilots who'd rescued the Tiger 923 survivors; and the sundry other gifts that, when added up, have exceeded in dollar terms what all but a few other survivors have received.

When it comes to quantifying emotional injury, money is a poor medium of exchange. This is why it took so long for victims to start receiving compensation for so-called intangibles, according to Gary Fromm, the leading aviation economist in the 1960s. But while the Brookings Institution's senior fellow said that "putting a specific monetary value on human life may seem immoral, if not monstrous," he also noted that by the mid-1950s juries had started doing just that. The average wrongful death award was $150,000. One plaintiff who thought he was drowning received $35,000 for *two and a half minutes* of "pain and suffering."[27] It's hard to fathom why Tiger 923's victims received so much less, even though many suffered so much more, but it was at least partly a reflection of the times and the not-yet-commonplace bigger award precedents.

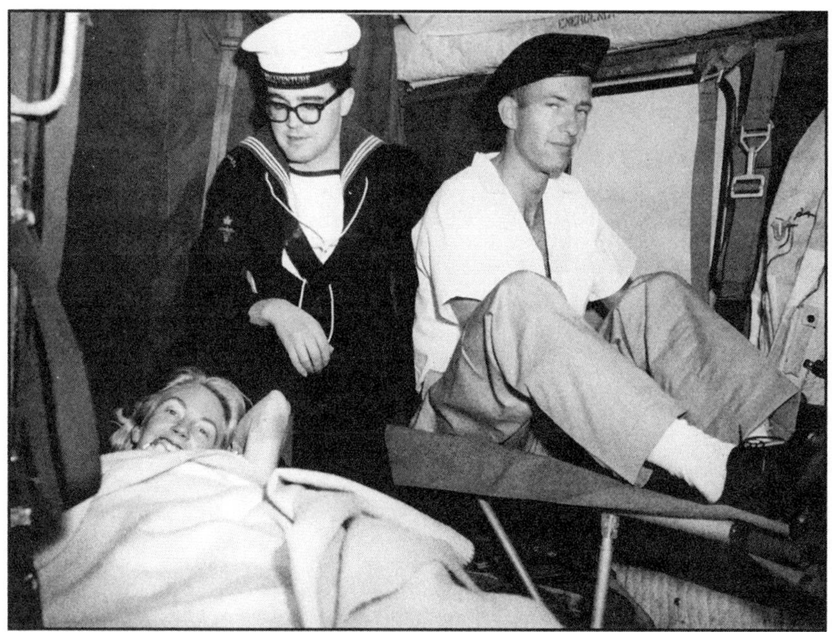

Certain people did their best to suppress and spin the official Tiger 923 story, but they hadn't planned on an inquisitive U.S. Army major or a canny private first class. (Top) September 26, 1962: Lois and Dick Elander on a Canadian Navy helicopter, en route to the U.S. Air Force hospital in Swindon, England, by way of a press conference at Ireland's Shannon Airport. COURTESY ROYAL CANADIAN NAVY, ELANDER FAMILY. (Bottom) December 4, 1962: After Art Gilbreth spent weeks at the same English hospital, Opal Gilbreth visits her son at the U.S. Army hospital at the Presidio, in San Francisco. COURTESY ART GILBRETH.

Chapter 12

Crew Legacies

There haven't been many research studies that have tracked the emotional toll on ditching survivors because there haven't *been* many ditching survivors. By the time PTSD had become an accepted psychological disorder in 1980, prompting longitudinal academic studies, jets had by and large supplanted props and the Department of Transportation, National Transportation Safety Board, and Occupational Health and Safety Act were 13 years old.[1] The combined effect was a dramatic decrease in aviation casualties. There have been a few illuminating studies, however, including of ditchings and other aircraft accidents, and certain findings rise to the top.

First, the "reactions [to disasters] vary dramatically."[2] Some survivors seem never to tire of talking about their ordeals, while others never want to talk about it. Some can't recall a thing about a disaster minutes after the fact, while others recall things in vivid detail decades later. Some people find that fear presents quickly but dissipates, while others develop late-onset symptoms. Some fly more after an airplane accident in the belief that God has their back, while others suffer immobilizing panic attacks at the mere thought of setting foot on a plane again.

Second, most survivors say they suffer from guilt to some degree. The psychoanalyst and Holocaust survivor who coined the term "survivor guilt" said it's unavoidable. "The very fact of survival always causes severe guilt," said William Niederland, MD. "Always."[3]

Third, the vast majority experience persistent, harrowing nightmares. The big difference seems to be that some don't suffer as much while awake, Carl Jung's "shadow" (that murky facet of our personality that at times protects us, at times harms us) mercifully sequestering the horror in the subconscious.

Fourth, many lives change for the better. Professors Richard Tedeschi and Lawrence Calhoun of UNC-Charlotte coined the term "post-traumatic growth" to mean a "positive change experienced as a result of the struggle with a major life crisis or a traumatic event."[4] The benefits often manifest in "changes in self-perception, interpersonal relationships and philosophy of life."[5]

Fifth, it's often the victims behind the victims who struggle the most. The survivors' loved ones can be heroes too. Their resilience is often the real story.

John Murray

In his closing statement at the 1962 CAB hearing, before thanking his crew and blaming himself for expecting too much of them, he said, "I am not an articulate man."[6] But he was. He just wasn't "much of a talker," says elder son, John Patrick.[7]

More accurately, Murray appears to have been selective in whom he talked with, about what. He spoke at length with Swiss deckhand Pierre-André Reymond, who would later say: "We all know that it is a normal reaction after a PTSD not to talk about such an accident (please do not call that an incident). Time has no meaning for these persons: past, present and future is all the same one thing. The notion of time doesn't exist for them, they are inside the trauma and the trauma is in their mind."[8]

Reymond wasn't alone. John Patrick recalls how "Dad talked about the ditching from time to time and was contemplating writing a book. He even taught himself to touch-type using a Sears electric typewriter and wanted to capture the right details."

Some details continued to trouble him. "Of course they did," says John Patrick. "Who wouldn't have thought about certain things? Dad always wondered if there was more he could have done. He didn't say so, but I could tell. I don't know if survivor's guilt is the correct term. I think it was more second-guessing guilt. 'Could I have done something different?'; things like that. He did everything he could but the loss of life bothered him."[9]

The death of his friend and ally Captain Bechtold conflated his ruminations. "That really affected Dad. He said something to the effect of 'I'm sure glad I had Ed on my side. They really came after me during that hearing. I don't know what I would've done without him.'"[10]

But he "never suffered from panic attacks. That kind of reaction was totally outside his personality. When Flying Tiger Line president and WWII Ace Robert Prescott asked: 'Well, you haven't lost your nerve, have you?' Dad smiled and said 'I never had any to begin with.' But he was a bit ruffled by the question." Although his father never boasted, "Dad knew he had done everything as well as it could have been done. He did his job well and, with all modesty, knew it."

His most prominent attitude was gratitude. That Bechtold—a highly decorated combat aviator and New York's top safety expert—died while attempting to land on a smooth runway in New York in late November underscored how fortunate Murray had been to "land" in the middle of 20-foot waves two months prior. Still, as the New Year rolled around, because Murray knew regulators were political animals, and there were forces at play beyond his pay grade, he knew there was a chance he could be faulted, however unjustly. He knew there was a chance the FAA could strip him of the licenses and certificates he needed to fly for a living.

Some good news finally arrived in March 1963, in the form of the Coast Guard's "Search and Rescue Study." The unequivocally supportive 279-page analysis by seasoned pilots and first responders put some wind at his back.

No one can recall when Murray read the CAB's "Aircraft Accident Report" on Tiger 923, but he probably read it the day of or soon after its release on September 13, 1963. As to where he read it, his good friend and fellow Tiger pilot Larry LeFever guesses it was in the Newark Airport parking lot, in his car, where he could read it in peace.

He likely took note of its brevity: at 19 pages, just 7 percent as long as the Coast Guard's study; and its sloppy beginning, in the form of a "Synposis [*sic*]."[11] But the first paragraph was nonetheless heartening:

"The Board determines that the probable cause of this accident was the failure of two of the aircraft's four engines, and the improper action of the flight engineer, which disabled a third engine, thereby necessitating a ditching at sea."

Some of what followed the synopsis comported with the 31 hours of the Commerce Department's hearing testimony and the Treasury Department's study. But there were also disagreements. The CAB said that "preparations for the ditching were not completed," Murray "did not recite . . . the checklist . . . as required by the company manual," and he was "not aware" or was "unable to recall" certain items in the Tiger manual and/or the proper sequence of events.[12] The CAB took special exception to Murray's ditching maneuver. "The procedure he used is, as a matter of fact, warned against in the manual. Based on witness testimony concerning the absence of the left wing . . . it is apparent that considerable impact force was encountered in the ditching. Failure of the left wing deprived survivors of the life rafts stowed therein."[13]

But the conclusion was unequivocally laudatory. "Under the circumstances of darkness, weather, and high seas, which prevailed in the North Atlantic at the time of this ditching, the Board believes that the survival of 48 occupants of the aircraft was miraculous, however, had lights been provided on the lifejackets, even more would have survived."

While Murray was relieved that even the remote risk of losing his license was gone, he wasn't looking for vindication. John Patrick recalls: "Despite criticism of the procedure he used, Dad did not think the CAB had skewered him and saw more positives in the report than negatives. He never, *never* doubted the wisdom of his approach to the ditching, thoroughly convinced that it was exactly the correct thing to do. The fact that the aircraft survived a ditching intact in such rough seas, at night, on one engine is phenomenal and testimony that he got it right, critics notwithstanding."

The CAB also made some recommendations, most of them obvious. "Consideration should be given to improving the basic design of [the life] jackets," requiring that they all have lights, and storing all the rafts internally, to protect them better, given none of the four main rafts was where it should have been. The report closed by saying that all U.S.

airlines needed to train their crews better in emergency procedures in general, and in the event of ditching, particularly.

Murray's reaction was more equable than that of others, like Super Connie–rated Tiger pilot Larry LeFever, who feels the CAB took some cheap shots.[14] He agrees with the RAF and Canadian Navy pilots cited in the Coast Guard study: "Given the winds and seas, it's a miracle anyone lived. Remember: everyone got off 923 alive. That was no swimming pool John landed in." LeFever also notes that the CAB's saying the evacuees were "deprived" of the four main rafts is false, as all of the rafts were retrieved, and two of them had been occupied.

Layman-survivor Art Gilbreth says, "I got a copy of the report. What I remember is he did a hell of a job with the turning controls locking up, landing between those big swells, with it raining like mad, not clipping the waves with the broad wings. It was obvious to see, at least to anyone on-board, what an incredible job he did."[15]

Murray didn't stew in the negativity. He knew he was lucky to be alive. He could live with a few ignorant assessments or unreasonable opinions. What he couldn't live with, however, was wasting his last chance. He knew it wasn't a second. He was up to his ninth chance, at least, maybe nineteenth, after eluding death over the skies of Tel Aviv, in the deserts of Yemen, during the winters of Detroit, and along 3,000 potholed, pre-Interstate miles on his Indian Junior Scout, his aviator goggles often covered in bug guts, when such trips weren't for the faint of heart.

The pilot used his chance to be a better father and husband. According to John Patrick, the trained chemical engineer

> *encouraged me when I experienced great difficulty in General Chemistry my first semester at Georgetown, suggested I consider rowing crew (which I did, and we won the Dad Vail regatta in Philly in '68), talked to me about his adventures flying guns into Palestine while helping me build a fence at home and teaching me how to replace a cracked piston in our lawnmower, got me started in my summer job as a commercial clam digger, took us all to Ireland for an unforget-*

> *table summer in 1964, where he took Steve and me on many flights to Europe and took us all to Greece and Italy, was a doting father to Ellen and Barbara, took Mom on several vacations, and along with Mom, was a strong influence on my Catholic faith and, after he passed, he was the inspiration that got me involved in flying.*[16]

He also took "Barbara and me fishing a lot," Ellen recalls. "The first time I caught anything it was a big black eel. I was so excited and yelled 'Daddy! Daddy, I caught snake!' I brought it home and put it in the bathtub, hoping to keep it as a pet. As you can imagine, that didn't pan out."[17]

The Murray family arrived in Limerick in June 1964, renting a home close to Shannon International Airport. They were well received. The role Irish hospitals and helicopters, nuns and fishermen had played in Tiger 923 was still relatively fresh in people's minds, and a source of Celtic pride, as was the fact that, of all the places he could have chosen to reside, the man whom Cork's *Examiner*, London's *Times*, and seemingly every other TV, radio or newspaper reporter called the miracle pilot elected to reside in their fair city.

In addition to transport flying, much of it from Shannon to Frankfurt, Captain Murray endeavored to put pen to paper. But he struggled to find the time.

Dorothy made friends easily on account of her old school Irish Catholicism and love of literature, though the butcher may not have been as welcoming, for she was a hard bargainer when it came to his cuts and prices.[18] A passionate rose lover, she toured every garden she could, painted every chance she got, and treasured the simple things that were so rare in the U.S., like just-caught salmon atop a schmear of fresh-churned Irish butter on a hand-cut slab of just-from-the-oven Irish brown bread.

While all five Murray children felt at home, like they belonged, Limerick was particularly enjoyable for the elder son. Though 16-year-old John Patrick had arrived thinking he wanted to practice medicine, his Irish internship planted a seed that would later sprout a new purpose and direction in life. Two incidents were especially formative.

I was in the jumpseat (inches behind the pilot's left seat) of a Lockheed Super Constellation taking off from Shannon. Seconds after takeoff, no higher than 500 feet, the loudest alarm I have ever heard in my life suddenly rang out. "Fire—number two engine!" shouted the engineer. Though it occurred fifty years ago, I can hear those words in my mind—volume, pitch, tone, and timbre of every syllable—as clearly as if it had happened this morning. Dad coolly and expeditiously led the crew through the emergency procedures checklist.

My job during this incident was to become invisible and utterly silent and it was the best emergency assignment I ever performed. Dad and his crew didn't need help and I wasn't about to ask questions. The landing was uneventful and it turned out there was no actual fire.

As intense as the fire warning, engine shutdown and feathering were, the incident wasn't so much alarming as dramatic. It was like I was watching a movie, starring my father. He never spoke of the incident, but I never forgot the sheer awe of seeing him command the response with such coolheaded, manifest expertise. Exactly how I knew he'd handle it.

Later,

I flew with Dad . . . into West Berlin (Tempelhof Airport). The nighttime flight, in a Super Constellation, took us over communist East Germany, through an air corridor that civilian flights were "permitted" to transit.

Halfway to Berlin, air traffic control called out (I'm recalling the approximate words) "Bogie (unknown aircraft) at nine o'clock," followed by "Bogie turning and closing to trailing position," and "Bogie at your six o'clock." Six o'clock—dead astern—is the classic position for a fighter about to commit an extremely unfriendly act.

"Bogie turning left, exiting corridor," was the last call. The fighter had left us.

I was only 16, but I knew enough to recognize this was a pretty unusual situation for a civilian airliner. Dad took it in stride—he

> *was amused if anything. Evidently, this was a little harassment the Soviets/East Germans found entertaining, launching one of their fighters to intercept a civilian airliner, just to show whose turf they considered the air corridor to be.*

Such an apprenticeship might have shocked certain people. But it was a common practice. "Pilots knew there was no better training than actual flying; the younger the better."[19]

In 1965, the U.S. economy was booming, exceeding the most bullish economic forecasts. Then again, few economists had predicted an eight-fold increase in soldiers serving in Vietnam in just 12 months, and with them millions of tons of K-rations, M-16 carbines and howitzer shells, much of it transported by Flying Tiger Line, Inc.

While TWA, Pan Am and other airlines were far better known to the average American, owing to their slick advertising and regularly scheduled routes, Flying Tiger had quietly become not just the country's largest cargo airline, but in some months the third-largest passenger carrier, on the basis of its low-cost student charters and, especially, its Air Force work, as the U.S. ramped up from 23,000 troops in January to 184,000 in December (peaking at 536,000 in 1968).

Fortunately, John Patrick Murray hadn't yet enlisted or been drafted, and so he wasn't an official passenger aboard one of his father's many flights. Rather, following in the footsteps of his grandfather, John Desmond Murray Sr., he'd applied to Georgetown University. When he was accepted, his Irish Catholic parents were thrilled.

Meanwhile, for Captain Murray, flying may have been tainted somewhat by the increasing number of Vietnam-related casualties. While the vast majority of deceased soldiers were flown by the Air Force, the Tigers did also from time to time.[20]

Yet it was clear Murray still loved to fly and spend time in the water. Larry LeFever tells of the time when he (as copilot) and Murray (as pilot) had flown nine straight hours from Newark to LA. After checking in and getting their room keys at their hotel, across from Santa Monica Pier, the men ran into two Tiger colleagues, about to head east.

We chatted for a few minutes, then John says, "I'm heading to my room. Safe flight." He shakes our hands, and leaves us to our hangar flying. Now though I'm still gabbing, I can barely keep my eyes open, and I'm really looking forward to hitting the sack. A few minutes later, I hear the elevator ding, look over and see John step off. He's wearing his swim trunks, shades, carrying a towel. He walks across the lobby as if oblivious to the fact that me and the guys are there, that he knows us at all, and heads across the street, and goes for a swim—in the ocean. In the morning. It was really cold![21]

While a few holdouts continued to question Murray's actions on the night of September 23, 1962, almost all such questions had stopped by mid-July 1965 after U.S. Air Force captain Murray Brady lost three engines and was forced to ditch his Lockheed Super Constellation in the North Atlantic.[22] (The plane was 1 of the 36 strung out across the northeastern sky to provide early warning of incoming Soviet intercontinental ballistic missiles.) Captain Brady hit the water 100 miles east of Cape Cod, in a warm summer sea, with waves at 5 feet, not 20.

While it's unknown whether Brady employed Murray's nonstandard ditching maneuver, it is known that rather than just the left wing snapping off, his Connie lost both. It's also known that, as compared to Hard Luck Sam salvaging one raft, the Air Force crew wasn't able to find any of its five. It's also known that rather than 48 of 76, only 3 of 19 survived, Captain Brady not among them.

As the war in Vietnam escalated in 1966, John Murray was busier than ever flying a mix of domestic, Asian, and European routes. He was making good money. But far more important: rather than fighting in a jungle thousands of miles away, John Patrick was just an hour away by plane, studying with the Jesuits.

The pilot did more than just fly. He took 5-year-old Barbara and 7-year-old Ellen to the World's Fair in nearby Queens. One highlight was Disney's It's a Small World ride, in its debut. He also continued planting saplings on his 240-acre farm in upstate New York. It wasn't fancy, but the Christmas trees would be a cash crop and require very little in the way of ongoing expenses or oversight. The farm would really start to bring in good money when he reached 60, the mandatory retirement age.

Whenever he had a spare moment, which was usually late at night, in the ready room at Newark Airport or while driving along the Long Island Expressway, he'd turn his attention to the memoir he'd begun. Sometimes his emotions got the better of him.

He couldn't get a lot of the images and other recollections out of his head. The look on Garrett's face when he said "I goofed." The high, furious water that stood between him and the cockpit, and the flashlight. Feeling certain the raft would capsize, again and again. Falling off the Swiss ship's rope ladder, back into the sea.

It was really hard locating all the source material (domestic and international, official and unofficial), making sense of the many gaps and contradictions, then knitting it together into his version of an incident report. He had notes lying all around the house, in the glove compartment of his Ford, in his locker at Newark.

But as things starting coming together, he decided to move forward on a long-deferred dream of owning his own plane. Technically it was an amphibian: it could take off from and touch down on land or water. He tried to justify purchasing the preowned Seabee to Dorothy by saying he could take the kids up in it for a spin as well as up to the farm.[23]

Dorothy wasn't sold, but she was tolerant. Her husband had worked hard. She didn't begrudge him his flying frog. He kept the plane's idiomatic Southern name painted on the side by the previous owner: *Honey Chile*.

Though his elder son had said he wanted to be a doctor, not a pilot, and he'd declared biology as a major (premed), his father knew that collegiate intentions rarely locked one onto a career path. (The transport pilot had majored in chemical engineering.) So the father continued the flight instruction he'd begun in Limerick.

Fifty-three years later, the apprentice recalled his

Dad driving to Deer Park Airport on Long Island to pick up Honey Chile. The Airport made it clear that the Seabee wasn't welcome as a

> *permanent resident (it was too loud on takeoff and risked incurring the ire of neighbors), so, wanting to be a good neighbor, Dad agreed to fly it to a more accommodating airport (Zahn's in Amityville). He drove both of us to Deer Park in his Ford convertible, then handed me the keys so I could drive it to Zahn's and pick him up after he landed. The Sunliner was a stick shift which I had driven only once or twice, and I was a little unsure of myself. "I think you'll do fine," he said to me. He was right.*
>
> *His flight in the Seabee was his first solo in that aircraft and the thought that struck me is that he and I were in similar situations: I was a novice in driving a stick shift, he was a novice in the Seabee. We both made it of course but the similarity of our situations is something I still think of from time to time.*[24]

All five Murray kids loved spending time with their pilot-father in his loud and ungainly aircraft with the silly, endearing name. As it had room for a pilot and three passengers, there were numerous outings. "I'll never forget what a thrill it was flying over the Statue of Liberty with my Dad," Ellen recalls.[25]

Murray Residence
Oyster Bay, New York
Christmas Eve 1966

While memories have faded, it's likely that five stockings hung from the mantle, the aroma of hot apple cider from the kitchen competed with that of crackling wood in the fireplace, and there was a crèche beneath the tree the family bought at the A&P parking lot because the pilot-moonlighting-as-a-Christmas tree farmer could only offer sprigs. Though Captain Murray was in Vietnam or somewhere en route back home, it was still a happy, festive scene.[26]

Sometime that afternoon, while he was out driving, John Patrick heard the following on the car radio:

> *There are reports of a Flying Tiger Line military charter crashing in Da Nang, South Vietnam. The death toll is in excess of a hundred people, including the entire flight crew.*[27]

He returned home immediately and told his mother, and she called Tiger's Newark office.

As he had when she'd called him after the ditching, Chief Tiger pilot Carey Bowles answered. This time he assured Dorothy it wasn't John.

No one can recall her specific words, but her profound relief was obvious. Also, the stress likely underscored her desire to continue discussing how she and John were going to adjust and realign certain priorities.

She had aspirations too, that she'd put on hold. In addition to her passion for painting, Dorothy was looking forward to resuming a long-postponed career in journalism. (She had written for the University of Detroit paper and taken courses on Long Island.) But she couldn't hit the resume button on her life if John was always halfway around the world and then, once home, off to the farm to plant saplings that wouldn't bring in any money for years, if at all.

She respected her husband's work ethic. He was a good provider. But life was too short. Rather than fly and farm, she encouraged him to finish his book about Tiger 923. It had been more than four years, yet he'd only written 167 pages, many culled from government reports.

Shortly after dinner, as Dorothy and the children were milling about, the phone rang. John Patrick walked over and lifted the receiver. He distinctly recollects having heard: "Please let me speak with your mother." He also recognized the voice on the other end: Father Soave, pastor at their church, St. Dominic's. The son eyed his mother.

"Mom took the phone, listened to the news, and quietly hung up."

The news was: Captain Murray was dead.

He'd not been on the plane that went down in Da Nang. He'd drowned off Wake Island during a refueling stopover while bringing some U.S. troops home for the New Year. He'd gone snorkeling alone in the Pacific with his underwater camera. His body and camera were found washed ashore.

"She announced the news to us at that moment," John Patrick recalls, "cushioning the blow with as gentle words as she could muster on such short notice." Beyond that, "all I can recall is a somber silence we all experienced. I had no doubt it was true. I was more stunned than anything. How could it be? How could he be gone?"

John Patrick doesn't know how the family's parish priest got word, just that "Father Soave apologized to me for delivering the news over the phone, saying he was immersed in Christmas activities and couldn't get to our house to deliver the news in person. Mom thought he should have found a way." Soave "obviously regretted it. However, his failure to convey the news in person was not something that troubled me, since I was overcome by the fact of Dad's death."

He tried to console his mother, his older sister, Kathleen, and his three younger siblings: Steven, Ellen, and Barbara. But how could they be consoled? Could there be a less welcome Christmas present? "Shock is the best description. Followed a few days later by grief."

That a great swimmer died in the Pacific after having survived the violent North Atlantic for seven hours was tragically unexpected. Had he suffered a heart attack, like the Tiger 913 pilot? Murray's colleagues who flew the same route said sometimes a vicious undertow could appear out of nowhere and get the better of even the best of swimmers, and that a tiny, highly poisonous mollusk was indigenous to the area, and its sting was essentially undetectable.

The Murray household sunk into deep sadness. Everyone's faith was tested.

Word got out. Well-meaning people called, visited, sent cards. As the just-turned 19-year-old was now the man of the house, he helped his mother prioritize the cascading repercussions:

> No will;
>
> The obituary;
>
> The funeral arrangements;
>
> Disposing of an odd aircraft;
>
> Deciding what to do with a Christmas tree farm that was years away from generating any revenue but was incurring taxes and mortgage expenses;

Five traumatized children;

His father's remains.

The day after Christmas, late in the evening, he stood beside Francis DeVine of DeVine Funeral Home inside the Flying Tiger Line cargo hangar at Newark International Airport as the Lockheed Super Constellation bearing his father's remains taxied toward him. "I saw the casket unloaded from the plane and placed in the Cadillac hearse. Mr. DeVine drove back to Oyster Bay, dropped me off at home, then took the remains to the funeral home."[28]

The funeral service was "small, quiet," followed by a burial at St. Patrick's Cemetery in Huntington, with a "large Celtic cross over his grave. There was no wake."

> *Since everything happened over Christmas break, I returned to Georgetown either on schedule or maybe missing only a few days. Given the situation, I got the OK to delay taking final exams—something I needed and really appreciated. Although crew didn't row during the winter, we had early morning workouts and weight lifting in McDonough Gym six days a week and I found that routine comforting.*
>
> *I learned the meaning of the word grief in the aftermath of Dad's death and it stayed with me for exactly one year, vanishing forever on the following Christmas Day. It was a heaviness that accompanied my days but wasn't overpowering or all-encompassing, just something I would feel from time to time, regret, loss, sadness.*

These days, John Patrick adds, 54 years after the fact, "I don't mind recounting the event. It's not hard or painful."

Dorothy Murray never remarried. She moved to Wicklow, Ireland, in 1969; the two eldest, Kathleen and John Patrick, stayed behind. "No doubt the summer we spent in Ireland in 1964 was the main reason for Mom moving there with the three youngest of our clan," says John Patrick, "since she knew what Ireland was like after living there for two months. A key reason for the move was the cost of living in Ireland was far cheaper (it's not anymore!) and she could send the kids to Irish schools taught by Catholic nuns. That was a far better option than the tumultuous Sixties in the U.S."[29]

Steven, Ellen, and Barbara weren't sold, not by a long shot. "What about all our friends?"

"You'll make new friends," Dorothy assured them. She downsized, buying the converted stone mews that had stabled the horses used by the monks who'd once lived in the cloisters across the street. For the next 31 years Dorothy was an avid gardener, painter in oil and watercolor, and explorer of Ireland's beautiful back roads. The paintings that didn't sell at her exhibitions were given to visiting American friends.

Over the years, the clan scattered and germinated, as the Irish have always done: to LA, Dublin, Tenerife. Kathleen moved to Ireland, but John Patrick remained in the DC area.

He'd eventually invite Ellen to join him, after her graduation from University College Dublin in 1981.[30] As for his aspirations, "although I liked biology, I came to realize that medicine was not my calling. It just wasn't what I wanted to do. So . . . what career could I follow? Having spent many hours flying with Dad (both with Flying Tigers and in his Seabee amphibian), it seemed a natural choice and I ended up spending 18 years flying fighters for the DC Air National Guard."[31]

He rose to the rank of lieutenant colonel. While on a two-week deployment to Iceland flying the F-4 with the DC Air National Guard, John Patrick had the opportunity to sit alert, awaiting the call to intercept Russian Bear bombers that regularly passed by Iceland. To his regret, the Bears were hibernating that day and he never got the chance to intercept and fly alongside them. "They never came. I was very disappointed!" Then-Capt. John Patrick Murray knew Capt. John Desmond Murray would have loved being copilot on that sortie.

However, "sadly, Dad had died before I made my decision to pursue flying, so there was no Braveheart moment. He would have been thrilled that his son became a fighter pilot."

It's reasonable to assume that Captain Murray would have also been thrilled that Lieutenant Colonel Murray typically flew twice a week, plus the annual two-week deployment, because he worked full-time at FEMA, where, during 9/11, he showed President Bush the agency's Information and Planning activities. It's also safe to assume the Tiger pilot would have been proud and not at all surprised that his son had submitted a Suggestion Box idea that both saved money and averted "a minor disaster for the emergency preparedness agency."[32] It's equally safe to assume that the father would have laughed but not been surprised when, according to the *Washington Post*, FEMA tried to reward his son but he "declined, with thanks," returning the check along with a note that said "it was just part of my job." Wanting to avoid the limelight—put him in it.

The "miracle pilot" who'd so famously ditched, loved to fly Lockheed planes, and loved to sail would have also been delighted and amused by the life trajectories of his other progeny. His youngest daughter, Barbara, became a sailing judge for the Olympics. His eldest granddaughter, Maureen, John Patrick's only daughter, went to work for Lockheed, then became the fourth-generation Murray to solo.[33] And granddaughter Sarah, the only daughter of his second-youngest, Ellen, went to work for Washington Speakers Bureau, where she managed all of Capt. Chesley Sullenberger's speaking engagements.[34]

Sam Nicholson

When sitting beside Fred Caruso aboard the *Celerina*, curled up before the big mess hall stove in his underwear, Hard Luck Sam swore he was through with flying. Such sentiment was understandable. He was shivering and traumatized. His chemical burns were bad and growing more painful by the minute. He'd nearly died twice in the line of work over the past six months.

But despite his surgeries and a stint in a wheelchair, Sam didn't quit Flying Tiger Line, which enabled him to save dozens more lives.

As Capt. Larry LeFever recalls:

> *Four years after the ditching Sam was dead-heading on a flight to the west coast when I was captain. He was scheduled to be navigator on a trans-Pacific flight and, like many of the guys, he carried a*

sleeping bag stuffed in a knapsack, so he could lay down wherever, to try and grab some sleep in between flights. About twenty minutes out of Newark, I went to the back of the plane and found him sitting on his sleeping bag, reading a book. He told me he couldn't sleep because he didn't feel well. He also said he smelled a bad smell. Then I smelled it. Turns out we had an acetylene leak. It permeated the entire plane. I immediately declared an emergency and returned to Newark Airport. That was a close call. If anyone had lit up a cigarette? It would've been all she wrote.

Paramedics met us when we landed. They wanted Sam to go to the clinic at the Airport. But he didn't want to. He just wanted to go home, and did.[35]

Malfunctioning engines or gas tanks didn't end Sam's Tiger career. It was the inertial navigation system. The airline retired its entire roster of navigators in the mid-'70s. Now a piece of equipment could do what Tiger 923's navigator had been doing.

Well, not everything he'd been doing. Everyone lost track of Hard Luck Sam. But none of the Tiger 923 survivors or their loved ones have ever forgotten how lucky they were that their flight hadn't been navigated by a piece of equipment.

Carol Gould

The stewardess and pilot sat on opposite ends of the spectrum in terms of the willingness to discuss Tiger 923. While Murray was a man of very few words, Gould joked with reporters in Antwerp, New York and New Jersey; inspired the various groups who'd invited her to be their keynote speaker; captivated the people on the streets of Little Syria in Paterson, Lyndhurst and Brooklyn who recognized her; and held in thrall the ladies who sat beside her under the bulky permanent wave machines that looked like devices designed by a joint venture between NASA and the Spanish Inquisition.

Our Lady Queen of Peace Church
North Arlington, New Jersey
April 6, 1963

Gould had had a blast over the prior six and a half months. Everyone was so nice to her. She'd signed autographs galore and, though her free perms had ended, everyone still wanted to buy her drinks, the Central Bergen League had just recently given her a "huge trophy for valor," and she even met famed WWI ace Eddie Rickenbacker.[36]

Now the scene was reminiscent. This time, however, rather than a single Gould huddling with Hard Luck Sam and Murray in the corner of a Swiss freighter, gazing at the festivities, not feeling festive themselves, the just-married Carol Hansen was the focus of the gaiety, and only Murray stood apart, observing from the top right corner of the front steps of the Syrian Catholic church, as far away as possible from the thrown rice and gown's train.

Only this time he was smiling. He had reason to, Hansen knew. He'd been proven right after all. Had the pilot not done what he did back in September, Gould never would have married the man of her dreams; keeping it in the family, so to speak, as Eddie managed the Tiger cargo terminal where Murray's remains would arrive three years hence.

But Mrs. Eddie Hansen wasn't just thinking about how she'd managed to survive what experts called an unsurvivable ditching.[37] She was also thinking about how though she'd been credited with sustaining morale on the raft, Murray had sustained hers. Though she'd harbored grave doubts about ever seeing her wedding day, he'd said: "You're getting married."[38]

Hansen quit working as a stewardess. "Eddie's proposal had been a package deal: marry me, and stop flying."[39] Though she wasn't afraid of returning to the skies, he was, and "I was madly in love with him."[40]

They made a happy couple. They had a boy. They named him John. And a girl. Lauren.

One day in 1970, after having lunch together in Newark, Carol and Eddie were walking across the road. The first indication of trouble was an ominous rumbling roar, clearly headed their way. Carol turned just as a car came barreling toward them, at what she'd later learn was 100 mph, in a 30-mph zone. She dodged it, barely. But it hit Eddie, head-on. He flipped up and onto the hood in a horrific blur.

The car zigzagged more than slowed down, but as gravity had pinned Eddie's body to the windshield, the driver couldn't see, so he screeched to a halt. Carol took off running toward the car as the driver climbed out, stumbled over, and "tossed my Eddie off the hood like a sack of potatoes. I went berserk. I could tell the guy was drunk."[41] As she knelt down beside her husband, the driver yanked open the car door, knocking her to the pavement, climbed in and sped off.

The ambulance arrived to find her sobbing, cradling her beloved. The paramedic didn't need to tell her. She knew: he was gone. "He looked so peaceful. I'd always felt no Hollywood actor was as handsome as Eddie. Now I was sure.

"Later they asked me if I wanted to see my husband. I said, 'No, I'd prefer remembering him how he was when he was alive.' The guy who killed Eddie was caught, and it was like his third DUI, but as he was the son of some judge he got off with a slap on the wrist."

After her husband's death, Carol returned to the skies, though not as a stewardess. She worked as a travel agent. "I loved it. I'd missed it. I got to travel all over the world."[42]

Today, at age 80, she harbors no ill will. She's as ebullient as ever.

> *I think we've all got a choice: to be bitter or happy in life. I choose to be happy. Maybe I'm a little crazy, but that's okay. Whenever anyone asks me why I'm not mad, I tell them: What good would it do? When a psychologist in Antwerp asked: "Are you angry with anyone?" I said, "Just at the ocean."*
>
> *I tell people: Don't sweat the small stuff. I didn't die that night in the North Atlantic. I could have, easily. I should have. I didn't die in that hit-and-run, either. Instead, I married the man of my dreams. He's still in my head, and in my heart, and in the eyes and smiles of my two wonderful children. I've made lots of new friends. I've been blessed.*[43]

She admits to being sad that her children didn't get much of a chance to know Eddie. "He was such a sweet man! And a great father." One of the things she'd most wanted was for her 6-year-old son and 5-year-old daughter to have what she hadn't had growing up: a father. (He'd left home when Carol was 5.) But it wasn't meant to be.

Spending time with animals has helped her stay positive. "With so many people around me dying, I figured it was probably safest for all concerned that I stick with animals, instead of humans." She's become a one-woman animal welfare league, knowing full well that the welfare is a two-way street. Carol rescues stray and abused animals, and cares for the pets of friends and family while they're flying around the world.

(Top) November 1962, Carol Gould holding the trophy "For Heroism" given to her by New Jersey's Central Bergen League. (Bottom) April 6, 1963: Carol and Eddie Hansen on the steps of Our Lady Queen of Peace Church in North Arlington, NJ. The bride's mother, Paula Ziegler, is in the upper-left-hand corner. Capt. John Murray (who on the raft had assured Carol she'd marry) is in the upper right. COURTESY CAROL HANSEN.

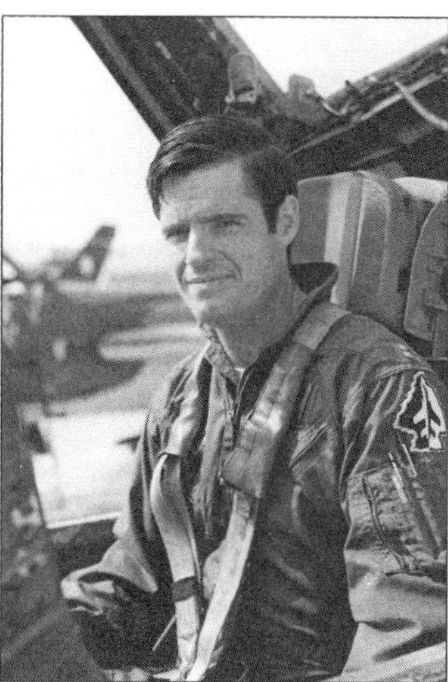

Like father, like son. (Top left) Pvt. John D. Murray in U.S. Army uniform, circa 1945. (Top right) DC Air National Guard Capt. John P. Murray in an F-105 cockpit at Andrews Air Force Base, MD, 1978. (Bottom) John P. Murray briefs President Bush on the federal response to 9/11. COURTESY JOHN P. MURRAY; DC AIR NATIONAL GUARD; U.S. DEPARTMENT OF HOMELAND SECURITY.

Chapter 13

Passenger Legacies

Lois and Dick Elander

Lois' dislocated shoulder was fully healed within days of the ditching, and the vertebrae in her back weren't far behind owing to the fact that she'd suffered a stress fracture and a bad sprain. But as the U.S. Air Force doctors at the hospital in Swindon, England, didn't want to take any chances, they kept her bedridden much of the time in semi-traction.

Her husband's situation was different. His first operation cut away a fair bit of dead leg tissue. It hadn't gone well. He was running a really high fever. The ophthalmologist wasn't a general surgeon, but he had two eyes, so after the dressing was removed, Dick said: "It didn't look like there's much left of the leg."[1] The prognosis wasn't good.

Six days after the first surgery, an Air Force doctor again operated on the Army doctor. He removed a flap of skin from Dick's upper left thigh, cut it into swatches, and grafted them onto the burned areas. The results were inconclusive. The bandages had to be changed every few hours. "It was very painful. As the dressing dried, it would pull away the attached muscle and flesh."

He was administered penicillin and powerful narcotics. The latter "didn't help the pain much but it made me feel good." He drew strength from the cards and letters sent by strangers from hither and yon, as well as friends and family in Seattle and West Point, saying "how much my story meant to them."

The prognosis remained uncertain. The only certainty was that the delay in treatment occasioned by the Pentagon's detour to Ireland for a press conference had made matters worse.

A few days later, in the afternoon, when Lois was resting, Dick used his walker to wander into the common area, where he struck up a conversation with Bob Eldred. While Eldred's burns weren't as severe, the Cape Cod resident was distraught at having lost his wife, Edna.

Someone saw a chess board. Elander fancied himself a decent player but Eldred was a step above, writing the chess column for his local paper, *The Cape Codder.* Eldred's grief was a handicap, the major knew, but as the eye doctor was really competitive, he didn't cut the retired captain any slack. He told Lois: "We each won once, so I thought that was pretty good."

The two officers also set up a mock chain of command, "ordering" Acevedo, Caruso, and other lower-ranking survivors to bring them Cokes and stand sentry to watch for the beastly nurse. "We had a lot of fun with them, and the young soldiers played right along and enjoyed our little game, too."

The friendship conferred additional benefits. "Sir Charles Somebody visited Bob from London, bringing him a bottle of Canadian Club disguised as a box of chocolates. So we were all set for the night."[2]

A week later, Elander was out of the woods. He and Lois were told they could head home October 28. Though he still needed a cane, he could walk. Lois was fully recovered.

They sent word to their family. Everyone was thrilled. "I had the best show-and-tell of anyone in kindergarten," says Jill, who was five at the time. "Just sixteen days til my mommy and daddy get home. . . . Just fifteen days. . . . Each day I said the same thing."[3]

On the day of departure, Lois and Dick flew to an Army base in Germany, were debriefed again and given their plane tickets. When they stepped onto the tarmac and saw what they were about to board—a Lockheed Super Constellation—they stopped walking and eyed one another. Dick made inquiries: Was there no other way? Afraid not, he was told, unless he and Lois wanted to wait another week or so. Feeling the PR-obsessed Army would make sure this Connie wasn't defective, they decided: We'll just knock a few back and forget the make of plane we're on.

Lois didn't forget, however. Right after boarding she entered the cockpit and said to the pilot, "Now you are going to get us there this time, aren't you?"[4]

Much about the journey was discomfiting and emotional. The printed ticket with the "McGuire AFB" staring back at them once again. Looking down over the same stretch of sea where their lives had hung in the balance and their good friends had lost theirs. Disembarking in New Jersey: only this time via steps, in the light of day, on land. A few hours later they boarded a DC-8 and flew to West Point. They arrived home at night.

When Lois popped her head into Jill's bedroom and stood in the doorway, her daughter stirred, rolled over, and said, "Mommy, is that you? Are you real?"

"She came over and sat on my bed. I touched her face. 'Yes,' she said. 'I'm here.'

"It'd seemed forever. Five weeks is a long time for a five-year-old."[5]

Three days later, on Halloween, in response to his father's incessant questions, Dr. Elander sat down to begin a tape-recorded memoir, but 3-year-old Troy was having none of it. In the background, he can be heard talking about something far more important than his parents' ordeal: his Superman costume. Dick sounds delighted to be interrupted. "Yes, I agree, your costume's the winner."

But eventually Troy ambled off, and Dick began: "Hello, Dad . . . I'd like to give you a chronicle of the events that happened a little over a month ago. . . . This is the last time I'm going to tell the story."[6]

His nine cassettes are clinical. He sounds very humble. He prefers facts to opinions.

Sometimes his voice catches, like when he describes the atmosphere in the cabin right after Murray announced he'd have to ditch: "All you could hear was the silence and the whining of the plane going down."[7] If judged by the halting delivery, it was even scarier a half hour after impact, when "we knew we were completely alone. The sea was extremely rough. It would sweep over the raft and completely drench everyone."

But he doesn't dwell on the downside. His joy is patent as he recounts the "wonderful homemade soup and Dutch beer" on the Swiss freighter, and every moment aboard the Canadian carrier. "This really began," he says, in a voice thickened by emotion, "the most delightful period in our whole adventure, really. It was really quite delightful. The Scottish surgeon who'd flown in from a destroyer was a marvelous fellow. Everybody came down to see us."[8] (The *Bonaventure* crew numbered 1,200.) "One of the little cabin boys even sent in two bars of scented soap for Lois. He felt he wasn't really worthy of coming in but he sent them in."

While the sort of research into "shell shock" Major Elander's deceased Tiger 923 travel companion Major Devlin once studied at West Point talked in terms of a monolithic "aftermath," more discriminating studies in the 1980s began to reveal, typically, three quasi-discrete stages: the reaction, triggered and driven by nerves and adrenaline; the response, when the brain and the body try to recuperate; and the long-term phase, where the shadow psyche often lurks and rules. The length and nature of the phases vary dramatically, survivor by survivor.

Dr. Elander's phases were more crisply delineated than most. Judging from his words and tone, the first, aboard the Swiss and Canadian ships, was for the most part enjoyable, while the second was very rough.

As for his third and final aftermath phase, it's another illustration of the sort of positive outcome professors Tedeschi and Calhoun uncovered in their research. According to his son, Troy, though his father had always been the adventurous sort, it was now directed in a different way: he clearly wanted to make the most of God's gift of survival. For starters, the major felt he was being called out of the Army. It had been good to him, but helping people see wasn't its core mission. It was now time to beat his sword into a plowshare. But how?

After his commitment expired in 1963, the major-doctor was all set to return to Seattle, near his parents, where his well-connected father could help kick-start his private practice. However, after a final pre-move visit, a friend suggested he swing by LA en route back to West Point in order to see Jules Stein's vision of a new eye institute. After touring Dr. Stein's UCLA clinic, Dick phoned Lois. "Change your tickets. There's something I'd like you to check out."[9]

He didn't have to ask twice. When Dick had proposed to Lois in 1954, the Enumclaw, Washington, native (population 3,300) said: "Yes, but get me out of here. I want to travel. I want adventure."[10]

Lois got her LA adventure alright. First aboard Tiger 923, then an emergency raft adrift in Odyssean conditions, now by joining her husband as he became the right-hand man to one of Al Capone's buddies.

Capone had taken a liking to Stein when he booked talent at Scarface's Chicago speakeasies, after Stein had put himself through college and med school by playing the sax and violin at weddings and bar mitzvahs. When Stein moved to LA, rather than practice medicine, he pursued his real passion: music. Though he didn't have Lois' talent he was a music business savant: he founded the Music Corporation of America, then acquired Decca Records, plus its subsidiary, Universal Pictures.

Later in life, Stein wanted to give back, so he poured much of his fortune into his clinic. While he spent most of his time schmoozing the stars he managed, like Bette Davis and Frank Sinatra, he attracted the likes of Elander to pioneer refractive eye surgery and other innovative techniques. Cataracts weren't just a scourge and the world's leading source of blindness in 1963: 55 years later, many health experts still consider them "the largest unaddressed disability in the world today."[11]

Though Dr. Elander helped thousands see over the subsequent 12 years, he still felt like he wasn't making the most of his survivorship. So in 1975 he decided to go from one of the most modern cities in the world, LA, to one of the most archaic: Kabul. Once again, the woman who'd wanted adventure was right beside him, helping him perform hundreds of free operations on the poorest of the poor, enabling them to see their first toddling grandchild or first kite running. They teamed up on a second pro bono trip to Nigeria, in 1980, where the working conditions were even more primitive and remote. Rather than work on movie stars in a glitzy air-conditioned surgical suite in Santa Monica, they sweated in a thatched hut several hundred miles from Lagos on patients who'd never seen a movie.

This time Lois and Dick were accompanied by their youngest, Troy, who was 20 years old. The experience helped persuade the ex-Superman and then–Williams College junior to apply to medical school at Cornell, and follow in his dad's footsteps.

Lois died in 2009 at age 79 of systemic organ failure. With her family gathered around, just before passing, she smiled and said: "It's all been borrowed time, really."[12] Though she didn't elaborate at the time, everyone knew what she meant: she could have died in 1962.

Dick died in 2014, after a bout with Parkinson's. The *Los Angeles Times* said he'd "loved challenging himself, caring for patients, [and] trying new adventures."[13]

Troy picked up where Dick left off, based in the Santa Monica office he shared with his father for 19 years. In addition to performing over 9,000 surgeries, many pro bono, the former president of the LA Medical Association has also fought for better health insurance, more eye research, and best practices in the public health arena, including by awarding scholarships to medical students who pledged to return to practice in underserved parts of Los Angeles.[14]

And in a wonderful bit of synchronicity, much of his free medical care has been delivered aboard a plane: the Orbis Flying Eye Hospital, which has treated more than 25 million people and trained more than 325,000 health care professionals in 92 countries. And . . . who provided the plane? FedEx, which acquired Flying Tiger Line in 1989.

At age 61, nearly twice as old as his parents were when they'd boarded Tiger 923, Troy's reminiscences are equally informed by filial love and professional respect: "Dad was not afraid to explore new avenues in medicine." He "often faced lots of resistance, but he refused to cow to convention that was no longer supported by the evidence. Though by nature conservative, if he saw something that showed promise, his thought was, 'Why not?' And when people told him in the mid-1970s that shaving off layers of the cornea, freezing them, and then re-inserting them sounded like science fiction, he'd respond, 'Just like flying to the moon was once science fiction, you mean?'"[15]

The eldest of the three siblings, Tom, 67, clearly blends his parents' DNA. As a senior architect with RBB (a leader in health care design), he's married his mother's aesthetic sense and father's knack for architecture, which is, Troy says, what cornea surgery is fundamentally about.

Jill, 63, shared the same office with her father and younger brother. She leveraged Lois' renowned panache into Jill Young Designs. While her interior design firm specialized in LA residential projects, her stylish sensibility also received rave reviews from her many medical office, law firm and country club clients. In a tragic, almost inconceivable double irony, Jill died in a plane crash on September 11, 2020.[16]

Raúl Acevedo

Physically, Raúl Acevedo was again strong and strapping two months after the ditching, so he was deployed to the Army base at Gelanhausen, West Germany, about 25 miles east of Frankfurt, where, as originally planned, he was assigned to the quartermaster's office, but doing much less medical work than he'd hoped. The main residual effects of his chemical burns were occasioned by the swatches of skin doctors had had to remove from his abdomen and graft onto his legs. The sutures itched. The differing hues made him feel self-conscious about the way he looked, especially in the shower and his skivvies.

Emotionally Acevedo was a mess. Tormented by PTSD (called "shell shock" at the time), he suffered from vivid nightmares, often bolting up out of his bunk in the middle of the night, waking his unit-mates, sweating despite the German winter, yelling "No!" and believing he was just about to be engulfed by another "wall of water."[17]

He also worried about his father's health.

> *His heart was not good to begin with. Then he got the news I was missing after the ditching, on top of thinking I was in Mexico, representing the Zacatecas basketball team at the national tourney in Monterrey, instead of being a soldier in the US Army, on my way to a two-year posting in Germany. And though I did get to speak with him on the phone, and said I was getting better, he got it into his mind that I was lying to him, to not hurt his feelings. He felt I was really*

crippled for life, and that's why I hadn't returned home, because I knew that his seeing me in a wheelchair or something would kill him.

Raúl felt he needed to see Roque. Or, rather, that his father needed to see him, and see with his own eyes that his son was in one piece, albeit reassembled.

His superiors didn't agree. The Army adjutant didn't even bother to look up from his desk outside the CO's office as Acevedo said, for the third time, as deferentially as he could, while standing at attention and holding a crisp salute, that he'd really appreciate "just one minute" to speak with the base commanding officer.[18]

The assistant replied: "I told you I'd tell him, private. The CO's a busy man."

Acevedo wanted to ask: *Have you told him?* But he figured that would make the guy mad. "I was prepared to make it up, the leave. I suppose the CO felt all the time I'd spent in hospitals should be treated as vacation time. Or maybe his assistant never passed along my requests."

A week or so after the third rebuff, Acevedo got an idea: If not my base commanding officer, how about my commander in chief: JFK?

He tried to compose a letter, but it was hard. He wasn't sure how to begin. His English was not as good as he'd have hoped. It was a very emotional exercise. He crumpled up draft after draft and tossed them in the trash. He wondered if he was just wasting his time.

Finally, he felt he'd struck the right tone: "Dear Mr. President, I know you served your country, and you have a father, too. I know you did your duty. I want to do my duty, but I am here in body only, not mind. My mind is back home in Mexico, where my father is very ill."[19]

The next day, Acevedo visited the base post office, handed an envelope to the clerk, and asked: "How much to mail this?" The letter was addressed to "President John F. Kennedy, at 1600 Pennsylvania Avenue. The clerk looked at me like I was nuts."

Several weeks later, while Acevedo was playing a bit role in a massive NATO war game along the West German–Czechoslovakian border, readying medical supplies in advance of the expected flood of mock casualties, the geopolitical situation didn't seem like a game at all. Though the

Soviets had blinked during October's Cuban Missile Crisis, many people still felt Armageddon was imminent. As the East Germans continued to fortify the Berlin Wall and shoot anyone who tried to scale it, Premier Khrushchev said he'd cut off all access to West Berlin, and that if NATO tried to stop him Americans would soon be able to look up and see not snow falling but his 58-megaton H-bombs, the world's most powerful nuclear weapon, each one 3,000 times as destructive as the bomb dropped on Hiroshima. JFK talked just as tough.

"I can still see the hill," Acevedo recounted, 57 years after the fact, "with all the Soviet tanks lined up, as far as the eye could see, their red flags flapping on top of the turrets. Across the barbed wire fence were our tanks, with the American flags flapping."

I saw at the distance a helicopter making a cloud of dust as it landed. I didn't pay much attention to it. I heard someone say: "It must be a bigwig, wanting his picture taken for Stars and Stripes."

About thirty minutes later I heard two soldiers calling out somebody's name. When one got closer I could hear clearly who they were looking for, a soldier named "Avocado." Then one of them looked at my name tag and said, "Is it you who we are looking for?" I said, "It's Acevedo, not Avocado."

The guy scratched his head, and looked down at a piece of paper. "Whatever," he said. "Gather your gear."

I was really confused. I didn't know what was going on. I'd sent the letter to JFK so long ago and hadn't heard a peep that I'd assumed someone had just thrown it in the trash and ignored me again. I thought I was maybe in some sort of trouble. "Where am I going?" I asked.

"Home, soldier."

I was in shock. I froze.

"First, back to base, at Gelanhausen. President Kennedy has granted your request for leave, for thirty days."

"When?" I asked.

"Right now," he said. "With us," he added, "in that." He nodded at the helicopter up on the hill. Then he handed me a thick envelope.

I looked inside, and there was a plane ticket from Frankfurt to New York, via military Air Force, along with another to Mexico City. Plus a wad of cash.

"You'll have to buy the last ticket to your home town once you get to Mexico City."

Acevedo felt it best not to alert his father ahead of time, "in case Uncle Sam changed his mind. If I said I was coming, and then didn't? His heart couldn't take that."

His mother and sister he told, however. He could trust them to keep it a secret, and make all the necessary plans.

It was very hard for me to be able to get on that helicopter, and to fly from Frankfurt to New York. My heart and brain felt like they were going to explode, and I was sweating a lot, but the idea of visiting my parents and letting them see me in person, that my body was all in one piece, although my mind wasn't, gave me strength to bear the pain and fear of flying again. Everything was still fresh in my mind.

I flew New York to Mexico City, where my sister, her family, and some friends were waiting for me at the airport. I stayed with Ofelia for two days; then I took the bus to Zacatecas.

It was around noon when I finally arrived to the city. Knowing that my father would be at his store at that time, I went there to surprise him, and as I thought, he was there as usual.

My father saw me, opened his eyes so big and with his opened arms walked as fast as he could toward me. We embraced very hard and cried like little kids for a long time. He couldn't believe I was there and alive.

Then we walked home to meet my mother and brothers. Everybody happy![20]

Two months after returning to West Germany from his home in Zacatecas, Raúl was in Stuttgart at the home of Helga Groves because, though he'd be forever grateful to JFK for allowing him to see his father, family and friends, he'd returned to base even less interested in cavorting and carousing with other soldiers his age with whom he had so little in common.

But he had something in common with the 18-year-old widow who

> *invited me twice to visit her and I stayed two days at her home each time. I met her parents. They were very nice and thanked me for helping their daughter, by pulling her into the raft from the horrible sea. We would spend most of the time talking. She was very sad, stressed, and traumatized since she lost her husband in the plane crash. She cried often, she would hug me and thank me over and over again.*
>
> *I lost contact with Helga. I have always wondered whatever happened to her. [No one in the Tiger 923 community has been able to establish contact.]*
>
> *I was discharged in mid-1964 in New York City, stayed there for two months visiting my uncle, then I went to the Port of San Pedro.*
>
> *But instead of packing tuna I decided to have a new beginning . . . so I drove to Los Angeles and in the same day placed three work applications, at the telephone company, the gas company, and RCA Records. Three days later RCA called me and offered me a job, training at various positions. Long story short, right away I relocated to Hollywood.*[21]

RCA helped Acevedo reacquire a sense of purpose and accomplishment. Voted union shop steward, "I took part in many negotiations and helped bring about salary increases, better insurance and other benefits." Then "I became a Company man, going from lead supervisor to second in command."

But his biggest success had nothing to do with work. "While at RCA in 1971, I was lucky to find and meet the love of my life, Vicky Bloomfield, born in Bolivia of English and Bolivian descendents. She worked at Prudential Insurance. We met at the famous Beverly Hills restaurant Casa Escobar, that had famous bands."

Ten years later, when RCA realized that vinyl records were going the way of the horse and buggy, they shuttered the Hollywood plant. However, as Acevedo was in line to be California plant manager, New York headquarters offered him the same job in Rockaway, New Jersey. But as he and Vicky loved the LA area, he resigned and started selling homes for a living, translating depositions and medical records on the side.

His own medical record continued to perplex him, however, until he received a PTSD diagnosis in 1982. He was told that he'd held up amazingly well given what he'd been through. The diagnosis helped him understand why he couldn't sleep or control the emotional roller coaster of joy and despair. Gradually things made more sense, were invested with positive meaning. The flowers in his garden were more fragrant. The bird-song was funnier, more melodic, uplifting.

Yet PTSD is chronic. It can't be cured, just mitigated. Discussing Tiger 923 has not been easy. Sometimes during our interviews Raúl would be overcome and have to take a break.

The triggers remain ubiquitous, sudden, and can hit like an emotional freight train. Just hearing a plane overhead or smelling fuel vapors while filling up his car.

As for air travel . . . "Ever since the accident happened, it has been very hard on me. I hardly ever fly unless it is an emergency and if so, I have to take medication. As soon as I sit on a plane, I feel very nervous and start sweating. My heart feels as if it wants to come out of my chest, it hurts, and everything comes back fresh in my mind as a flashback of everything that happened."[22]

He copes by spending time in his La Brea garden "oasis" with Vicky, their children and grandchildren, and with his parrots and chihuahuas, Cookie and Biscuit.[23] In 2020, at age 80, he's still going strong as a residential broker with Century 21.

Fred Caruso

In late October 1962, though Caruso had hoped to be one of the paratroopers selected to attend the CAB Board of Inquiry hearing, he wasn't at all surprised he was confined to Germany. "I knew too much," like "28 poor devils were killed by the lowest bidder."[24]

He was convinced that the ditching, the problems with the life vests and life rafts, and his being spirited away on short notice in the middle of the night to three hospitals in three separate countries were somehow related. "I tried to forget the seemingly disconnected incidents, but I couldn't."[25] While he was still seeing a psychiatrist and exhibiting symptoms of what would later be called PTSD, his vague theory had at least some basis in fact.

First, the U.S. military did have a troubling history of awarding troop charters to lowball bidders, irrespective of quality considerations.[26] However, Flying Tiger Line typically lost such bids to Riddle and Slick Airways. While the Tigers could fly at a fraction of the cost of the Air Force, they grew and succeeded on the basis of performance and customer satisfaction metrics.

Second, Caruso was right to be confused by "the high-priority, rush orders to Germany—no days off to go home, even though we were only 60 miles away." Every other Jump School graduating class had been granted leave before deployment.[27] His work in the battalion press office that plugged him into the Pentagon grapevine supported his theory: just prior to the Crisis, while JFK had asked Congress for permission to mobilize 150,000 U.S. troops, and said they were headed to Germany, this was a feint, as it was later acknowledged the troops were being readied for an invasion of Cuba.

> *When I was working for* Stars and Stripes, *Russian reporters would come by for our daily edition, like we did for theirs. They were always monitoring the Air Force flights. Never commercial. Not until they ramped up in Vietnam. But in 1962, paratroopers like us shouldn't've been flying alongside Hawaiian elementary kids. The situation at Checkpoint Charlie was tense, so we did have a legitimate mission. But as for how we got there, the brass was trying to slip us in under the radar. We were pawns being used by the Pentagon.*

Though discharged from the U.S. Army hospital in Germany after the Crisis had ebbed, "I couldn't let my guard down" because "Agents . . . were stalking me."[28] However, his conspiracy theories began to lose their potency. It dawned on him that it made little sense to dwell on the past or attempt to decipher Cold War geopolitics. "I was starting to feel better. I was soon producing more and better work than the base had seen in years. I was happy."

The move from the 8th Infantry *Arrow* to *Stars and Stripes* was key to his recovery. He was over the moon to be "sharing a legacy with Ernie Pyle, Lowell Thomas, Andy Rooney and other journalism greats."[29] He started taking photos. In a contest, one of his was chosen from more than 200 that had been submitted for a special *Stars and Stripes* cover.

Just before his three-year stint was up, the Army tried to entice him to reenlist. Though he got a raise and a promotion, he didn't take the bait. He returned to New York, reconnected with friends, then, in 1966, headed west to Big Sky Country and the University of Montana to study the journalism he'd already been practicing for years. He got his degree courtesy of the GI Bill.

He also lassoed a rancher's daughter. In 1967, he married Margaret Ellen Broadus in the village of Lame Deer in Montana's Northern Cheyenne Indian Reservation. His $7,000 Tiger 923 settlement paid for their honeymoon to Ireland.

Over the years, his PTSD waxed and waned. He bounced around a number of jobs, finally settling into helping Ellen run her successful association management and lobbying business, which connected companies and nonprofits with state and federal lawmakers. Ellen gave birth to two lovely girls: Andrea and Tanya. The family moved to Eagle, Colorado.

When his darkest thoughts resurfaced via the sound of a howling wind or the sight of a burning fire in some ski lodge, he'd sink into ennui, depression, rage, or self-loathing, sapping the joy and pride of fatherhood, marriage to a wonderful woman, his professional accomplishments; living.

The nightmares were so real, so horrible. Insomnia and sleep apnea made things much worse. Surgery to repair a deviated septum didn't help. The slightest, most benign, often imagined provocation would trip an incendiary fury.

He returned to psychotherapy. He was wary, dodgy, in denial, as if he'd never achieved catharsis decades earlier in Frankfurt. His psyche had closed back up.

His therapist was great. He helped usher Caruso back to face the truth:

> *Some poor devil came to me out of the darkness and raging sea, screaming, horrified and drowning . . . eyes wide open. Panic and desperation. His grasping, icy, gasoline-soaked fingers were reaching for me and got me by the neck. He was pulling at me and begging me for help . . . and . . . I pushed his face down and under the water. I drowned him right there, in an instant, to save myself, then I proceeded to put him and anyone else who might have been a witness right out of my mind.*[30]

Wow, his therapist said. He'd seen few people exhibit such courage in dredging up the shadow from its darkest recesses and wrestling it into the light of consciousness. In order to consolidate the therapeutic traction, he suggested Caruso consider writing a memoir. After consulting the 1962 letter to his parents and some writing he'd done for a class at Montana, the dormant journalist fretted. It was one thing to talk with his therapist behind closed doors, and not be judged. Just talking about it with his incredibly compassionate wife was really hard. But Ellen encouraged him. The writing was grueling: the craft, coupled with the emotional thicket. Developing and sustaining a narrative was a lot different from the punchy nature of journalism. You could get away with burying the lead, not burying the arc. And what was the lead, anyway? And the story arc? What was he trying to say? To whom? Why?

It helped that he and Ellen kept returning to Ireland to vacation, and that they'd made so many friends, like the man who at 5 had found the parachuted provisions that were intended for Caruso but which had washed ashore off Galley Head. Ellen and Fred fell in love with and bought a fixer-upper vacation-retirement cottage 85 miles west of the Mercy Hospital that had admitted him on September 26, 1962.

Still, the muse was elusive and recalcitrant, fomenting bad memories and fears. Caruso would get overwhelmed, and he'd have to give it a rest. He'd fret: *How will I be judged?*

He was adjudged a very good writer, and a very brave man. Published in 2007, *Born Again Irish* garnered many plaudits, including an award from the State of Colorado.

Art Gilbreth

After 10 weeks of surgeries and rehab related to his mangled leg, shattered back, and chemical burns, Gilbreth returned stateside. After a brief stay at the Presidio Army base hospital in San Francisco, followed by some R&R at home in Big Bear Lake over the holidays, in early January 1963 he shipped out to Fort Bragg, North Carolina, where he was assigned to the 82nd Airborne and told that, owing to his injuries, he wouldn't be jumping out of another plane any time soon, if ever; and he'd best forget about applying to the Green Berets, which was the only reason he'd enlisted in the Airborne in the first place, as a stepping stone.

After discharge in 1966, flush with the settlement money equal to more than a decade of Army wages, he moved to Sunriver, Oregon, where, even though he couldn't skydive, he could still ski, enjoy the great outdoors, and do things that gave him a rush, like riding his motorcycle on the high desert highways with no one around for miles, just rattlesnakes and pronghorn elk. Like Acevedo, he also figured he'd try his hand at selling residential real estate.

He had a knack for it. His low-key manner appealed to fellow Army vet Phil Knight, who, in 1988, though his Nike IPO had "only netted him about four hundred million" (circa 2020, he's worth about $40 billion), was looking for a vacation home outside of Portland.[31] When Knight began to refer other clients, it took some of the sting out of Gilbreth's not being able to join the Green Berets. (Gilbreth had heard that fellow Tiger 923 survivor Frank Bazell had joined the Berets, only to die in March 1967 in Binh Dinh Province, Vietnam, the victim of small-arms fire. He was 24.[32])

Though Gilbreth was diagnosed with PTSD, and still suffers nightmares and flashbacks, during our interviews he recounted his ordeal in a strikingly subdued manner. No survivor was in worse physical shape. Emotionally, he endured a harrowing sequence of events on the plane, underwater, on the raft, on the helicopter hoist, and on several operating tables. Yet he talked about them as casually as if he were discussing a baseball box score.

He still looks rugged at age 80, like he can handle himself. "I still like doing things that give me a rush." His main takeaway has been awe: "The miracle of the body. How your body reacts to trauma . . . it's very reassuring."

He's clearly mellowed since his days of coiled ferocity as a swaggering devil in baggy pants. He manifests the sort of "changes in self-perception, interpersonal relationships and philosophy of life" professors Tedeschi and Calhoun cite in their research.[33] Tiger 923 has "given me a different outlook. I've never been an over-religious person. I've always believed that something created us. Of course I prayed during the incident. It's made me a bit more religious."[34]

He also exhibits some survivor's guilt, though he doesn't appear overwhelmed by it. He says he has but two regrets. First, he never got the chance to thank Fred Gazelle for saving his life on the raft. "Had Little Animal not pulled that guy off me, I'd have drowned, for sure. I was drowning."[35] Second, he wishes he'd searched longer for the woman he helped in the sea. "It bothers me to this day."

Bob Eldred

Five weeks after the ditching, *The Cape Codder* printed a dramatic interview with the former artillery captain and then-antiquarian that took up the entire front page, second page, and concluded on the back page with a biting Op-Ed about how the Normandy vet was intent on being of further service to his country by "put[ting] all his considerable energies to work for air safety."[36] His energy didn't get him added to the Board of Inquiry witness list, however.

It's not hard to fathom why the CAB called a half-dozen green teenage Army privates, many who said the same thing, many who couldn't remember much at all; yet not him. First, he'd praised Murray, criticized the civilian regulators, the Air Force, and the sort of politicians appointed to the CAB. Second, Eldred had great and germane credibility as a shrapnel-filled hero of D-Day who, like Captain Murray, had also overridden explicit instructions. Third, given he'd walked with a pronounced limp even before the crash, he'd been badly burned, and he was prone to cry when recounting his ordeal and the loss of his beloved, courageous wife, he'd have been a dramatic, highly sympathetic—thus effective—witness.

As it was clear he was going to be ignored, and he had bills to pay, Eldred tried to move on with life: to recuperate from his wounds, transition from retail antiques to auctioneering and estate sales, and especially be a good single parent. But the loss of Edna was crushing, on many levels.

After his interview in *The Cape Codder* on November 1, 1962, he never said another word about Tiger 923 to his family. And while the taciturn Murray made the ordeal the fulcrum of his 167-page memoir, it's never mentioned in Eldred's 58-page memoir.[37]

In it he writes about being severely injured by Nazi tanks, seeing his friend get shot in the head by a sniper while seated beside him in a Jeep, and U.S. bodies piling up on Omaha Beach; collecting snakes; being taught "the needle trick" by his illusionist uncle's best friend, Harry Houdini; riding "the rails as a hobo"; memorizing the 101 quatrains in *The Rubaiyat of Omar Khayyam*; working as a "toilet bowl model" (he test-drove wooden seats to detect splinters); and selling cemetery plots.[38] When Eldred pivots to his "day of destiny," one suspects he's teeing up Tiger 923, but he means the day he first wielded an auctioneer's gavel. He calls the 1960s "a continuous whirl of auctions, sea clamming, antique shows, house calls, square dancing, and, above all, learning. I loved every minute of it."

Eldred's warm recollections are starkly at odds with his emotional newspaper interview, where he described his feelings while in the water, unable to locate a raft: "I knew I was going to die"; and on the ship, which "was the worst time of all," when told Edna hadn't survived.[39]

However, at age 68, the Purple Heart recipient found love again, in the person of Louise Westwood, who'd been his secretary for decades. As his daughter, Karen, recounts: "They didn't have many years as a married pair (five), but it was a time of healing for him."[40] (Bob died of a heart attack in 1986, Louise of bone cancer in 1987.) "She was a beautiful soul.

I believe that my father had at last found his happiness for the first time since the crash."

Karen Eldred was devastated by the loss of her mother and haunted by the visions of what both parents had endured. Consistent with the research, her aftermath sequence was nonlinear and combustible.

The news that she'd never again see or spend time with her mother sent the 17-year-old high school senior into a tailspin of disbelief, anger and grief, that resulted in confinement in her school's infirmary and the home of close family friends. Mercifully, for the first seven weeks, the Cuban Missile Crisis and the standoff in Mississippi between the governor and federal troops JFK had sent in to integrate Ole Miss overshadowed Tiger 923, so even though the CAB's three-day hearing was public, covered in *The New York Times* and most other media outlets, it was no longer headline news. However, in mid-November, when she was back at school, Karen recalls: "I was in the line at the dorm, waiting to go into dinner. On a table to the side were some newly arrived magazines, one of which was the *Saturday Evening Post*. I opened it and found myself looking at a full two-page spread with an artist's impression of my father and 50 other souls writhing in a horribly overcrowded raft in a hellish sea. That was difficult," she adds, in a big understatement. "I went through most of my senior year in a daze."[41]

> *I was of an age where my mother and I were trying to find a way through my insecurities and we were often at odds, although I was never an active "rebel." Just lost. And she was doing her best to reach me. Afterwards I used our disputes to punish myself. These were hard times. I had no one to talk to and no way to find relief or escape from my enormous guilt feelings over our fights. Despite our problems, she really was my rock and support, which I didn't recognize. And then it was too late. She would never be able to be a "friend" for me, something I wept over for decades afterwards (I could weep even now when I think about it). She was a strong, energetic and highly intelligent woman. I missed her terribly.*

Plus, some advice I was given by two mothers of classmates "to be strong for my father and brother" was well meant but destructive. Especially at the beginning, when I was basically alone, and my father was half a world away. Although later I discovered he had little awareness that I needed help. I could never have understood what he was going through (also without help). I felt even more alone and forgotten. Nobody ever asked what I needed for support, and the next years became a time of losing trust in myself because I was unable to help my brother or father.

I used to dream that I was in the house on the Cape and there was a knock at the front door (nobody uses the front door on the Cape, always the back door). I would open it and find my mother standing there, having washed up on the coast of Portugal somewhere. I had that dream for years . . .

I didn't go off the rails really till I was about 30, but it had been inevitable. Luckily I was able to, bit by bit, put myself back together.[42]

Falling in love was key. Though her parents never made it to Germany, she did. She met the internationally acclaimed opera singer Erwin Stephan in New York and impressed him with her voice during a dinner party in 1992; when he returned to New York in 1996, he said he hoped Karen might join him in Germany. She did. They still live in the Westerwald (northwest Germany), where they give voice lessons and concerts, and perform opera and operetta with their students.

(Top) June 1963: Soldier journalist Fred Caruso on assignment for *Stars and Stripes* outside Mainz, West Germany. (Bottom) June 17, 1967: the civilian journalism grad marries Margaret Ellen Broadus in Lame Deer, on Montana's Northern Cheyenne Indian Reservation, 10 miles south of the Broadus Ranch.
COURTESY ELLEN AND FRED CARUSO.

Santa Monica, November 25, 2019: Jill Young (née Elander) models the actual outfit fashioned from an aircraft carrier's State Room curtain so her mother, Lois, would have something "proper" to wear at the dinner in her and Dick's honor aboard the Canadian Navy's *Bonaventure*. COURTESY ELANDER FAMILY.

In WWII, the German High Command called the 82nd Airborne (the first U.S. combat troops to fight on German soil) "devils in baggy pants." At 80, former Airborne paratrooper Art Gilbreth says, "I still do things that give me a rush." Here, Gilbreth is riding his 131-JIMS Harley past Devils Tower, en route to Sturgis, South Dakota. COURTESY ART GILBRETH.

Chapter 14

Not So Tight Security

National Archives II (NA2)
College Park, Maryland
October 2, 2017

While the U.S. National Archives and Records Administration comprises dozens of storage facilities scattered across the country, NA2 is home to all National Transportation Safety Board (NTSB) and Civil Aeronautics Board (CAB) files. Security is tight when I arrive, in part because, from time to time, people try to make off with the archival treasures.[1] Pens and water top a long list of proscribed items. I pass through four checkpoints with screeners, wands and pat-downs, all the while under the watchful eye of omnipresent cameras.

At the second floor Reading Room reception desk, I'm handed a rugged leather bag; its padlock is opened; I'm told it will be searched when I leave, and it had better not contain contraband. The room has 60 workstations quartered into 240 cubicles, no interior walls, and big windows. While from the outside NA2 looks modern, the room is like the Land That Technology Forgot: squeaky old carts ferry cardboard boxes fabricated by defunct companies; small wooden dishes lie about with torn scrap-paper and miniature-golf-course-size pencils with no erasers. I catch myself looking about for typewriters but see only incongruous desktops and laptops.

The yearlong Tiger 923 investigation uncovered a trove of information, ranging from Captain Murray's personnel file and the 8-mm film shot at sea by a first responder to 47 survivor affidavits and 12 autopsy reports, most of which I expect to find in the 1961, 1962, or 1963 files of the CAB's Office of General Counsel or Bureau of Compliance and Consumer Protection. Since less complex accidents like Tiger 913 and US Air 1549 generated up to 4,500 pages of backup, my sense is the Tiger 923 files will run at least 5,000.[2]

Though 35 exhibits were referred to during the CAB's 1962 public hearing, I've not spoken with anyone who's laid eyes on a single exhibit, then or since. However, a dazzling team of archivists, investigative reporters and aviation experts from *The New York Times*, the John F. Kennedy Presidential Library, the NTSB and the Federal Aviation Administration has assured me that, by law, NA2 must retain the CAB Safety Bureau files.

Though the reference desk manager says my files would normally require several hours to pull, in 45 minutes they're on a cart with a banjaxed wheel. It's quite a haul: 11 valises, each the size of a microwave oven; enough for 30,000 pages.

I wobble to my workstation, place three valises on my desk, unwrap their elastic cords, and open them. As by now warm sunshine has found its way through the windows and over to my cubicle, I reach into my official NA2 bag, fish out my baseball cap, don it, doff my blazer, drape it over a chair, then remove two folders from one of the valises and lay them on my desk.

A monitor arrives in a silent flash and hovers over me. She doesn't smile. She says I've just violated protocol, thrice. It's impermissible to wear headgear, remove jackets, or have more than one valise on a desk at any given time.

"Sorry," I whisper. I balk, not sure which of the infractions she wants me to redress first. She offers no guidance. I remove my cap, put my jacket on, then return two of the valises to the cart. As she walks away, I begin rooting around inside an auspicious-looking valise from 1962.

There's one cache of materials, on top of which sits the same sort of floppy plastic binder I used for book reports in junior high school in the early 1970s. As I rifle through the files and folders, it's clear they all pertain to one crash: Tiger 913, which plowed into Hollywood homes and buildings on December 1962, killing everyone on board, plus others on the ground.

After a thorough review of the other 10 valises, it's clear that the Hollywood crash is the NA2's only Tiger file between 1961 and 1963, even though I know:

> There were at least three more disasters within a 13-month time frame;
>
> All three were U.S. Army missions;
>
> All three were U.S. Air Force charters; and
>
> All three flew Lockheed Super Constellation planes.

Instead of 5,000 pages, there are none. This is no innocent mistake, according to former Marine aviator, Connie pilot, and CAB Safety Bureau crash report writer Dick Rodriguez, who'd been hired just one month before Tiger 923. "If it was legit, there'd be a signed and dated IOU saying 'My name's so-and-so, I'm with XYZ, and I've borrowed these files for such-and-such a reason."[3] I found no such IOU. By way of corroboration, chain-of-custody notations are sprinkled throughout the Coast Guard's 1963 search-and-rescue study, such as the typed "Directive Clearance Sheet" on page 152, which every reader had to sign or initial, and the handwritten "Attach this article to Flying Tiger case" on page 179.[4]

More baffled than angry, I head over to the open-air, glass-enclosed Consultation Room, where lead volunteer Joe Schwarz approaches and asks if he can help. Based on his tone of voice and body language he seems like a nice guy, an earnest public servant. He also seems the perfect person to help me: he began his 38-year career with the National Archives and Records Administration at the Declassification Unit; then he moved over to the Office of Presidential Libraries, where he was the White House liaison.[5] I tell him what I'm looking for, what I've found, and what's missing.

His response is instantaneous. "That's strange. That tells me it's CIA."[6]

I ask: "You've seen this sort of thing before?"

"Oh, yeah."

However, despite Schwarz's initial reaction, he admits that who took the records and why will likely forever remain a mystery. Former CAB accident report writer Rodriguez agrees: "I can't imagine who would've taken the files."[7]

The case of Sandy Berger illustrates the difficulty of ascertaining the truth. Even the U.S. House of Representatives (with 435 members, thousands of support staff, and subpoena powers) couldn't get to the bottom of *why* President Clinton's former national security advisor stole some files from the National Archives and destroyed them.[8]

The *how* is less of a mystery. One didn't have to be a former national security advisor to steal documents. While a congressional study found that "lax procedures at National Archives created an environment where [Sandy] Berger easily removed highly classified documents" in 2003, when I was a student in the early 1980s, I was allowed to roam freely amidst boxes of official sealed governmental records in DC, Chicago, and Seattle, and I'd bet things were far less secure in the mid-1960s.[9]

September 24. Rettung der abgestürzten Flugzeuginsassen, morgens 3⁰⁰ Uhr bis 7⁰⁰ Uhr siehe special Bericht.

that the alarm is

SOULS ON BOARD

weather forecasting domestic + overseas

The Navigator's remarkably accurate position plotted to the time of trouble showed three hours and ~~twenty~~ thirty minutes to Iceland. This estimate later proved to have been within one minute.

Just a tiny fraction of the crew records not found at the U.S. National Archives, where by law they belong. (Top) *Celerina* carpenter Walter Wunderlin's logbook (likely recorded within 24 hours): "Rescue of the passengers from the crashed airplane from 3:00 a.m. to 7:00 a.m. See separate report" (refers to the letter to his parents); translation courtesy Peter W. Frey. COURTESY WALTER WUNDERLIN, PETER W. FREY. (Bottom three images) Just a few of Captain Murray's recollections (undated, so they could have been recorded hours or years after the ditching), found amongst his memoir-related papers. COURTESY JOHN P. MURRAY.

Pfc. Paul R. Stewart
RA15644006

The Plane Crack Up

Sept. 22, 1962 – Fort Dix New Jersey

Sept 24, 1962
Monday

Dear mom & dad,

Thank God! The Lord is truly with me. Miracles do happen.

The nearly impossible happened last night. Our plane crashed out at sea at night, with 78 persons on board, mostly soldiers.

of the 49. Thank God!

Right now we are headed for Belgium. I don't know what is going to happen from there. I hope back to the state. Please help me pray to God to thank him. Let Em read this account. I love you all. I can't wait to see you all again.

Love,
your son,
Fred

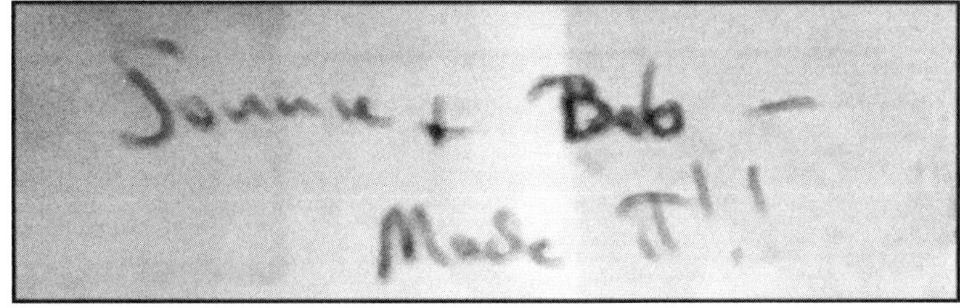

Sonnie + Bob —
Made It!!

Some of the passenger recollections not found in the National Archives files. (Top) "The Plane Crack Up," PFC Paul Stewart's handwritten account (note Army ID number beneath his name), undated. COURTESY U.S. DEPARTMENT OF TRANSPORTATION. The middle two excerpts are from the letter PFC Fred Caruso wrote to his parents, September 24. COURTESY FRED CARUSO. (Bottom) Army major Dick Elander's letter written to his friends, composed September 26, was short but sweet: "Sonnie and Bob—Made It!!" COURTESY ELANDER FAMILY.

Chapter 15

The Healing Hand of Friendship

In the initial hours and days after their rescue, survivors on Swiss and Canadian ships, in Irish hospitals and German barracks, and at a Belgian hotel swore they'd never forget and never lose touch. But most lost touch, and most wanted to forget.

Until March 2007, when Fred Caruso published *Born Again Irish*. After reading the book in his home town of Russellville, Arkansas, Gordon Thornsberry rang Caruso in Denver, where he was helping his wife, Ellen, build a lobbying-consulting practice.

Both now in their late 60s, the men had first met in their early 20s in Georgia during Advanced Infantry training. They shared a tent on a night maneuver. They'd not seen each other or communicated since their time together on the *Celerina*, from which Caruso was medevacked to Ireland on a British helicopter while Thornsberry continued on to Antwerp.

"It was really pretty funny," says Caruso. "After the past 45 or so years, we had both put on a few extra pounds and neither of us looked like tough combat paratroopers. Before even finishing our greetings, Gordon started going through our offices, telling everyone to come up to our reception area. He wanted them all to see something."[1]

Once everyone had assembled, the mobile home resort developer said, "Look here at two paratroopers who jumped out of airplanes in the Army. See what decades of civilian life can do to you?" "The way he did it," Caruso recalls, "was an absolute comedy."

More people heard about the book, contacted Caruso, and sent him telegrams, vintage photos and letters. Other Army pals he'd not heard from for 40-plus years got ahold of him, as did a Brazilian lawyer, Swiss architect and Irish farmer. The most common question: Can you connect me with anyone who maybe knew my father, brother or uncle? They were survivors too, but they never talk about it. Ever.

All the interest and questions led Caruso to wonder if he should try and do more. Before long he was reading up on how to design a website. Flyingtiger923.com went live on October 28, 2011, with this inaugural post written by Caruso:

> *Nearly 50 years ago, a four-engine Lockheed Super Constellation with a very distinctive arched tail accented by three vertical tail fins resembling predatory sharks swimming in close formation launched from McGuire Air Force base in New Jersey, headed for Frankfurt, Germany. The flight was to take about 19 hours. The aircraft never made it.*
>
> *It crashed some 500 miles off the coast of Ireland during an attempt at a late night water landing (ditching operation). It was all happening in the midst of a massive wind storm which was pushing waves to nearly 20 feet in height. Of the 76 persons on board, 68 were passengers and eight were crew. Of that number, 48 survived and 28 perished. Under the circumstances of the event—the distance from shore, the strength of the winds, and the turbulence of the seas—it was a miracle that anyone survived at all.*
>
> *This site is about that crash, the people who comprised the crew and staff, the various rescue crews who made any sort of salvation of human life even possible, the families and friends who feared for their loved ones, and anyone else who was involved in any possible way.*

Three weeks later, Swiss journalist Peter W. Frey first learned about Tiger 923 from a friend he ran into during a veterans association meeting in Zurich. As former front-page editor and correspondent for the prestigious daily newspaper *Tages-Anzeiger*, Frey couldn't understand how he'd never before heard about such an intriguing story.

Having retired in 2009, Frey had time on his hands and a desire to stay active. He did some digging. When he found Caruso's website, even though there hadn't yet been many posts, he wondered: *Should I make a documentary?*[2]

The field was getting crowded: Swiss journalist Marc Decrey heard about Tiger 923 from his friend and fellow yachtsman Pierre-André Reymond after the former *Celerina* crew member had also come across Caruso's site. A trip to interview Caruso was arranged. On April 15, 2012, as Decrey stood on the stoop, set to tape-record the first meeting between the survivor and first responder in nearly half a century, Reymond rapped on the bright red front door of the cottage Fred and Ellen bought and renovated in Glengariff.

When Caruso opened his door and laid eyes on the former deckhand, who had gained about 30 pounds, he smiled and said: "You haven't changed a bit."[3]

Reymond replied: "You either," though Caruso had gained maybe forty. "Well, maybe you look more clever, don't you?" As they shook hands and patted each other on the back, their glistening eyes were the only outward sign of what may have been going on emotionally.

The three men headed down the road to what Reymond described as a "genius evening in the pub."[4] While the interview of Caruso is sometimes hard to hear over the "laughing and beer and the very best whiskey I ever had," Decrey began by asking how it all felt after 50 years.

Caruso struggled to answer. "It's a big emotion. I try not to get . . . I could but I try not to. . ."[5] While most of the pub photos show Caruso smiling, there's something strained about them. There's a hint of irritation in his eyes and posture, consistent with *Born Again Irish*, where he recounts losing "the ability to experience exhilaration, elation and delight," and how "far too often I found myself smiling while my brain proceeded to process an entirely different script."[6]

A week later, Decrey's 16-minute interview with Caruso and Reymond was broadcast on French-language Radio Télévision Suisse. It was well received.

The second Swiss journalist arrived in Ireland one day after the first left. Over the course of four days Frey interviewed Caruso five times and Reymond three times for a documentary he was making to commemorate the 50th anniversary of the saga, with a special focus on the Swiss role.[7]

As one listens to the interviews, Caruso's voice never cracks. There's no throat-thickened wavering, only intermittent pauses as he tries to retrieve the details to answer Frey's insightful questions. Caruso sounds confident, open, forthright. He wisecracks. The overall impression? Relief. That he's finally getting the ordeal off his chest.

When asked about the last few minutes before hitting the water, Caruso says, "It was frightening looking into the dark, glued to the window; the view gave me a horrid chill." The man who today has more Irish than American friends speaks of how his mind has broadened since the accident. He says, "As a New Yorker I was on top of a very big world: I didn't know anything about Germany or anywhere else and I didn't want to know."

Reymond spoke of how the disaster was an inflection point for him too. For instance, it catalyzed his interest in maritime safety and naval architecture, as revealed on https:/www-navigare-necesse-est.ch, his great website.

Three months later, Frey flew to the U.S., where he interviewed Carol Hansen in New Jersey, Sammy Vasquez in Phoenix, and Art Gilbreth in Oregon. Frey spent the next several months dredging up additional source material, then weaving it all into a 45-minute German-language documentary, which aired on Swiss National Public Radio on September 20, 2012.[8]

It was very well received. Some of the things that fascinated the listening public included how there was so little panic during the terrifying ordeal, how 54-year-old retired schoolteacher Edna Eldred and 32-year-old retiring chief stewardess Betty Sims were among the coolest under pressure, how it was a neutral country's ship that rescued the mostly military survivors, and how the name of the 8-mph freighter translated as "the speedy one," or "the quickest."[9]

Three days later, Caruso and Reymond were the star attractions at two 50-year anniversary commemorations in Cork, whose organizers included Michael Flahive, who, when 5 years old, saw the "giant" aircraft carrier pulling into the Shannon Estuary below his home; then, months later, found washed ashore one of the many plastic-sealed emergency kits ineffectually dropped by planes during the search and rescue effort.[10] (The kit contained rations, first-aid supplies, and a saltwater-to-fresh-water converter.) The hundred and thirty attendees also included the current operator of Galley Head lighthouse, which had guided the *Celerina*; Switzerland's ambassador to Ireland; the former head of the Cork Airport rescue team; and Caruso's favorites: "the beautiful red-haired lassies who cared for me at Mercy Hospital. They were so amazing. There's still five of them."[11]

Over the years, Caruso's website has spawned many new relationships and rekindled old ones. Reymond first met the Tiger pilot's youngest daughter in Tenerife, Spain, after Barbara Murray had posted that she'd be interested in connecting with anyone who had any information about the flight or her father. Similarly, Art Gilbreth contacted Carol Hansen in response to one of her posts, while she reunited with former colleagues at a Flying Tiger Line convention in San Diego after another ex-stewardess had reached out to her.

In 2014, when he learned that Fred and Ellen Caruso were planning to rent a car and tour southern France and northern Italy, Reymond reached out to Frey to see if he might be able to arrange a reunion with Walter Wunderlin, the carpenter who'd saved dozens of lives in 1962, at great risk to his own. The Swiss journalist said: "What better venue to celebrate the exploits of the *Celerina* and two of its heroic crew than the village after which the ship had been named?"[12] The five Swiss and two Americans met in Celerina, in the Engadin Valley near St. Moritz. They shared several meals together, took an excursion to the top of Muottas Muragi mountain, and reminisced. "The memory of you and the other desperate survivors in the life raft still makes me jittery today," said Wunderlin over dinner in the garden at Hotel Chesa Rosatsch. "Often times during the evening," noticed Monika Merki Frey, Peter's wife, "sturdy Walter had wet eyes."[13]

On June 8, 2018, in Vail, Colorado, Fred and Ellen Caruso first met me and my wife, Ellen, the second-youngest of Captain Murray's five children, who was just shy of 3 years old at the time of the ditching. Before dinner arrived, after a sip of his beer, the ex-paratrooper turned to his former pilot's daughter and said: "I want to thank you for what your father did that night. I wouldn't be here if it wasn't for him." Ellen shut her eyes, just for a moment. "Thank you for saying that."

Three months later, Caruso posted the following on his website: "This year on 9/23 it will be our 56th anniversary, which places the disaster some 20,454 days in the past. For the survivors who are still alive today, those 20,454 days are all extra days alive on this planet, thanks to Capt. John Murray and a lot of others."[14]

Since its launch, Caruso's website has averaged more than 28 views a day. That only 48 survived (and 28 died) suggests that Tiger 923 still resonates with those involved and is compelling to strangers. The cyberspace repository includes the *Saturday Evening Post* sketch of the raft; the photo of a daredevilish looking figure (a survivor or first responder) suspended 30 feet in the air between the deck of a Swiss freighter and a Canadian Navy helicopter; many photos of badly injured survivors being rushed to hospitals in Cork; and countless other touching stories and ironies. For instance, survivor Paul Stewart's father, Henry, kept a cardboard box of clippings and mementoes. His daughter inherited it; she bequeathed the box to her daughter. By the time Paul first saw the box, 55 years after the fact, the "real shocker" finding was the friendly postcard sent by the Swiss freighter's searchlight operator Markus Janka, which lay atop the terse U.S. Army telegram sent to Stewart's parents informing them their son was alive.[15]

Caruso and his website have helped to console scores of Tiger victims, including himself. "How many people get the chance to help hundreds of others not just find closure but joy, after decades of suffering?"[16]

While he knows his PTSD is a foe that won't ever relent, Caruso nonetheless now looks at Tiger 923, and life, through a different lens. "I never run out of cocktail party conversation. My wife tops the list."[17]

He'd not have gone to the University of Montana to study journalism, and thus not met Ellen in line during class registration, had he not been an Army journalist. That never would've happened had he not ditched. Nor would Caruso have honeymooned in Cork, bought an Irish cottage, gotten an Irish passport, adopted the name O'Caruso, or had 130 friends and family attend his and Ellen's 50th wedding anniversary in Cork—had an RAF helicopter not rushed him there on the afternoon of September 26, 1962. "Darn you, Eric, I try to be a curmudgeon, but you keep reminding me how the rewards have been fantastic."[18]

Tiger 923's survivors haven't been the only ones to benefit paradoxically from the tragedy. Family members have too. Including me.

This book is undergirded by nearly 1,700 interviews conducted over five and a half years; 94 in-person. By way of illustration, in 2017, Peter W. Frey very kindly flew over from Zurich just to meet with me for three days in Washington. In 2018, my wife, Ellen, and I flew to meet Fred and Ellen Caruso in Colorado; then Art and Susan Gilbreth in Oregon; then Raúl and Vicky Acevedo at Los Angeles International Airport. Raúl kindly braved the emotionally triggering venue in order to facilitate our challenging logistics. In 2019, I met all three of Lois and Dick Elander's children at the Santa Monica office Troy and Jill shared with their father. I'm honored to call many of the 117 people I've interviewed friends, even though I have yet to meet many of them in person. (We met on Skype or Zoom.) Our relationships have expanded beyond this book. While everyone I've met during my research has taught me something, four people have been my primary instructors.

According to experts, about nine out of ten Americans have suffered or will suffer at least one traumatic event during their lifetime.[19] Persistent post-traumatic stress is less common: about one in eight. Combat veterans, first responders and abuse victims are hit hardest: about 30 percent. Though not a "statistically significant sample," about three quarters of the Tiger 923 victims I interviewed still suffer from PTSD.

According to the logic of inferential statistics and common sense, Carol Hansen should have suffered considerably. She should still be suffering; at a minimum, one would think, being "jittery" the way rescuer Walter Wunderlin says he still feels all the time.

Yet I detected no jitters or dark flashes the three times we met. She was exactly as I'd imagined based on our many phone and email interviews: grateful, relaxed, unpretentious; a pure delight. Rather than dwell on sad memories, she was quick to pivot to talking about how her tiny French bulldog, Ruka, dominated both her pit bull, Brandy, and her Rottweiler, Angel. I'm not sure I've ever known a happier person.

"What's your secret?" I asked over the phone in the fall of 2020.

"I'm a bit crazy. But what's wrong with that?"[20]

She illustrates lesson 1: crazy is often our best coping skill. The former stewardess has taught me that to be a good steward of my life I sometimes need to embrace crazy.

Hansen loved both her parents and lived in a beautiful home in New Jersey: "Everything was going great."[21] Then, when she was 5, her father skipped out and she and her mother began an itinerant existence."We moved a lot but first into an abandoned shoe store across from a plant that emitted bad chemicals. I have asthma." Hansen laughed while recounting this. Suddenly uprooted from her friends, she endured muttering ostracism and the bratty light-skinned boys who'd ask, "What's it like riding a camel to school?" Then, while on layover in Cleveland, en route to Tiger stewardess training in Burbank, she got thrown by a horse, ended up in the hospital for nine days (a broken kneecap among her injuries), and was told she could no longer be a stewardess. (She sweet-talked the personnel manager.) Then, just before boarding Tiger 923, her best friend was killed by a hit-and-run driver while trying to help someone fix a flat along the New Jersey Turnpike. Then, after hours of anxiety, she hit the ocean at 120 mph in an aluminum plane. Then she frantically struggled to work the raft release and get off the plane before it sunk.

Then she was petrified because she couldn't find any of the five life rafts. Then she endured seven hours of horror in a badly overcrowded upside-down raft that seemed like it was going to capsize every few minutes; and when others were in the depths of despair, freezing and shivering, she'd say things like "Anyone want a cup of coffee?" Then she barely made it up the wildly whipping rope ladder to the deck of the rescue ship; then she dangled 30 feet in the air, at the mercy of the faltering grip of one man. Then she couldn't sleep for 90 hours because she had to stay alert to ensure a traumatized just-widowed teenager didn't leap to her death to join her husband. Then Hansen's husband was hit by a drunk driver. Minutes later, the man of her dreams died in her arms.

Yet somehow Hansen is an 80-year-old tower of strength and inexhaustible font of good cheer. I'm a very lucky man for having made her acquaintance in the summer of 2015, for she's reminded me how being a little crazy can sometimes be the key to happiness.

Friends tell me, "We're only as sick as our secrets." Storied indeed are the annals of the 82nd Airborne: what Sergeant York did in WWI and the "devils in baggy pants" did in WWII. But I wonder how many paratroopers have equaled Caruso in the courage department: first by facing his demons, then by sharing his battle with others, to help them slay their tormentors.

Fire had terrified Caruso ever since a neighbor's home nearly burned to the ground and the kids next door wore face masks to hide their gruesome scars and patchwork skin. So he was predisposed to the trauma of witnessing—nearly at arm's length—the gut-wrenching sequence of engines catching fire and failing from four miles up in a nighttime sky, 1,000 miles from land. Then he endured the same ditching-evacuation-raft ordeal as Hansen. Only his special circle of hell also included the vivid, searing memory of struggling with and being unable to save some scared guy who'd latched onto him for help.

Born Again Irish is an hilarious and at times disturbing window into the psychology of faith, family, and military recruiting. Caruso talks of how his "devout" Catholic great-aunt Elizabeth would charge a pretty penny to cast an evil eye, "overlook," or other hexes behind the parish priest's back; how his 4'8" tall godfather, Dominick, was never seen not in the presence of his two 4'10" Great Danes; and how the Army ensnared teenagers with *The Mark of the Man* promising an adventure of a lifetime and *Airborne!* taunting "Unless you thrive on excitement—rugged living and bullet-fast competition—better back out right now, because, buddy, this just isn't for you."[22] Caruso's lesson has inspired me to do a better job of facing and sharing my demons, understanding their lairs, and being much more honest about what I thrive on.

After Dr. John Warren Axline posted on Caruso's website how he'd treated Lois and Dick Elander in the U.K. and mentioned in passing how their "son Troy continues the Medical practice they shared for 19 years," I emailed the Elander Eye Clinic, introduced myself, and asked Troy if we might meet and he might help me reconstruct some of the events pertaining to Tiger 923.[23] He replied: "I had to re-read your email. We've met."[24] (I'd completely forgotten that Troy and my best friend attended medical school together and that we sat at the same dinner table at our friend's wedding reception.) The ophthalmologist taught me lesson 3: the right way to do things is often right before our eyes. Only by stumbling upon Troy three years into my research did I realize I'd gone about things all wrong: haphazardly, as opposed to systematically poring over every Caruso website post and reply from day 1, then running down leads.

Troy, his wife, Diane, and his siblings, Tom and Jill, have been of monumental help on the research front. First, they had assembled a Tiger 923 archive second only to Caruso's, which included not just newspaper clippings and magazine articles that few knew existed but many private letters, press releases, telegrams, photographs, and contemporaneous tape recordings, and even a custom outfit and the beret worn at the gala held in Lois and Dick's honor aboard the Canadian aircraft carrier. Second, in yet another striking coincidence, four months after Troy and I first spoke but before we met in person, while he and his siblings were cleaning out one of their father's remote storage cabinets five years after his passing, they found what may be the only extant copy of the U.S. Civil Aeronautics Board hearing transcript, which I'd expected to find at the National

Archives but was missing. The "official" 959 pages comprise a vital though not always dispositive source.

My father-in-law taught me lesson 4: in service of a good cause, it's often imperative to ignore convention. John Murray risked his life to defy President Truman's short-lived (and inhumane) executive order not to help defend the Holocaust survivors as they faced yet another round of butchery, persecution, and indifference. By flying humanitarian missions into war zones, he seemed to be flying in the face of conventional good sense. He gave generously to the widows of pilots he barely knew. Over the objections of his flight crew, he insisted they leave the most dangerous part of the plane prior to impact. He was the only one aboard who refused to brace before slamming into the concrete-like North Atlantic at 120 mph because were he to do so, he knew, would have severely impaired his ability to stick a 1-in-10-million "landing" on water. Then, defying any sort of conventional algorithm—despite a bad head gash, likely concussion, frightful conditions, and atrocious odds—he went back to look for and retrieve the half-submerged flashlight that was the main reason 48 people survived.

Yet by all accounts Murray passionately disdained being called a hero. He called Sam Nicholson a hero, Betty Sims a hero, Carol Hansen a hero, Joe Lewis a hero, Domenico Lugli a hero, Walter Wunderlin a hero, the Canadian helicopter pilots heroes. Murray's reticence wasn't the mark of false humility. It's the hallmark of true heroism.

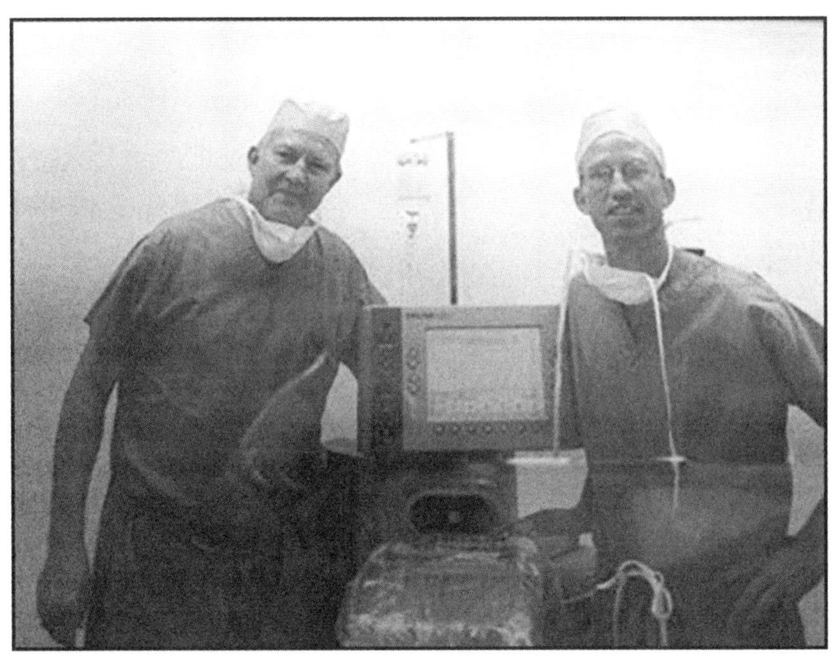

Like father, like son. (Top) Dick and Troy Elander operating together, circa 2000. (Bottom) Troy continuing the pro bono ethos his parents instilled via Orbis Flying Eye Hospital, in the DC-10 aircraft donated by FedEx, which acquired Flying Tiger Line in 1989. COURTESY ELANDER FAMILY.

July 18, 2014, Celerina, Switzerland: former *Celerina* deckhand Pierre-André Reymond (left) and former ship's carpenter Walter Wunderlin flank the man whose life they helped save: former paratrooper Fred Caruso. It was the first time the three saw each other in nearly 52 years. COURTESY GIANCARLO CATTANEO, PETER W. FREY, PIERRE-ANDRÉ REYMOND.

Acknowledgments

I'd like to thank the Murray family first. Getting to know and be adopted by this clan has been one of the highlights of my life. True to the memory of the Tiger 923 pilot, they are not showboats, but humble. They were all traumatized by Captain Murray's sudden and bitterly ironic demise, and the sadness has to some extent lived with them all for 54 years. As such, rather than insistent, they were hesitant that this story be told, despite their father's unfinished memoir being evidence of his unfulfilled desire. I thank them all for their courage; for recognizing the value of this story; and for their pivotal assistance in the form of so many interviews, letters, photographs, clippings, the memoir, and much more. In addition to Ellen, I must single out John, who devoted so much time to this project, including reading the manuscript many times, doing corroborating (and sometimes rebutting) research, and writing hundreds of incisive comments. No Murray asked me to add or delete a word. They wanted the facts to speak for themselves.

My birth family has also been really supportive, especially my wonderful, incredibly well-read mother, Mary Jean, the Lindner clan's resident Cold War historian (hired by the CIA in 1948), and my late, beloved father, Tad, who served as an Army private in Occupied Japan five years after the Flying Tigers first took to the skies against Imperial Japan in 1941.

Thank you, Fred Caruso. Without *Born Again Irish* and your website, this book would not have been possible. Thank you, Ellen Caruso, for playing such a vital role for more than half a century and for being such a gracious host in Eagle, Colorado.

Thank you, Pierre-André Reymond, for your prescient decision to bring both an 8-mm movie camera and a still-photo camera on your trip from Port Churchill to Antwerp, for your inspired use of the devices, for helping Fred sustain the Tiger 923 flame, and for always responding so quickly and graciously to my every request for information.

Thank you, Peter W. Frey, for realizing retirement is a silly construct, for being such an amazing journalist, for being so creative and resourceful, and for your warm friendship. Thank you, Monika Merki Frey, for being Peter's rock, and for also venturing to the U.S. for such an enjoyable visit.

And to complete the Swiss triumvirate: thank you, Walter Wunderlin. Though this story is replete with Homeric heroes, how you risked your life and knocked out your front teeth to save 51 desperate strangers in nightmarish conditions 58 years ago will forever resonate. Thank you for allowing Peter to interview you as my proxy, and for your many records and reminiscences.

Crossing the Rhine river at Laufenberg, Switzerland, and continuing north into Germany's Westerwald: thank you, Karen Eldred-Stephan. I marvel at the speed with which you were able to uncover so many rich sources, from your father's 1962 interview in a Cape Cod newspaper to his remarkable memoir, posthumously edited in 1987.

Thank you, survivors: Raúl Acevedo, Art Gilbreth, Carol Hansen, Juan Figueroa-Longo, Paul Stewart, Gordon Thornsberry, Sammy Vasquez, and everyone else aboard Tiger 923. You are all inspirations. Thank you, family members, especially Vicky Acevedo; Robert Burnett, Esq.; Diane, Tom, and Troy Elander; Susan Gilbreth; and the irreplaceable Jill Young.

Thank you, Tigers—of every stripe. This book would not have been possible without your passion, heroism, and dedication. Flying Tiger Line Pilots Association president and captain John Dickson beat the bushes on my behalf, which yielded myriad invaluable sources. Capt. Larry LeFever and Association historian Capt. George Gewehr have been unbelievably generous, insightful, and responsive. Thank you, also, Cynthia Bowles; Helena Burke; Lydia Rossi; Dawn Seymour-Adams; Marshall Meyers, Esq.; and captains Elgen Long, Gary Luccio, Doug Shaw, Al Silver, Starr Thompson, and Guy Van Herbruggen.

Thank you, aviation first responders, safety gurus, and related aerospace experts: Scott Dunham, Scott Fechnay, Alan Mulally, Harro

Ranter, Jim Record, Dick Rodriguez, and Steve Smith. Each of you has played a key role in this book.

Thank you to my army of gifted and generous artists, archivists, historians, journalists, librarians, photographers, and researchers: Bryan Azorsky, Kat Burns, Whitney Breeden, Adam Clymer, Marie Carpentieri, Giancarlo Cattaneo, Micheal Dabin, Michael Desmond, Ernst Frei, John Hammond, Lloyd Hand, Melissa Jones, Amy Kueffler, Rich LaMarca, Ed Leslie, Urs Mattle, Mark Mollan, Warren Nowlin, Rick O'Fee, Amy Reytar, Harry Rhoads Jr., Rodd Ross, Miguel Salcedo, Joe Schwarz, Robert Stonerock, Lisa Strattan, Sylvia Van Craen, Mike Walling, and Gordon Witkin. A special thank you to Joe Wight for his magnificent cover illustration and design assistance.

Thank you, Rowman & Littlefield! No author could hope for a better publisher-partner. CEO Jed Lyons saw this story's potential from day one and urged me to shelve two other projects. Though every other acquiring editor on the planet passed, Lyons Press Co-Editorial Director Gene Brissie took a chance. Neil Cotterill's exterior design work was fabulous, as was the interior layout by the coincidentally named Wanda Ditch. Mark Via's copyediting was superb, Project Editor Ellen Urban's production stewardship insightful and patient, and Candace Hyatt's index exacting and concise. Marketing and PR Director Shana Capozza was wonderful, as was Publicist Jessica Kastner.

Thank you, Lucinda Dyer, for being such an insightful advisor over the past nine years. Thank you, David Ebershoff and Robbie Goolrick, for your candid mentoring regarding the craft of writing. Thank you, Jeff Kleinman, for your savvy agenting. Thank you, Sam "Bruno Sammartino" Caggiula for being such a great tag-team PR partner. And thank you, Alexandra Shelley, for being such a kind, brilliant, and uncompromising editor.

Notes

Part I. Missing Planes

1. John D. Murray memoir (unfinished, undated). No page is cited here or elsewhere because few of the 167 typed sheets or handwritten notes are numbered or otherwise sequenced. The papers didn't have a title or table of contents.

Chapter 1. Trouble above the North Atlantic

1. "Aircraft Accident Report: The Flying Tiger Line, Inc., Lockheed 1049H, N 6923C, Ditching in the North Atlantic" (Washington: U.S. Civil Aeronautics Board, 1963), 16. All official times are Greenwich Mean; so, for example, when Tiger 923 left Gander, it was 1:09 p.m. in New York.
2. "In the Matter of: An Aircraft Accident Involving the Flying Tiger Line, Inc., Lockheed 1049H, N 6923C, Which Ditched in the Atlantic Ocean Approximately 500 Miles due West of Shannon, Ireland, September 23, 1962" (Washington: U.S. Civil Aeronautics Board, CSA Reporting Corporation, 1962), 59.
3. Larry LeFever interview, April 13, 2019. LeFever first soloed in 1957 at age 16 and received his license at 17. Flying Tiger Line, Inc. hired him in July 1962 as a Super Constellation copilot. He "checked out" as captain in 1966. He later flew DC-8s, DC-10s and 747s before retiring (from FedEx) in 2001, at 60.
4. "SAR [Search and Rescue] on Flying Tiger N 6923C" (Washington: U.S. Coast Guard, 1963), 229.
5. Interview with George Gewehr, Flying Tiger Pilots Association historian, March 2, 2016. Also see LeVerne J. Moldrem, *Tiger Tales: An Anecdotal History of the Flying Tiger Line* (Chelsea, MI: Sheridan Books, 1996), 82; Art Chin, *Anything Anytime, Anywhere: The Legacy of the Flying Tiger Line 1945–89* (Seattle: Tassels & Wings, 1993), 26–49; Guy Van Herbruggen, *Flying Tiger Memories* (Surrey, UK: Astral Horizon Aviation Press, 2019).
6. "In the Matter of," 86–87. It's impossible unequivocally to reconstruct the feathering, fire suppression, and engine shutdown sequence. Only two of the four eyewitnesses survived, and none is alive today. Captain LeFever has attempted to fill in some of the gaps, but it's only best guesses.
7. Murray memoir.
8. "Aircraft Accident Report," Supplemental Data, i–ii.
9. See www.aviation.safety.net.
10. One hundred eleven out of 556, or 19.96 percent. Interview with Harro Ranter, Aviation Safety Network CEO, April 28, 2018. Also see www.aviation.safety.net.

11. "Sea Search Abandoned," *Eugene Register-Guard*, March 23, 1962.
12. "Plane, 107 Sought," *Evening Independent* (St. Petersburg, FL), March 16, 1962; "2 State Soldiers on Lost Airliner," *Milwaukee Sentinel*, March 17, 1962.
13. See, e.g., Ernst Frei, Urs Mattle, and Katsuhiko Tokunaga, *Super Constellation Backstage* (Zurich: AS Verla, 2014), 9.
14. www.lockheedmartin.com/us/100years/stories/vip-planes.
15. The L-1049H wasn't equipped with a voice data recorder in the cockpit, nor the latest, *fully* automatic deicers, on the exterior. But Murray was no Luddite. All "innovations" weren't helpful, at least not in their early incarnations. For instance, former CAB and NTSB aircraft accident investigator Dick Rodriguez said his work was often more *difficult* when a plane had a black box, because, as it ran nonstop, it was filled with "coughing, etc." Rodriguez interviews, September 25 and October 2, 2017. Also, analogous to how it can be dangerous in 2020 to set a car on cruise control, in 1962 it could be dangerous to assume a deicer was doing its job properly. Seasoned pilots relied more on "stick-and-rudder" flying than technology.
16. *Detroit News*, September 24, 1962.
17. Sammy Vasquez, interview by Peter W. Frey, October 30, 2011.
18. The "923" in Tiger 923 came from the tail number: "N6923C." That the ditching occurred on September 23 was pure coincidence.
19. Robert Calvin Eldred, *Bob's Story* (unpublished, Louise Westwood Eldred, ed., 1987), 45.
20. "An Exclusive Interview," *Cape Codder*, November 1, 1962, 1.
21. "An Exclusive Interview," 1.
22. Richard Elander's 79-minute audio memoir, recorded October 31, 1962, tape #1 (of 9 cassettes).
23. He wasn't wearing his "Dewey for President" necktie because Al Silver wasn't his navigator. "I was your typical Jewish liberal from Brooklyn. John was an Irish Catholic from Chicago. Though we seldom agreed on anything he was always polite when arguing, treating me as his equal, even when he was my superior by many years and several ranks. He was one of the nicest men I'd ever met." Silver interview, April 13, 2017.

Murray dressed neatly and professionally, but no one ever called him dapper. Once, when piloting a flight that was approaching departure time, he couldn't be found. A search-and-rescue effort ensued. His legs were spotted in the Newark parking lot, jutting out from under his Ford. He was trying to reattach his muffler with a coat hanger. When Murray shimmied out, his uniform was splotched with gunk and grime. Though his copilot suggested he take a few minutes to clean up, Murray couldn't finish his repairs, depart on time, and tidy up, so he slid back under the chassis and finished his work.

When he stepped aboard, looking like he'd been working at a muffler shop all day, his passengers did double takes, wondering if the state of the pilot's clothes was any indication of the state of the equipment or his preparedness. But the flight proceeded on time, without a hitch.

Shortly after the incident, at one of the pilots union meetings Murray rarely attended because he felt they were often just excuses to bitch, moan, and gossip—in absentia, he was nominated and unanimously elected as chairman of the union's newly created Uniform Committee. LeFever interview, June 2, 2016.

24. John P. Murray interview, July 27, 2015.

25. Murray memoir. It was a miracle he survived. With his teacher sprawled on the ground, unconscious and bleeding profusely, the quick-thinking student slogged his way through thick snow to the closest road and flagged down a passing motorist, who drove Murray to the hospital.

26. *Detroit News*, September 24, 1962, 2-A; Ricky-Dale Calhoun, "Arming David: The Haganah's Illegal Arms Procurement Network in the United States 1945–1949," *Journal of Palestinian Studies*, Vol. XXXVI, No. 4 (Summer 2007), 22; Murray memoir.

27. Murray memoir.

28. Composite of interviews with Cynthia Bowles, May 8, 2017, and John P. Murray, July 27, 2015; also see Moldrem, 207.

29. John P. Murray, letter to his daughter, Maureen, March 20, 2008.

30. John P. Murray interview, September 11, 2020.

31. Murray memoir.

32. https://www.cbc.ca/news/canada/newfoundland-labrador/gander-airport-mural-significant-1.5253318; also see www.ganderiaport.com.

33. Art Gilbreth interview, June 11, 2017.

34. Carol Hansen (neé Gould) interviews: February 26 and March 14, 2016; interview by Peter W. Frey, November 1, 2011.

35. Hansen interview, November 21, 2016.

36. Fred Caruso interview, May 21, 2019.

37. Similar to Tom Hanks' hatred as a FedEx manager, in *Cast Away*. So it's no wonder FedEx acquired Flying Tiger Line, Inc., in 1989.

38. Wayne G. Johnson, ed., *Chennault's Flying Tigers* (Paducah, KY: Turner Publishing, 1996), 199.

39. Chennault called his squadron "the All-Volunteer Group" (aka "AVG"), but Madame Chiang Kai-shek referred to the AVG pilots as "my boys, my tigers." Gewehr interview, May 4, 2017.

40. The Super Constellation's landing gear was painted flat black so as not to reflect moonlight. Marshall Meyers, Esq., interview, April 19, 2020.

41. Gewehr interview, August 23, 2018.

42. Gewehr interview, July 3, 2019.

43. LeFever interview, September 19, 2019.

44. Murray memoir. Also, as regards what "only" 30 Army paratroopers were capable of, in WWI, six, led by Sgt. Alvin York killed or captured 132 German soldiers and disabled 12 machine-gun nests. The most recent source is Douglas V. Mastriano, *Alvin York: A New Biography of the Hero of the Argonne* (Lexington: University of Kentucky Press, 2014).

45. Murray memoir.

46. "In the Matter of," 59; "CAB Accident Investigation Report: Crash Spurs Ditching Recommendations," *Aviation Week and Space Technology*, January 6, 1964, 96; "Philadelphia Paratrooper, 18, Aboard Downed Plane," *Evening Bulletin* (Philadelphia), September 24, 1962.

47. "In the Matter of," 220–21.
48. He was supposed to be on the Tiger flight that disappeared after departing Guam in March 1962.
His friend Larry LeFever tells of another near-miss. "Hard Luck Sam bought a Harley-Davidson, and he loved that bike. One day, he flew around a curve and there was a dog smack in the middle of the road. He did all he could to avoid the dog but he plowed into it, killing it, on the way to a nasty wipeout into a ditch, beside the road. He was out cold, in bad shape, and his beloved Harley was wrecked. When he came to, a priest was beside him, on one knee. Hard Luck murmured: 'No . . . not the Last Rites . . .' The priest replied: 'You just killed my dog, you son of a bitch!'" Interview, September 15, 2017.
49. "In the Matter of," 47.
50. LeFever interview, June 24, 2020. (As with the feathering and fire suppressing, the record is spotty.)
51. Vasquez interview by Frey, October 30, 2011.
52. "In the Matter of," 47, 809–15.
53. LeFever interview, June 24, 2020.
54. Gilbreth interview, November 18, 2017. Though unsettling for the uninitiated, orange flames and smoke were routine prior to an L-1049H departure, by-products of oil being heated by the engine.
55. Frederick Caruso, *Born Again Irish: A Story of Disaster at Sea, the Joy of Ireland, and the Vortex of Fate* (Eagle, CO: CGI Books, 2007), 35.
56. During one of his two interviews with Peter W. Frey, retired paratrooper Sammy Vasquez talked about a class where only 18 out of 130 volunteers (13.85%) graduated Jump School. Given the fact that guys like Vasquez and Gilbreth were fit, tough, and self-selecting, that's quite a failure rate. "It was a rough course, for seven months. It was hot, and miserable." Vasquez interview by Frey, October 31, 2011. Corroborated by interview with Robert A. Stonerock, 82nd Airborne Division Association historian, April 5, 2018.
57. Gilbreth interview, June 11, 2018.
58. "Gathering Storm": The Philly riots of '64," Will Bunce, *Philadelphia Inquirer*, August, 2014.
59. Raúl Acevedo interview, June 29, 2015.
60. "5 Southlanders Aboard Crashed Plane Rescued: Relatives of Army Men Receive Word They Are Among Survivors," *Los Angeles Times*, September 25, 1962.
61. Acevedo interview, July 5, 2015.
62. "H.M.C.S. *Bonaventure*, at Sea, 26 September 1962." (Recorded by unnamed member of the crew, much is excerpted in later media accounts.)
63. "Lois was the original stacker. She wore pounds of bracelets on her wrists years before doing so was de rigueur." Jill Young interview, August 13, 2019.
64. Hansen interview, June 20, 2016. Also see Walter Hamma, "Always a Heroine: Her Name Forgotten, but Deeds Remembered," *Herald-News* (Passaic, NJ), September 23, 1968.
65. Hansen interview, August 8, 2019.

66. For an excellent overview, see Katherine LaGrave, "From Stewardess to Flight Attendant: 80 Years of Sophistication and Sexism," *Condé Nast Traveler*, March 8, 2017. For a fuller treatment, see Kathleen M. Berry, *Femininity in Flight: A History of Flight Attendants* (Durham, NC: Duke University Press, 2007).
67. Airline founder and CEO Robert Prescott changed the Tiger policy in 1966, when WWII ace and Tiger pilot Dick Rossi told him he wanted to marry Tiger stewardess Lydia Cowgill. Gewehr interview, June 23, 2020.
68. Hansen interview, August 16, 2020.
69. Hansen interview, July 25, 2019.
70. Hansen interview, June 25, 2016.
71. It wasn't just the women who felt this way. Capt. Al Silver, one of Murray's best friends, called some of his male colleagues "pigs." Silver interview, March 31, 2017. (He'd "cycled through the seats": as a Tiger navigator, copilot, then pilot.) On the other hand, one of the industry's first female commercial pilots was a Tiger: Capt. Diane Bixby, aka "Miss Flying Tiger." Moldrem, 64, 65.
72. Hansen interview, October 1, 2020.
73. Hansen interview, February 7, 2018.
74. Hansen interview, February 7, 2018.
75. Caruso interview, June 27, 2016.
76. Caruso, 31.
77. Caruso interview, March 8, 2016.
78. Gilbreth interview with Peter W. Frey, October 31, 2011.
79. Caruso interview, April 1, 2017.
80. Caruso interview, December 4, 2015.
81. Caruso interview, April 7, 2016.
82. Caruso interview, May 9, 2017.
83. Murray memoir.
84. "Crash Survivors Reach Antwerp," *Times* (London), September 29, 1962.
85. Gewehr interview, April 9, 2017.
86. "In the Matter of," 133.
87. LeFever interview, June 24, 2020.
88. "CAB Accident Investigation," 104.
89. That is, what they'd need to make it to Frankfurt, plus the standard cushion for unexpected contingencies. While *pound* seems an odd unit of measurement for fuel, in aviation, weight is a more important metric than volume. The origin of the term "Grandma's gas," denoting reserve fuel, is apocryphal. Perhaps it's traceable back to some early aviator who siphoned fuel from his grandmother's Model T.
90. "SAR on Flying Tiger N 6923C" is the source of all cockpit communication.

Chapter 2. Anything That Could Go Wrong

1. Ranter interview, April 29, 2018; www.aviation.safety.net.
2. The Military Air Transport Service was a unit of the Air Force's logistical division. MATS decided when to use an Air Force plane versus a charter, how much to pay the contractor, etc. Composite of interviews with Joe Schwarz, October 2, 2017, and Hansen, July 18, 2016.

3. "In the Matter of," 87; Murray memoir.
4. Murray memoir.
5. "In the Matter of," 87.
6. Though "I am sorry, John, I goofed" hardly seems commensurate with the gravity of the situation, it's very well corroborated. See, e.g., "In the Matter of," 119.
7. "In the Matter of," 120, 247.
8. Federal Aviation Regulation 93.3 accords a pilot's "feel for the plane" the presumption of propriety over any other regulation.
9. Murray memoir.
10. Murray memoir.
11. The official term for "ditching."
12. Interview with Peter W. Frey, November 2, 2017. Also see "An Atlantic First," *Philadelphia Inquirer*, September 25, 1962; Paul Bertorelli, "Ditching Myths Torpedoed!" last revised August 19, 1999, www.equipped.com/ditchingmyths; and Olaf Lindenau and Thomas Rung, *Review of Transport Aircraft Ditching Accidents* (Stuttgart, Germany, KRASH Users' Seminar, June 2009).
13. "In the Matter of," 521.
14. Caruso interview, July 1, 2016. Also see https://flyingtiger923.com/2012/07/08/peter-foley-tells-the-world-of-terror-and-survival/.
15. Eldred, 22; 55.
16. Caruso, 31.
17. "In the Matter of," 221.
18. "In the Matter of," 583.
19. "In the Matter of," 792–93.
20. "In the Matter of," 595.
21. Elander memoir (tape #1).
22. Elander memoir (tape #1).
23. "In the Matter of," 89–90.
24. Of six permutations, the "best loss" was the 2 and 3 combination. Tied for worst were the 1 and 2 and the 3 and 4 combinations.
25. Murray memoir.
26. Murray memoir.
27. According to Dick Rodriguez, crashes usually involved an inscrutable mix of "acts of God" and "human error." It was extremely rare for human error to be the lone cause. Rodriguez interview, October 2, 2017.

Retired Coast Guard officer Michael Walling fleshes out many of the forensic challenges in his terrific book *In the Event of a Water Landing* (Middletown, DE: Cutter Publishing, 2015).

28. Each "level" equated to 100 feet.
29. Hansen interview, June 25, 2016.
30. "Good Show," *The MATS Flyer*, February 1963, 16.
31. "SAR on Flying Tiger N 6923C," 20.
32. https://flyingtigersavg.com/avg-aces/. Rossi was credited with 6.25 kills in Burma.
33. Hansen interview, July 11, 2019.

34. LeFever interview, October 4, 2020.
35. "In the Matter of," 573, 594; also see "An Exclusive Interview," 3.
36. Hansen interview, March 17, 2016.
37. Hansen interview, March 17, 2016.
38. "An Exclusive Interview," 2.
39. Eldred, 21.
40. Hansen interview, June 20, 2016.
41. Hansen interview, January 4, 2018.
42. Hansen interview, April 25, 2017.
43. Acevedo interview, April 21, 2018.
44. Caruso interview, June 27, 2015.
45. Elander memoir (tape #2).
46. Murray memoir.
47. Murray memoir.
48. Murray memoir.
49. "In the Matter of," 314.
50. Composite of interviews with Acevedo, April 16, 2019; Gilbreth, November 3 and 8, 2017; Hansen, June 6, 2016; and Caruso, January 1, 2019.
51. "In the Matter of," 783.
52. "In the Matter of," 525.
53. Hansen interview, July 6, 2015.
54. Hansen interview, January 4, 2018.
55. Hansen interview, February 7, 2016.
56. Hansen interview, July 14, 2016. Also see Senior Master Sergeant Peter A. Foley, "We Ditched at Sea," *Saturday Evening Post*, November 17, 1962.
57. Murray memoir.
58. Composite of interviews with Acevedo, June 22 and 29, 2016, and Hansen, June 23 and 26, 2016.

Chapter 3. Fixin' to Die

1. Its lethality hasn't lessened over time. For instance, the *Andrea Gail* (of *The Perfect Storm* fame) sank in the North Atlantic in 1991.
2. See "Anxious Area Families Await Life-or-Death News," *Philadelphia Inquirer*, September 25, 1962.
3. Murray memoir.
4. Hansen interview, November 21, 2016.
5. *Cork Examiner*, September 26, 1962.
6. "In the Matter of," 563.
7. Murray memoir.
8. "Aircraft Accident Report," 8.
9. Murray memoir.
10. Steve Smith interview, February 23, 2017. Though the senior air traffic controller has spent most of his 25-year career in the field, keeping the skies above Maryland, Virginia, and the District of Columbia safe, he's also worked at FAA headquarters, helping to improve the DC area's traffic management.

11. Murray memoir.
12. Murray memoir; Pierre-André Reymond interview, August 1, 2019.
13. The typical glide slope was 3 degrees. Murray memoir. Though counterintuitive, it is dangerous not only if the plane is going too fast in its final approach, but also too slowly. The "glide angle" is key. (It's akin to how a precise Acapulco cliff dive from 30 meters, traveling at 50 mph, can be far less painful than a bellyflop, from 5 feet, traveling at 10.)
14. "In the Matter of," 111.
15. "In the Matter of," 793.
16. "In the Matter of," 594.
17. "In the Matter of," 588.
18. "In the Matter of," 780–83.
19. Paul Stewart affidavit, 2: "The Plane Crack Up." Courtesy Peter W. Frey.
20. Hansen interview, June 27, 2016.
21. "In the Matter of," 530.
22. "In the Matter of," 754.
23. Caruso, 43. Slightly amended during Caruso interview, March 10, 2017.
24. Caruso interviews, July 1, 13, and 20, 2016.
25. Caruso interview, March 10, 2017.
26. Gilbreth interview, November 8, 2017.
27. Elander memoir (tape #2).
28. "An Exclusive Interview," 2; also see Paul Sargent Hines, "Crash Landing in the North Atlantic," *Man's Magazine*, March 1963.
29. Hansen interview, June 26, 2016.
30. Hansen interview, July 4, 2016.
31. Acevedo interview, November 30, 2017.
32. Acevedo interview, November 5, 2018.
33. Acevedo interview, June 29, 2015.
34. "48 Survive: Heroism Marked Crash-Landing in Atlantic," *Seattle Daily Times*, September 25, 1962.
35. "Heartbreak Ends Day's Wait By Delaware Valley Families," *Philadelphia Inquirer*, September 25, 1962; "Anxious Area Families Await Life-or-Death News," *Philadelphia Inquirer*, September 24, 1962.
36. "Local Woman Among Missing," *Philadelphia Daily News*, September 24, 1962.
37. Reymond interview, August 1, 2016.
38. "In the Matter of," 684.
39. "CAB Accident Investigation," 104.
40. Murray memoir.
41. "In the Matter of," 95; Gilbreth interview, October 27, 2020.
42. "Good Show," 17.
43. "Good Show," 17.
44. Hansen interview by Frey, November 1, 2011. The veteran Swiss journalist said, "It's so interesting that there was no panic." Many survivors corroborate Hansen's account, including Dr. Elander (tape #1), and Lieutenant Colonel Dent ("In the Matter of," 573).

45. A synoptic composite of a dozen slightly different versions of his final PA announcement. See, e.g., https://flyingtiger923.com/2013/11/15/forgiven-disaster-carol-hansen-and-the-ditching-of-flying-tiger-923/.
46. Murray memoir.
47. Murray memoir.
48. Hansen interview, April 20, 2018.
49. "In the Matter of," 347.
50. Acevedo interview, November 5, 2018. See "We Faced Death in the Atlantic," in "Family Weekly" supplement in *Asbury Park Press*, December 2, 1962.
51. "In the Matter of," 464.
52. Gordon Thornsberry interview, July 25, 2020.
53. Murray memoir.

Part II. Missing Life Rafts

1. Murray memoir.

Chapter 4. Trouble in the North Atlantic

1. "An Exclusive Interview," 2.
2. Murray memoir.
3. "We Faced Death in the Atlantic."
4. "An Exclusive Interview," 2.
5. Caruso interview, March 10, 2017.
6. "In the Matter of," 361.
7. "In the Matter of," 527.
8. *Middleton (NY) Times-Herald*, September 25, 1962.
9. "In the Matter of," 508; 599–600.
10. "In the Matter of," 599.
11. Hansen interview, March 3, 2016.
12. Acevedo interview, July 6, 2015.
13. Gilbreth interview, November 8, 2017. See "Here Is My Story of Flying Tiger 923, by Art Gilbreth, Survivor," at https://flyingtiger923.com/2012/02/19/out-of-body-experience-guides-trooper/.
14. Murray typically called it a "torch," not a flashlight, as in Ireland and England. Murray memoir; "In the Matter of," 156.
15. Credible official reports cite temperatures between 44 and 52 degrees (at various points and times).
16. "In the Matter of," 352.
17. "In the Matter of," 367.
18. "In the Matter of," 397–98.
19. Vasquez interview with Frey, October 31, 2011.
20. "In the Matter of," 471–72.
21. "In the Matter of," 601–2.
22. "An Exclusive Interview," 2.

23. Hansen interview, August 20, 2019.
24. Elander memoir (tape #2). Also see "HMCS *Bonaventure* - Operations 1962" (anonymous author: Canada Aviation and Space Museum, Ottawa.)
25. "In the Matter of," 531.
26. "In the Matter of," 574–75.

Chapter 5. Invisible

1. "The navigator's remarkably accurate position plotted at the time of trouble showed three hours and thirty minutes to Iceland. This estimate later proved to have been within one minute." Murray memoir.
2. Murray memoir.
3. "Rescuing a Super Constellation in the North Atlantic Ocean, 1962" 1–2, at www.navigate-necesse-est.ch.
4. Walter Wunderlin, interview by Peter W. Frey, July 27, 2017.
5. Hansen interview, March 3, 2016. (While not yet aboard, she heard all about it from Nicholson during their five days together at sea, in Antwerp, and en route to New York.)
6. Vasquez interview by Frey, October 30, 2011.
7. Vasquez interview by Frey, October 31, 2011.
8. "Plane Survivors in Ireland," *New York Daily News*, September 26, 1962. Also see *Detroit Free Press*, September 27, 1962; *Man's Magazine*, March 1963.
9. Caruso interview, December 4, 2015.
10. Fred Caruso's letter to his parents, written aboard the *Celerina*, dated September 24, 1962. The letter he'd written aboard Tiger 923 on September 23 was lost at sea.
11. Caruso interview, December 4, 2015.
12. Caruso interview, April 4, 2016.
13. Caruso interview, May 9, 2017.
14. Hansen interview, July 6, 2015.
15. Hansen interview, August 29, 2019.
16. Hansen interview, November 21, 2016.
17. "In the Matter of," 531.
18. Hansen interview, January 3, 2017.
19. Other reports refer to it as an "under-slip." See, e.g., "Pilot Describes His First 'Ditch' in 24 Years," from clipping of unidentifiable provenance courtesy of Elander family that reads only "From Our Special Correspondent: Antwerp, Friday [September 28, 1962]."
20. Hansen interview, August 20, 2019.
21. "In the Matter of," 574.
22. "An Exclusive Interview," 4.
23. Acevedo interview, June 24, 2015.
24. Acevedo interview, July 6, 2015.
25. Acevedo interview, June 24, 2015.
26. Gilbreth interview, November 8, 2017.
27. Caruso interview, April 27, 2017.
28. Caruso, 48.

29. Caruso interview, March 8, 2016.
30. Elander memoir (tape #2).
31. Lee Belser, "U.S. Major Describes Ditching of Airliner," *New York Journal-American*, September 29, 1962; also see "In the Matter of," 604.
32. "Fire Breaks Out aboard Plane's Rescue Ship," *New York Daily News*, September 26, 1962.
33. Hansen interview, May 17, 2016.
34. "In the Matter of," 531.
35. "In the Matter of," 531.
36. "In the Matter of," 534.
37. Murray memoir.
38. Murray memoir.
39. Murray memoir.
40. Given the darkness and chaos, it's not surprising Murray said, "I couldn't identify this woman." See "In the Matter of," 157. She's not *named* in any of the extant records. However, based on all the facts, forensics, affidavits, hearing testimony, and by process of elimination, it had to be Helga Groves.
41. Murray memoir.
42. Vasquez interview with Frey, October 30, 2011.
43. Hansen interview, April 20, 2018.

Chapter 6. All We Had Was Hope

1. Reymond interview, August, 2018.
2. For a 2:27 clip, see: https://www.navigare-necesse-est.ch/sea-stories-en195.html (Reymond's in it). Reymond interview, August 1, 2018.
3. "Georg Stöckli: Ship Radio Operator Adds New Insight to Rescue," *Strom & See* [*Current & Sea*], October 1962, 60 (translated from German by Karen Eldred-Stephan), https://flyingtiger923.com/2013/06/13/ship-radio-operator-georg-stockli-adds-new-insight/. Also see Michael G. Walling, *In the Event of a Water Landing* (Cutter, 2010); Michael O'Toole, *Cleared for Disaster: Ireland's Most Horrific Air Crashes* (Cork: Mercier, 2006); Edward E. Leslie, *Desperate Journeys, Abandoned Souls: True Stories of Castaways and Other Survivors* (Boston: Houghton Mifflin, 1988).
4. "In the Matter of," 574.
5. Caruso, 47.
6. Elander memoir (tape #2).
7. "In the Matter of," 702.
8. Hansen interview, March 7, 2016.
9. Hansen interview with Frey, November 1, 2011.
10. Caruso, 52
11. Hansen interview with Frey, November 1, 2011.
12. Caruso, 52.
13. Murray memoir.
14. Hansen interview, September 9, 2019.
15. Hansen interview, February 11, 2016.

16. Acevedo interview, June 24, 2015.
17. Murray memoir.
18. Acevedo interview, June 22, 2020.
19. Vasquez interview with Frey, October 30, 2011.
20. "Eyewitness Depicts Rescue Saga: Flares Spot Rafts in Pitch-Black Sea," *Philadelphia Inquirer*, September 25, 1962.
21. "'Specks' in a Foamy Sea: Incredible Rescue Story," *New York Herald-Tribune*, September 25, 1962.
22. *Times* (London), September 25, 1962. Also see *Seattle Daily Times*, September 24, 1962.
23. *New York Herald-Tribune*, September 25, 1962.
24. *Times* (London), September 25, 1962. Also see *Seattle Daily Times*, September 24, 1962.
25. *Times* (London), September 25, 1962. Also see *Seattle Daily Times*, September 24, 1962.
26. https://flyingtiger923.com/2012/08/07/just-trying-to-do-the-right-thing/.
27. See, e.g., "SAR on Flying Tiger N 6923C," 40, 44, 51, and especially how the exact same "Facts" on page 229 became "Apparent Facts" on page 203, then "Apparent Facts based on limited information" on page 156.
28. "SAR on Flying Tiger N 6923C," 53.
29. "SAR on Flying Tiger N 6923C," 26.
30. Interview with Robert Burnett, Esq., March 16, 2016.
31. Burnett interview, October 3, 2017.
32. Hansen interview, January 3, 2017.
33. "An Exclusive Interview," 2.
34. Elander memoir (tape # 2).
35. Acevedo interview, June 24, 2016.
36. Acevedo interview, April 26, 2018.
37. Hansen interview, August 21, 2019.
38. The reported waves varied more than the temperature, from a low of 15 to 20 feet (Captain Murray) to as high as 50 feet (Major Benson). Both could have been accurate, just recorded at different times.
39. "Good Show," 17.
40. Walter Wunderlin's letter to his parents (written in Antwerp, September 29, 1962), 3. Translation from German courtesy of Peter W. Frey.
41. Wunderlin letter, 1.
42. LeFever interview, September 15, 2017.
43. "SAR on Flying Tiger N 6923C," 21; and basic arithmetic, given the fact that the swells were rolling in every nine seconds or so and Murray had reached the raft an hour earlier.
44. Larry LeFever is the source of Murray's thinking (August 23, 2020 interview). Some accounts list the raft occupancy at 25, but most say 20. In fact, the L-1049H Super Constellation operating manual says rafts "can be 10, 20 or 25-man" ("In the Matter of," Exhibit 4-B).

45. Art Gilbreth said in a June 11, 2018, interview, "Eveready [the battery maker] missed its chance for a great ad." See, e.g., Foley.
46. Elander memoir (tape #3).
47. Richard O'Fee interview, June 6, 2020. Formerly with the U.K. Defence Intelligence Staff (roughly the equivalent of the Pentagon's Defense Intelligence Agency), the NATO expert is especially knowledgeable as regards Soviet theater nuclear capabilities and the U.S. Air Force capabilities. Also see Seymour Topping, "Kennedy Assailed. Moscow Asserts Bid to Call Up Reserves Is Aggressive Step," *New York Times*, September 12, 1962.
48. Hansen interview, October 22, 2019.
49. Domenico Lugli, "Report Concerning the Rescue of 51 Passengers from a Super-constellation Ditched in North Atlantic" (composed and signed "At Sea September 25th 1962," later submitted to and stamped by the Swiss Maritime Office, in Basel, on October 3), 3.
50. Lugli, 3.

Chapter 7. Speechless

1. Synthesized from the 41 telegrams received by the U.S. Coast Guard (stamped "Priority," "Operational Immediate," or "Emergency"), see "SAR on Flying Tiger N 6923C," 239–79.
2. Hansen interview, May 12, 2017. Also see "'Specks' in a Foamy Sea."
3. Elander memoir (tape #5).
4. Murray memoir.
5. Murray memoir.
6. Murray memoir.
7. Hansen interview, August 20, 2019.
8. Elander memoir (tape #5).
9. "Good Show," 17.
10. Hansen interview, May 3, 2016.
11. Caruso interview, March 14, 2016.
12. Hansen interview, July 4, 2015. Also see "Plane Survivors—Their Grim Story," *New York Herald-Tribune*, September 27, 1962.
13. Lugli, 1.
14. Reymond interview, August 3, 2018.
15. "An Exclusive Interview," 2.
16. Hansen interview, July 11, 2018.
17. Hansen interview, June 7, 2017.
18. Lugli, 1.
19. Wunderlin letter, 2.
20. Reymond interview, August 1, 2019.
21. Hansen interview, June 25, 2016.
22. "Rescuing a Super Constellation," 2.
23. Wunderlin letter, 2.
24. Hansen interview, February 7, 2018.
25. Wunderlin interview with Frey, July 27, 2017.
26. Reymond interview, August 12, 2019. Also see "Rescuing a Super Constellation," 3.

27. "The Story of Major and Mrs. R. Elander." Unattributed 4-page incident report prepared by someone aboard the HCMS *Bonaventure*. Courtesy Elander family.
28. Wunderlin interview with Frey; Reymond interview, June 5, 2017.
29. Caruso interview, March 14, 2016.
30. Caruso interview, May 18, 2017.
31. Elander memoir (tape #5).
32. Caruso interview, May 18, 2017.
33. Gilbreth interview with Frey, October 31, 2011.
34. Gilbreth interview, November 8, 2017.
35. Gilbreth interview with Frey, October 31, 2011.
36. https://flyingtiger923.com/2012/07/26/thank-god-im-alive/. Caruso's letter to his parents, dated September 24, 1962, was printed in full in the *Daily Mail*, September 27, 1962, 3.
37. Reymond's "Sea Story" (#69), entitled "Captain John Murray," 1; at www.navigare-necesse-est.ch.
38. Also see Reymond's translation (from Italian) of Captain LC Lugli and Chief Engineer Anthony Neumann, "Reminiscences and Complications of a Rescue at Sea," *Nautica*, Vol. 528, April 2006, 3.
39. After reading the account in a German maritime periodical, Karen Eldred-Stephan concluded that "the success of the first phase of the rescue operation was principally thanks to the *Celerina*'s radio operator." See https://flyingtiger923.com/2013/06/13/ship-radio-operator-georg-stockli-adds-new-insight/.
40. Reymond interview, August 12, 2018.
41. Reymond interview, August 2, 2018.
42. Murray memoir.
43. Reymond's "Captain John Murray," 1.
44. Wunderlin letter, 3.
45. Gilbreth interview, June 11, 2018.
46. "An Exclusive interview," 3.
47. Elander memoir (tape #5).
48. Elander memoir (tape #5).
49. "Georg Stöckli," 60.
50. Caruso, 56.
51. Caruso letter, 4.
52. Vasquez interview with Frey, October 30, 2011.
53. Caruso interview, June 27, 2015.
54. Caruso letter, 4. While the syntax is a bit odd ("how much my parents think of me" versus "how much you think of me"), this is how the actual letter reads. Plus, Caruso wasn't in the best frame of mind.
55. Reymond interview, June 5, 2017.
56. Wunderlin interview, August 20, 2020.
57. Acevedo interview, November 30, 2017.
58. Elander memoir (tape #5).
59. Wunderlin letter, 4.
60. Hansen interview, November 21, 2016.
61. Wunderlin letter, 3–4.

Part III. Missing Persons

1. Murray memoir.

Chapter 8. I Don't Know What We'll Do Without Her

1. The media mistakenly reported that a fire had broken out on the ship, though the Mayday pertained to the burns incurred on the raft. "Air Crash Rescue Ship Sends Out SOS for Help: 2 Reported Burned as Swiss Vessel Sails for Belgium with 44 Disaster Survivors," *Los Angeles Times* (unattributed), September 26, 1962; "Fire Breaks Out."
2. "SAR on Flying Tiger N 6923C," 43.
3. Belser.
4. "Pilot's Wife: 'Wonderful, Wonderful,'" *Long Island Press*, September 25, 1962.
5. *Detroit News*, September 24, 1962.
6. John P. Murray interview, January 21, 2020.
7. Implied by their reporting of their interview with Dorothy, coupled with the fact that a *Press* reporter for sure broke the news to another Long Islander. See Rhoda Amon, "Mother's Vigil at the Phone—And Finally, the Good News," *Long Island Press*, September 25, 1962.
8. John P. Murray interview, October 5, 2020.
9. See Bob Dubill, "Air Victims' Families Flood M'Guire Base with Frantic Calls," *Philadelphia Inquirer*, September 24, 1962; "Relatives Flood McGuire with Calls for Names of Passengers on Plane," *Evening Bulletin* (Philadelphia), September 24, 1962.
10. "SAR on Flying Tiger N 6923C," 179.
11. Telegram courtesy of Tom Elander. The telegram to Gordon Thornsberry's parents had the exact same wording.
12. Thornsberry interview, July 28, 2020.
13. Acevedo interview, June 24, 2015; and see "5 Southlanders."
14. Acevedo interview, July 6, 2015.
15. Acevedo interview, June 24, 2015.
16. Belser.
17. Belser.
18. Karen Eldred-Stephan interview, August 23, 2020.
19. Elander memoir (tape #3).
20. Gilbreth interview with Frey, October 31, 2011.
21. Gilbreth interview, November 8, 2017.
22. "SAR on Flying Tiger N 6923C," 12.
23. "In the Matter of," 749.
24. "More Survivors Seen on Raft," *Seattle Daily Times*, September 24, 1962.
25. https://flyingtiger923.com/2014/09/18/crew-members-to-be-remembered/.
26. "Ditched Plane's Last Moments a Story of Drama and Pathos," *Philadelphia Daily News*, September 25, 1962.
27. These 425 hours represent maybe one half of 1 percent of the actual time spent. For instance, while the Canadian Navy spent 89 hours in *flight* operations, the search and rescue also tied up 1,200 sailors on the carrier for 36 hours, and hundreds more on five of the accompanying destroyers. (Just 1,200 × 36 = 43,200 hours.) All of the planes had

crews and passengers. "SAR on Flying Tiger N 6923C," 28; "Atlantic Rescue," *FLIGHT International*, October 4, 1962, 552.
28. Vasquez interview with Frey, October 31, 2011.
29. Reymond interview, February 25, 2018. Also see Lugli and Neumann.
30. Elander memoir (tape #4).
31. Elander memoir (tapes #4 and #6).
32. Elander memoir (tape #6).
33. Elander memoir (tape #7).
34. Elander memoir (tape #8).
35. Acevedo interview, June 12, 2018.
36. https://flyingtiger923.com/2012/02/11/acevedo-tells-of-crash-aftermath/.
37. Caruso, 58-60.
38. Caruso, 60.
39. Caruso, 61.
40. Sandro Galea, Arijit Nandi, and David Vlahov, "The Epidemiology of Post-Traumatic Stress Disorder after Disasters," *Epidemiologic Reviews*, Vol. 27, No. 1, July 2005, 78–91.
41. Caruso, 77.
42. Caruso, 81.
43. Caruso, 82–85.
44. Caruso, 81–82.

Chapter 9. Praise Galore

1. Reymond interview, January 1, 2018.
2. Reymond interview, April 3, 2018.
3. *Daily Mail*, September 27, 1962.
4. Caruso letter, 1.
5. Richard Witkin, "Ditching Raises Vest-Light Issue: Refusal of U.S. to Require Lights Weighed as Factor in Atlantic Airliner Toll," *New York Times*, September 27, 1962.
6. In 1987, Witkin shared a Pulitzer Prize for helping to uncover why the NASA Space Shuttle *Challenger* blew up 73 seconds after liftoff.
7. Witkin.
8. November 1962 edition of *The Airline Pilot*; excerpted in Murray memoir.
9. During his 2011 interview with Sammy Vasquez in Phoenix, veteran Swiss investigative journalist Peter W. Frey said: "From what I've read and the research, 923 is the only [even] partially successful ditching in violent seas." Renowned maritime expert Pierre-André Reymond later added: "It was the most successful for an air crash in the northern Atlantic." See https://www.navigare-necesse-est.ch/sea-stories-en195.html ("Captain John Murray," 1). Also see "An Atlantic First," *Philadelphia Inquirer*, September 25, 1962.
10. "An Atlantic First."
11. "SAR on Flying Tiger N 6923C," 179. Also see "5 Southlanders."
12. "Course Studied," *New York Times*, September 25, 1962.

13. See "Stewardesses Tell of Safety Violations," *New York Times*, September 29, 1962.
14. Wunderlin letter, 4.
15. "Rescuing a Super Constellation," 7.
16. "Pilot Describes His First 'Ditch.'"
17. Vasquez interview with Frey, October 31, 2011.
18. Wunderlin letter, 4–5.
19. Hansen interview, August 20, 2019.
20. "Rescuing a Super Constellation," 7–8.
21. "C.A.B. Dispatches 6 Men," *Los Angeles Times*, September 25, 1962.
22. "2 State Soldiers on Lost Airliner," *Milwaukee Sentinel*, March 17, 1962.
23. Thornsberry interview, August 7, 2020.
24. Hansen interview, June 20, 2015.
25. Hansen interview, March 26, 2020.
26. Hansen interview, April 25, 2019. Also see Hamma.
27. Hansen interview, October 13, 2019.
28. Hansen interview, June 25, 2015.
29. Hansen interview, March 1, 2018.
30. John P. Murray interview, June 12, 2015. While Murray (who was 14 at the time) isn't certain that his father said these exact words, they are in keeping with Captain Murray's character and wry sense of humor.
31. "Survivors Tell of Ditching Drill," *Evening Bulletin* (Philadelphia), September 25, 1962.
32. Frank Cameron, *Hungry Tiger: The Story of the Flying Tiger Line* (New York: McGraw-Hill, 1964), 245.
33. Hansen interview, August 30, 2020.
34. "Oyster Bay Honors Heroic Pilot with Gala Welcome Here," *Oyster (NY) Bay Guardian*, October 5, 1962. Oyster Bay's most famous resident once wrote: "It is not the critic who counts. The credit belongs to the man who is actually in the arena, whose face is marred by . . . blood, who strives valiantly, who errs, who comes short . . . who spends himself in a worthy cause . . . daring greatly." (First delivered by Roosevelt in Paris, France, April 23, 1910, in a speech entitled "Citizenship in a Republic.")
35. Murray memoir.
36. John P. Murray interview, December 8, 2019.
37. John P. Murray interview, October 5, 2020.

Chapter 10. Having Second Thoughts

1. Thornsberry interview, July 31, 2020.
2. Rodriguez interview, October 2, 2017.
3. Mark Hansen, Carolyn McAndrews, and Emily Berkeley, *History of Aviation Safety Oversight in the United States* (Washington: U.S. Department of Transportation, 2008), 10, 12.
4. Rodriguez interview, October 2, 2017.
5. "In the Matter of," 6–7.
6. "5 Southlanders."

7. "In the Matter of," 5.
8. As is clear from a review of Embry-Riddle Aeronautical University's collection of hundreds of aircraft accident reports, at https://www.ntsb.gov/_layouts/ntsb.aviation/index.aspx, and the NTSB database, at https://www.ntsb.gov/_layouts/ntsb.aviation/index.aspx.
9. "5 Southlanders; Search Called Off for 16 Missing in Atlantic," *Philadelphia Daily News*, September 26, 1962.
10. More than 10 hours were devoted to forensically immaterial albeit poignant human interest accounts by other survivor-witnesses.
11. By way of comparison, William Brennan's 1957 Supreme Court nomination hearing lasted 3 hours; Thurgood Marshall's 1967 hearing, 7; and Robert Bork's failed 1987 nomination, 30.
12. In thousands of pages of secondary research and nearly 1,700 interviews, I encountered this pilot's name just this once. "In the Matter of," 58.
13. While going into the hearing four different people claimed to have been the last to board the raft, the testimony confirmed it was Murray, after he'd helped Helga Groves (with an assist from Raúl Acevedo).
14. "In the Matter of," 808–15.

Part IV. Missing Files

1. Murray memoir.

Chapter 11. Final Verdicts

1. The Flight Safety Foundation's Aviation Safety Network has been an invaluable resource: https://aviation-safety.net/statistics/period/stats.php (this lists accidents by period).
2. LeFever, in a June 2, 2017, interview, said, "Garrett was one of maybe 10 engineers trained by, and furloughed by, Eastern Airlines. We had to retrain them all."
3. Richard Witkin, "C.A.B. Lauds Life-Vest Lights for Role in Saving 57 in Pacific: Notes U.S. Airlines Need Not Carry Such Equipment on Sea Flights—Board Favors Mandatory Rule," *New York Times*, November 24, 1962. Also see Witkin, "2 Airlines to Add Life-Vests Light: Pan Am and Trans World Join Growing Safety Movement," *New York Times*, December 6, 1962.
4. "Navigation and Vessel Inspection Circular No. 2-63" (Washington, DC: U.S. Coast Guard, December 1962).
5. Close enough. The Coast Guard lists the time of impact as 10:12, Murray uses 10:13 p.m.
6. "Fiery Plane Crashes N. Hollywood Homes: Eight Buildings Set Aflame; Power in Area Blacked Out," *Los Angeles Times*, December 15, 1962.
7. LeFever interview, July 13, 2019.
8. Rodriguez interview, October 2, 2017.
9. "SAR on Flying Tiger N 6923C," 77. The CAB was clearly aware of this: the "CAB Senior Hearing Officer" asked the Coast Guard to provide a witness at the CAB hearing, and "has also requested a copy of these activities" (p. 153).

10. "SAR on Flying Tiger N 6923C," 28.
11. "SAR on Flying Tiger N 6923C," 54.
12. "SAR on Flying Tiger N 6923C," 55.
13. Hansen interview, July 29, 2020.
14. https://flyingtiger923.com/2012/08/07/just-trying-to-do-the-right-thing/.
15. Thornsberry interview, July 30, 2020.
16. Eldred-Stephan interview, July 30, 2020.
17. https://flyingtiger923.com/2012/08/19/sitting-in-the-right-seat-at-the-right-time/.
18. Caruso interview, August 29, 2020.
19. Gilbreth interviews, November 8, 2017, and October 27, 2020.
20. Gilbreth interview, July 30, 2020.
21. Gilbreth interview, November 8, 2017.
22. Gilbreth interview, June 11, 2018.
23. Thornsberry interview, July 21, 2020.
24. Caruso, 235.
25. Hamma.
26. Hansen interview, July 30, 2020.
27. Gary Fromm, *Economic Criteria for Federal Agency Expenditures* (Washington: FAA, 1962), 595, 607, 617–18. Also see Stanley Ingber, "Rethinking Intangible Injuries: A Focus on a Remedy," *California Law Review*, Vol. 73, 778, footnote 27, at www.scholarship.law.berkeley.edu.

Chapter 12. Crew Legacies

1. *Diagnostic and Statistical Manual of Mental Disorders, Third Edition*; https://www.ptsd.va.gov/professional/treat/essentials/history_ptsd.asp.
2. Galea et al.
3. Wolfgang Saxon, "Dr. William G. Niederland, 88; Formulated 'Survivor Syndrome,'" *New York Times*, August 5, 1993.
4. R. G. Tedeschi, J. Shakespeare-Finch, K. Taku, and L. G. Calhoun, *Posttraumatic Growth: Theory, Research, and Applications* (New York: Routledge, 2018). Also see Priscilla Alvarez, "The Post-Traumatic Psychology of Disaster Survivors," *Atlantic*, December 6, 2016.
5. Wenchao Wang, Xinchun Wu, and Yuxin Tian, "Mediating Roles of Gratitude and Social Support in the Relation between Survivor Guilt and Posttraumatic Stress Disorder: Posttraumatic Growth among Adolescents after the Ya'an Earthquake," *Frontiers in Psychology*, November 5, 2018.
6. "In the Matter of," 281.
7. John P. Murray interview, October 5, 2020.
8. Reymond interview, November 23, 2019.
9. John P. Murray interview, July 27, 2015.
10. John P. Murray interview, January 21, 2020.
11. "Aircraft Accident Report," 1.
12. "Aircraft Accident Report," 9–10, 13, 15, 17.
13. "Aircraft Accident Report," 16.

14. LeFever interviews, June 2, 2017, and October 5, 2020.
15. Gilbreth interview, November 8, 2017.
16. John P. Murray interview, October 5, 2020.
17. Ellen Lindner interview, October 5, 2020.
18. Ellen and I visited her mother in Ireland almost every summer between 1986 (the year of our wedding) and 2000 (the year Dorothy passed). We'd often have long, spirited philosophical discussions. Her intellect and rhetorical skills were formidable.
19. John P. Murray interview, January 21, 2020.
20. Including Tiger 923 survivor Fred Bazelle.
21. LeFever interview, July 20, 2018.
22. "8 Crewmen Die, 11 Saved by Armada as Otis Plane Ditches in Atlantic," *Cape Cod Standard-Times*, July 12, 1965; "Sea Survival Problematic," *Record-American*, July 13, 1965.
23. Coincidentally, the Seabee was built in Farmingdale, New York, where the Murray family attended Mass at St. Kilian's parish when they lived on the farm in Melville, before moving to Oyster Bay in 1961.
24. John P. Murray interview, December 10, 2019.
25. Ellen Lindner interview, December 20, 2020.
26. As to why he was flying over Christmas, he'd been assigned it based on the route(s) he bid. Few liked flying over the holiday, Murray probably less than most, but few Tigers tried to finagle out of it. He never would have dreamed of pretending he was sick. Gewehr interview, September 21, 2020.
27. John P. Murray interview, December 10, 2019. Though the plane was the glitch-prone CL-44, the cause was poor weather. While there were no passengers on board, in addition to the 4-member Tiger crew, 107 people died on the ground and 50 were injured, many seriously, when the plane "struck an obstacle, stalled and crashed in flames . . . a few dozen yards short of the runway. The aircraft disintegrated on impact, and several houses were destroyed." See www.baaa-acro.com/operator/flying-tiger-line.
28. John P. Murray interview, December 10, 2019.
29. John P. Murray interview, January 21, 2020.
30. Also in September (but 1983), while a passenger on board KAL 007, Rep. Larry McDonald (D-GA) was shot down by Soviet fighter jets, just after Ellen quit working for him, on Capitol Hill.
31. John P. Murray interview, December 10, 2019.
32. Mike Causey, "The Federal Diary," *Washington Post*, January 31, 1984.
33. She's now with Amazon.
34. The "Miracle on the Hudson" pilot. The assignment was pure coincidence. She'd not sought it out, and WSB cofounder Harry Rhoads Jr. knew nothing about Tiger 923 when he asked if Sarah would take on the assignment. Though working very closely with Sully for 15 months after his ditching, she never mentioned Tiger 923 or its pilot. Sarah now works for Cancer for College, which gives scholarships to cancer survivors.
35. LeFever interview, November 8, 2020.
36. Hansen interview, August 21, 2019. Also see Hamma.
37. Cameron, 244.

38. Hansen interview with Frey, November 1, 2011.
39. Hansen interview, June 20, 2015.
40. Hansen interview, March 7, 2016.
41. Hansen interview, August 9, 2020.
42. Hansen interview, September 2, 2020.
43. Hansen interviews, August 21, 2019, and August 14, 2020.

CHAPTER 13. PASSENGER LEGACIES

1. Elander memoir (tape #8).
2. Perhaps having met at Checquers, when Eldred met Sir Winston Churchill, just before D-Day. The great man "shook my hand . . . wearing a dressing gown, and smoking a cigar" (Eldred, 37).
3. Young interview, August 21, 2020.
4. Elander memoir (tape # 6).
5. Young interview, November 21, 2019.
6. Elander memoir (tape #1).
7. Elander memoir (tape #2).
8. Elander memoir (tape #3).
9. Troy Elander interview, June 2, 2019.
10. Young interview, November 21, 2019.
11. Ingrid Gonçalves, "Farsighted Venture," *University of Chicago Magazine*, Summer 2018, 9. Coincidentally, Stein got his undergraduate degree from Chicago.
12. Diane Elander interview, April 21, 2019.
13. *Los Angeles Times*, June 1, 2014.
14. Here's Troy's COVID PSA: https://www.dropbox.com/s/lkdmcd4sue8pte8/Masks_Fine_Full.mp4?dl=0.
15. Troy Elander interview, June 2, 2019.
16. Though I only knew her for 10 months, the news of Jill's death hit me hard. She was a special soul; a woman of verve, style, and wit; and fun to be around. She loved talking about her parents' remarkable journey. I spent several hours with her in her Santa Monica office and we spoke, texted, or emailed more than a dozen times, the last time a week or so before her passing.

The manner in which her long-time boyfriend, Jim Deverannes, landed was a stunning display of skill and do-the-least-harm-possible heroism: when he experienced problems shortly after takeoff from Van Nuys Airport, he steered his two-seater clear of homes and other occupied buildings, crashing in the middle of a parking lot, in the center of an aisle flanked by cars.

When I mentioned to Tom, Troy, and Troy's wife, Diane, that, given the enthusiasm I'd seen, it was my sense Jill would have wanted this story told, they agreed. Diane Elander summed up their sentiment nicely: "Oh yes, Eric, you are right—she loved her mom especially and she loved a good story!" (October 7, 2020).

17. Acevedo interview, July 6, 2015.
18. Acevedo interview, July 6, 2015.

19. Acevedo's approach was ingenious. JFK's own father, Joseph, was very ill at the time. The stroke he'd suffered in December 1961 had left him paralyzed and aphasiac (he had trouble speaking). The president also might have instructed some assistant to inquire about Acevedo's father, who was powerful in Mexico. The benefit of helping the Mexican bigwig would not have been lost on the politically astute JFK, especially given his desire to contain Communism in Latin America.
20. Acevedo interview, June 28, 2015.
21. Acevedo interview, February 11, 2020.
22. Acevedo interview, February 11, 2020.
23. See Debra Mims and Rhondda Waddell, "Animal Assisted Therapy and Trauma Survivors," *Journal of Evidence-Informed Social Work*, Vol. 13, No. 5, 2016, 452–57.
24. Caruso, 81.
25. Caruso, 70.
26. Cameron, 238.
27. Caruso, 70.
28. Caruso, 85, 91.
29. Caruso, 134.
30. Caruso, 112–13.
31. Gilbreth interview, July 22, 2020.
32. https://flyingtiger923.com/2012/06/29/frank-bazell-survives-crash-to-die-another-day-for-his-country/.
33. Wang et al.
34. Gilbreth interview with Frey, October 31, 2011.
35. Gilbreth interview, June 11, 2018.
36. "An Exclusive Interview," 1–2; "Was This Tragedy Necessary?," *The Cape Codder*, November 1, 1962, 12.
37. But he does allude to it: after having not smoked since his father forced him to smoke a pack (and get sick) in 1925 (age 11), "I took up smoking again . . . [in] 1962" (Eldred, 5). In his November 1, 1962, interview, he said Edna advised he light up to calm his nerves ("An Exclusive Interview," 2).
38. Eldred, 9, 16–17, 62, 66–67.
39. "An Exclusive Interview," 2.
40. Eldred-Stephan interview, June 10, 2020.
41. See https://archive.org/details/the-saturday-evening-post-1962-11-17/page/n95/mode/2up?q=ditched.
42. Eldred-Stephan interview, October 3, 2020.

Chapter 14. Not So Tight Security

1. See "Notable Thefts from the National Archives" at www.archives.gov.
2. The US Air 1549 files cover a six-minute ditching, two-hour search-and-rescue operation, and run about 4,000 pages, including a 559-page hearing transcript. Tiger 923's ditching took two hours, the search and rescue took two days, and the files included a 959-page transcript. As for Tiger 739, while the National Archives files I saw ran about 2,000 pages, they were not complete. For instance, there was only a list

of the 32 witnesses, not any affidavits. Being a much less complex investigation is part of the reason why the Tiger 739 investigation took a little over 2 months, as opposed to just under 12.

Helga Groves was the only survivor not interviewed. "Crash Survivors Reach Antwerp," *Times* (London), September 29, 1962.

3. Rodriguez interview, October 2, 2017.
4. Only the CAB–Commerce Department files are held at NA2. The Coast Guard–Treasury's SAR was at NA1 on Constitution Avenue in Washington, along with the Declaration of Independence.
5. Schwarz interview, August 28, 2020.
6. Schwarz interview, October 2, 2017.
7. Rodriguez interview, October 2, 2017.
8. "Sandy Berger's Theft of Classified Documents: Unanswered Questions," Staff Report, U.S. House of Representatives, Committee on Oversight and Governmental Reform, January 2007, https://fas.org/irp/congress/2007_rpt/berger.pdf. Also see https://www.archives.gov/research/recover/notable-thefts.html.
9. "Sandy Berger's Theft," 3.

Chapter 15. The Healing Hand of Friendship

1. Caruso interview, July 15, 2020.
2. Frey interview, August 17, 2020.
3. Decrey's broadcast can be heard at https://pages.rts.ch/la-1ere/programmes/le-12h30/3922609-le-12h30-du-21-04-2012.html#timeline-anchor-segment-3934625.
4. Reymond interview, July 18, 2020.
5. Caruso interview with Marc Decrey, April 15, 2012.
6. Caruso, 232.
7. The documentary can be found at www.srf.ch/sendungen/doppelpunkt/rettung-im-atlantik.
8. www.srf.ch/sendungen/doppelpunkt/rettung-im-atlantik.
9. https://flyingtiger923.com/2012/06/06/how-did-the-rescue-ship-get-its-name/.
10. https://flyingtiger923.com/2013/06/18/memorial-dedicated-at-browmore-cliffs/.
11. Caruso interview, July 20, 2020.
12. Frey interview, July 21, 2020.
13. Composite of Frey interviews, including July 15, 2019, and September 26, 2020.
14. "The Numbers: 923—923," at www.flyingtiger923.com.
15. https://flyingtiger923.com/2018/10/13/friendship-postcard-reaches-its-target-after-55-years-in-safekeeping/.
16. Caruso interview with Frey, November 1, 2011.
17. Caruso interview with Frey, November 1, 2011.
18 Caruso interview, August 20, 2020.
19. https://www.nimh.nih.gov/health/statistics/post-traumatic-stress-disorder-ptsd.shtml; https://www.apa.org/research/action/ptsd; https://www.therecoveryvillage.com/mental-health/ptsd/related/ptsd-statistics/; https://barendspsychology.com/mental-disorders-post-traumatic-stress-disorder-statistics/.

20. Hansen interview, September 29, 2020.
21. Hansen interview, September 30, 2020.
22. Caruso, 13–29.
23. https://flyingtiger923.com/2012/01/24/major-and-mrs-richard-erlander/.
24. Troy Elander interview, June 21, 2018.

Index

Italicized page numbers indicate illustrations.